P9-CBI-657

STAND UP AND SHOUT OUT

STAND UP AND SHOUT OUT

Women's Fight for Equal Pay, Equal Rights, and Equal Opportunities in Sports

Joan Steidinger

ROWMAN & LITTLEFIELD
Lanham • Boulder • New York • London

Published by Rowman & Littlefield
An imprint of The Rowman & Littlefield Publishing Group, Inc.
4501 Forbes Boulevard, Suite 200, Lanham, Maryland 20706
www.rowman.com

6 Tinworth Street, London SE11 5AL

British Library Cataloguing in Publication Information Available

Library of Congress Control Number: 2019038984

∞ ™ The paper used in this publication meets the minimum requirements of American National Standard for Information Sciences Permanence of Paper for Printed Library Materials, ANSI/NISO Z39.48-1992.

To the grandmother of sports psychology

Dr. Carole Oglesby

guide and mentor to
thousands of girls and women in sport,
sharing her hand with black and white,
for her kind and generous heart,
willingness to friend and befriend those others
neglected whose backs were turned on,
to recognize beyond our borders the need for outreach
to our global neighbors,
our gratefulness knows no bounds.

Dr. Carole Oglesby and Dr. Chris Sheldon. *Dr. Carole Oglesby*

CONTENTS

ACKNOWLEDGMENTS

Girls playing sports is not about winning gold medals. It's about self-esteem, learning to compete, and learning how hard you have to work in order to achieve your goals.
—Jackie Joyner-Kersee, former Olympian, heptathlon and long jump, and winner of three gold, one silver, and two bronze medals in four different Olympics[1]

Once again, the phrase "it took a village" applies to the development of this book. Because of the assistance I received from leaders in girl's and women's sport in the United States and throughout the world, this book grew in depth, scope, and excitement. The collaboration, cooperation, bonding, generosity, and openness of the interviewees was greatly appreciated in helping bring this book to fruition. Thank you for your insight, wisdom, and support. Thank you from the bottom of my heart to the following individuals:

John Eric Poulson, my intelligent, kind, generous, and thoughtful husband, who puts up with my mess and ordering dinner out when I'm in the midst of deadlines.

Susanna Solomon, my writing coconspirator, who was encouraging and supportive as we enjoyed our "Wednesday night outings" at Jason's, making trouble during happy hour and enjoying a break from writing the book.

Dr. Mary Lamia, my colleague and friend who has written five books herself, who served as a mentor, guide, friend, and hiking buddy.

Constance Hale, who offered sage advice about which direction to take with this book.

Dr. Janice De Covnick, who actually asked me, prior to this book, if she could be a reader of my next book before I'd even decided on a topic, for her undying love and support.

Peter Beren, my agent, for believing in me long before he was my agent.

Cheryl Krauter, my trusted writing group buddy, for sharing an interest in my writing. The feeling is mutual.

Dr. Carole Oglesby, who opened doors for me to begin the journey of creating this book. It is dedicated to her.

Dr. Becky Clark, who supported my first book and planted the seed for this one.

Nancy Hogshead-Makar, who generously introduced me to a wide range of women leaders in sport, providing invaluable information about the #MeToo movement and helping develop the richness of this book.

Dr. Alpha Alexander, who with her invaluable knowledge and contacts helped me better understand the issues facing African American females in sport.

Brooke Warner, who is an excellent book coach whose guidance has taught me how to organize and think more clearly.

Krissa Lagos, my editor, whose feedback on and guidance in my writing has made me a better writer.

Thomas Newkirk, an attorney, who gave me a more in-depth view of how the law relates to gender discrimination.

Charlene Bayles, for our runs and discussions, which made me think about the politics of sport work.

Cade Netscher, head of Neurun, who believes in me and my work, and showed his support for this project

Frances Steidinger, my mother, who would be proud of me had she lived to see the publication of this book.

Dean Steidinger, my father, who taught me to reach for the stars in sports.

A huge thanks to my readers: Dr. Janice De Covnick, Charlene Bayles, Holly Harris, and Mary Foston English.

INTRODUCTION

Sports build good habits, confidence, and discipline. They make players into community leaders and teach them how to strive for a goal, handle mistakes, and cherish growth opportunities.
—Julie Foudy, World Cup soccer winner and American sports leader[1]

Today, women have greater opportunities to participate in sport than ever before, particularly due to Title IX. As a pre-Title IX athlete, I experienced huge limitations and watched them being placed on women in sports throughout the years. This is reflective of the challenge to move toward further equality. My lifelong love of all sport has driven me throughout the writing of this book on women's inequality. Thanks to the hard work of Billie Jean King, the Women's Sports Foundation, and the Black Women in Sport Foundation, among numerous other individuals and groups, girls and women's participation in sport has increased exponentially. Despite this growth after Title IX, women have struggled more than ever to hold leadership positions, become coaches of both girls' and boys' teams, receive equal pay, and even receive adequate coverage in the media. Women coaching girls and women has fallen to 41.8 percent from the 90 percent it was prior to Title IX, and media coverage of women's sports is a pathetic 4 percent. As the "godmother of sports psychology," Carole Oglesby spoke at the Social Justice in Exercise and Sport Psychology conference in March 2019, stating, "Sport is more gender antagonistic than most job climates."

When I ran my first marathon in San Francisco in 1987, I observed every size and shape of runner. This process of observing the different types of athletes helped widen my scope about girl's and women's issues in sport. I wrote an article for the website Disruptive Women in Health that explored the topic of appearance versus performance, a process that further enlightened me about the modern world's narrow view of what a female athlete should look like.

Then, during the Rio Olympics in 2016, I watched the media repeatedly invalidate and ignore the stories of numerous female U.S. Olympians who received medals. One tweet went so far as to identify a female athlete who received a bronze medal only as the wife of a NFL player. Much of the media coverage during these Olympics attributed female athletes' receiving medals to the men in their lives rather than their own hard work, training, and determination. In the 2018 Pyeongchang Olympics, the U.S. women outperformed the men, receiving more gold medals. Both their strengths and capabilities emerged more than ever before. For example, in a great show of determination and fortitude, Olympic cross-country skiers Jessie Diggins and Kikkan Randall made Olympic history by winning the first cross-country medal by U.S. women and the first cross-country medal in 42 years for the United States. Watching these inspirational performances motivated me to write about this topic of inequality for women in sport. Women athletes are stepping forward with their mettle, courage, and determination.

In the past couple of years, I've presented at numerous conferences and conducted workshops about such inequality issues as leadership, pay equity, media coverage, appearance versus performance, and treatment of white women versus women of color in sports. My interest in and passion for supporting women in sport in gaining more equality has grown exponentially. As a sports and clinical psychologist, Certified Mental Performance Consultant, member of the United States Olympic Committee (USOC) Registry of Sport Psychology, director of Sports Psychology for Neurun, and author, my professional life focuses heavily, although not solely, on sports psychology and female athletes. In fact, through attending the International Working Group on Women and Sport in Botswana in May 2018, my eyes were opened even wider about the growing need for advocacy for girls and women throughout the world. The networking and exchange of ideas of women from many cultures and backgrounds were powerful and demonstrative of work being done to promote sport for girls everywhere. The experience was inspirational and enlightening. I decided that there has been too much written about white privilege and the black experience in sport separately, so this book is an attempt to discuss the experiences of black and white female athletes, leaders, and coaches in sport. I encourage anyone working in sport with girls and women to attend the next International Working Group (IWG) on Women and Sport conference in 2022, in New Zealand. This will provide an even broader perspective on the state of females in sport.

Certainly, a number of positive changes in sport have occurred since the passage of Title IX in 1972. In the United States today, more than 3 million girls participate in sports, as compared to a mere 300,000 in 1972. There is even one sporting league, the World Surfing League, that awards equal prize money to women and men. Yet, three crucial areas in sport—leadership, money, and media—remain huge stumbling blocks for women and girls in sport. Today, however, despite the increase in females participating in sports, media still only covers female athletes about 4 percent of the time, and *Fox Sports* manages even less than that.

In my research for this book, I have unearthed many more shocking statistics about the dismal treatment of women in sport. My goal with *Stand Up and Shout Out* is to inform readers about these important issues, create more discussion about the unequal treatment of women in sports, address racism and sexual orientation, and present readers with "action steps" so we can become active contributors in improving this situation—and, by extension, the world.

I

LEADING THE CHARGE

Sports teaches you character, it teaches you to play by the rules, it teaches you to know what it feels like to win and lose—it teaches you about life.

—Billie Jean King, former world number-one tennis player and winner of 39 Grand Slams[1]

Women in sport are passionate, hardworking, and persistent in their efforts to achieve equality. There were two major influences that began opening up doors. Billie Jean King led the way when she beat Bobby Riggs in 1973, in the "Battle of the Sexes." In addition, the passage of Title IX in 1972 paved the way for increasing girls' and women's participation in sports. Next, the Women's Sports Foundation, founded in 1974 by King, was—and remains—dedicated to creating greater access to sport for girls and women.

Female sports leaders of today speak out in clear and direct ways. They want and deserve to be recognized for the leadership skills they bring to the table. Primarily through watching female sports leaders throughout the years, the younger generation has begun to recognize the value of and need for mentors. What we've seen reported repeatedly is that girls who participate in sports are more likely to succeed in life. Some of the earlier generation still working to establish equality in sports for black and white female sports leaders include Billie Jean King, Rosie Casals, Donna de Varona, Tina Sloane Green, Elana Meyers Taylor, Wendy Hillard, Nancy Hogshead-Makar, Jackie Joyner-Kersee, and Julie Foudy, to name just a few. Today, young women see such role models as Venus and Serena Williams (tennis), Megan Rapinoe (soccer), Simone Biles (gymnastics), Misty Copeland (dance), and Breanna Stewart (basketball), who are bringing to light both the opportunities and challenges faced when it comes to gaining respect, credibility, power, experience, openness to new ideas, and self-confidence.

Leading is like any sport: It takes practice to get better. It requires strength, endurance, positive thinking, hard work, determination, and, most of all, persistence, just like climbing a steep hill does. It requires fortitude, commitment, and an ability to soar. It requires a greater degree of confidence. In many studies looking at confidence in women, the repeated findings are that women underestimate their confidence in their abilities and performance, whereas men overestimate their confidence.[2] Some of the younger leaders reach beyond sports to support social justice causes, for example, Black Lives Matter. In 2018, Breanna Stewart of the Women's National Basketball Association (WNBA) led the way in supporting a variety of causes both inside and outside of sport. But as far as female leadership in sport goes, we're still at the

Billie Jean King and Wendy Hillard (Gymnastics Foundation). Wendy was the first African American rhythmic gymnast on the U.S. Olympic team. *Courtesy of the Wendy Hillard Gymnastics Foundation*

bottom of the hill. For all the progress we've made, much work remains.

WOMEN PASSING THE BATON

Women in sports leadership are essential to furthering the important cause of equal treatment for female athletes. Strong women administrators and coaches serve as mentors and role models whom younger female athletes can admire, respect, and emulate. Female athletes benefit from viewing such leaders, in every level of sport, as powerful, assertive women who are not afraid to speak their minds. This means we need more female leaders, especially those who understand the most effective strategies for working with girls to help them become leaders themselves.

Female athletes, sports governance officials, journalists, and coaches struggle with gender equality issues. In fall of 2017, Cam Newton, quarterback for the Carolina Panthers, was asked a simple question about pass routes by female journalist Jourdan Rodrigue. Instead of answering the question, he responded by saying, "It's funny to hear a female talk about routes." He snickered while the room remained silent. Rodrigue, who reports for the *Charlotte Observer*, remarked in a Tweet, "I don't think it's 'funny' to be a female and talk about routes. I think it's my job." She maintains that Newton did not apologize for this remark, even though some media outlets reported that he did.[3]

Newton's treatment of this journalist speaks to a larger trend in which women are not taken seriously and not treated with respect. Despite some progress in business settings, female representation in sport lags behind, with women holding too few decision-making roles in sports management and sports in general. According to *Forbes*, "The glass ceiling for women may be lower in sports than in any other industry," and an examination of 450 NCAA Division I athletic departments and "Big Four" sports clubs found that less than 10 percent of women are heads of athletic departments.[4]

This constitutes minimal representation in significant decision-making and voting roles in sports management and sports in general. Two leading authorities and pioneers—Carole Oglesby, the "godmother of sports psychology," and Donna de Varona, the first president and chairwoman of the Women's Sports Foundation—both indicated in interviews for this book that the lack of women in sports leadership positions is an issue of utmost concern. Although at the advent of Title IX in the United States, 93 percent of female teams were coached by women, the figure now runs at about 41.5 percent. Men are increasingly occupying coaching positions for female teams now that good salaries are being offered for these jobs. They are also consistently offered significantly higher salaries than the women coaches filling equivalent roles.

Tracey Griesbaum was fired from her job as field hockey coach at the University of Iowa in 2014 because, according to the athletic director, the team needed a "change in leadership," despite Coach Griesbaum, who happened to be a lesbian, having led her team to three Big Ten Conference tournaments, one regular Big Ten Conference championship, six NCAA Tournament appearances, and a 2008 Final Four. She was fired without a formal complaint or cause. The school's athletic director, Gary Barta, hired a male, Gene Taylor, in August 2014, to take over some of the duties of the associate athletic director, Jane Meyer, paying him $70,000 more. Subsequently, Jane Meyer (Griesbaum's partner) was also fired. Griesbaum sued the athletic department for discrimination and wrongful termination, and she won an award of $2.55 million in 2017. According to a piece in the online publication *HawkCentral*, "Griesbaum hopes that her lawsuit will inspire change and open more opportunities for female athletes and coaches."[5]

Women leaders in sport are out there paving the way to help provide inspiration and mentorship to the younger generation. When recognized for their leadership skills, women in sport increase their power and abilities to promote change for the girls and women coming up in sports. Women are drastically underrepresented in positions of leadership in sport organizations, however, comprising only 34 percent of administrative jobs in college athletics, 19.3 percent of athletic director positions, and less than 9 percent of athletic director positions in Division I–level college athletics.[6] Some of the barriers to leadership that women face include being viewed as less competent than men, having limited networks of support and influence, and lacking mentors. Those few women who are recruited to hold positions at colleges or in professional sports often have less power, receive less pay, and are offered fewer and more limited opportunities for advancement than their male counterparts.[7]

Mentoring is a key element for females in sports in that it helps direct young females to achieve greater success in every area of life, including in the workplace, educational advancement, and their personal sphere. This mentoring occurs in both active and passive roles. One of the first female athletes to step into this kind of leadership role in the United States was Donna de Varona, a two-time Olympic gold medalist in swimming, former world record-holder, television sportscaster, and advocate for girls and women in sports. She served as the first president of the Women's Sports Foundation (1979–1984) and has since served in numerous other organizations and committees. In 2018, I spoke with Nancy Hogshead-Makar, an Olympic gold medal–winning swimmer, award-winning civil rights lawyer, speaker, and author, who shared with me how de Varona singled her out to be a leader. She described de Varona "choosing" to train her to become a leader in sports. This is an example of active mentoring.

For years, Hogshead-Makar told me, she was mentored and then guided by de Varona, first interning at the Women's Sports Foundation and later becoming a member of the board, before stepping into the vice president role and eventually becoming president, a position she occupied from 1992 to 1994. After law school, Hogshead-Makar served as the organization's legal counsel from 2003 to 2010, and as its senior director of advocacy until 2014. In 2015, she founded her own organization, Champion Women, providing legal advocacy for females in sport, where she currently serves as CEO and president. Her focus is echoed by the mission statement of Champion Women: "Access and equality for participants, sexual harassment, sexual abuse and assault, employment and pregnancy discrimination, and legal enforcement under Title IX."[8]

Hogshead-Makar's advocacy work has been vital to the cause of equality for women in sports. She has frequently served as an expert witness for a number of sexual assault/rape cases, including, most recently, the Dr. Larry Nassar case. Dr. Nassar was found by the court to have sexually abused 150 young gymnasts in his role as team doctor for the U.S. Olympic gymnastics team and physician for the Michigan State women's gymnastics team. Hogshead-Makar has also been a role model, encouraging young women to stand up and shout out against their own injustices. She provides inspiration for other young women to fol-

Wendy Borlabi and Nancy Hogshead-Makar. *Nancy Hogshead-Makar, JD*

low her example, showcasing through her actions what determination, hard work, and persistence can achieve.

Recently, I bumped into a female cycling friend, Katie Sarachelli, who told me that Hogshead-Makar inspired her to start swimming after the 1984 Los Angeles Olympics, when she tied for Olympic Gold in the 100-meter freestyle alongside U.S. teammate Carrie Steinseifer. I'd had a similar experience that year when I watched U.S. Olympian Joan Benoit run and win the first women's marathon. Her performance inspired me to run longer distances and eventually complete my first marathon in 1987. These personal anecdotes support the notion that role models do, in fact, inspire girls to become more involved in sports.

Where leadership in sport for black women is concerned, an even greater challenge exists. Sports in the United States are too homogeneous. The United States doesn't look outward enough. As Tina Sloan

Green, cofounder of the Black Women in Sport Foundation (BWSF), has stated, "One of my goals and one of the goals of the foundation is to mentor young black women who want to pursue careers in sport." BWSF strives to expand and grow the footprint of involvement of black and other girls of color in sport through participation in sports, coaching, and leadership opportunities. Originally founded in 1992 by four African American women—Tina Sloan Green, Dr. Alpha Alexander, Dr. Nikki Franke, and Linda Greene—at Temple University in Philadelphia, BWSF strives to teach girls and women of color about "competitive play, teamwork, and academic achievement."[9]

Sloan Green has had many mentors and has acted as a mentor to thousands more. In 1969, prior to Title IX, she became the first African American chosen to play on the U.S. women's national lacrosse team. In 1975, she pioneered again when she was named the first African American coach in the history of collegiate lacrosse.

When I interviewed one of Sloan Green's cofounders at BWSF, Dr. Alpha Alexander (vice president of the organization), she commented that there is still a lot of racism in sport. Dr. Alexander mentioned that even Jackie Joyner-Kersee, an African American Olympian who won six Olympic medals in four Olympic Games, was not put on the cover of *Women's Sports* magazine (now defunct) or *Sports Illustrated*, simply because she was a black female.

Dr. Alexander holds an incredible list of accomplishments herself. Yet, it's hard to find much information about her online. Her career began in 1972, when she played college basketball and volleyball at Wooster College in Ohio. This was the year Title IX passed. After that, she went on to get her MA and PhD in physical education at Temple University in Philadelphia, where she became a graduate assistant in the women's athletics department, a role she kept for four years. Next, she served as assistant director of athletics and acting women's athletic director from 1981 to 1983, director of health and sports advocacy for YWCA USA, and more than a decade on the USOC's Board of Directors. Named one of the 30 most significant professionals in the business of sports by *Black Enterprise* in 1995, Dr. Alexander has won numerous awards for her service, notably the Billie Jean King Contribution Award and the Olympic Shield Award. Throughout her life, she has inspired and served as a role model and mentor to women of color and others.

Yet, she has run relatively under the radar when it comes to the general public.

Dr. Alexander is a perfect example of the many relatively unknown black female leaders who have inspired many young women of all races through their dedication to professional and service-oriented sports leadership. She is an outstanding African American female in sport who people need to know more about.

While conducting research about black females involved in sport, I was dismayed, although not entirely surprised, to find how lacking the internet coverage of current and past female African American leaders in sport truly is. In fact, one of the "foremothers" of Title IX was social activist and attorney Pauli Murray. Murray was African American and a cofounder of the National Organization for Women (NOW). She pushed for the Equal Rights Amendment. In fact, we must not forget Congresswomen Edith Green and Shirley Chisholm, the latter an African American, who drew language directly from the Equal Rights Amendment for Title IX.[10] This failure to acknowledge African American leaders in sport needs to stop, and the only way that's going to happen is if the female sporting world begins to address these issues by posting more positive articles about both white women and women of color athletic leaders online and putting pressure on mainstream media to do the same. Additionally, more of us need to speak up about the existence of BWSF and other institutions devoted to the furtherance of African American women and other women of color in U.S. sports, as well as the Women's Sports Foundation.

As a female of any race, what does it take to become a respected and admired leader in sport? Through action and thought, female leaders must be better than the best men to gain respect and admiration from their peers. For African American females, the challenge is even greater. Many consider Michele Roberts, executive director of the National Basketball Players Association (NBPA), to be one of the most powerful women in sports. Both respected and feared for her shrewd negotiation skills, Roberts is the first female to head a major professional sports union. But this success has only come through hard work and determination. Roberts says clearly, "You've got to be in the room and when you get in the room, try to own the room."[11]

As the title of this book suggests, the time has arrived for women in sport to demonstrate greater pressure and aggressiveness by standing up and shouting out for the rights of women in sport. Muffet McGraw, coach of Notre Dame's women's basketball team, is a powerful leader and strong voice for women in coaching and sport in general. She created a significant controversy on April 4, 2019, when she declared, "Too many men are still being hired. . . . We don't have enough female role models. We don't have enough visible women leaders. We don't have enough visible women in power."[12]

The major hurdle female leaders in sport face in overcoming inequality is getting everyone to listen to their voices and ideas about attaining greater equality for female athletes. In fact, when women do speak up, they are often immediately attacked and reminded of how much men have done for women. In response to McGraw stating that she would only hire women going forward, the coach for her rival team, the University of Connecticut, Geno Auriemma, responded as such, saying, "Well, I hope she sends a thank you to all those guys that used to be on her staff that got her all those good players that won a championship." With gender discrimination oozing out of this statement, McGraw's Fighting Irish went on to defeat the Connecticut Huskies in the women's Final Four in 2019.[13] As one researcher aptly stated, "Despite increased participation for girls and women in sport, they are underrepresented in leadership positions at all levels of sport."[14] Nancy Hogshead-Makar has labeled this struggle "Sexism 101." There's an unconscious bias toward women in sports and a general perception that they are not equal to men. Unfortunately, this extends to women in sports leadership roles as well. In our culture, we mainly equate sports with *men's* sports, and this is a problem not only in the United States, but also globally.

LEADERSHIP AND THE BATTLE FOR EQUALITY

Two of the most visible and powerful sporting institutions in the world, the International Olympic Committee (IOC) and FIFA (football/soccer), have never seen a woman in a top governance position. Established in 1894, the IOC has always had a man in charge. Similarly, FIFA has always been led by men since its establishment in Paris, France, in 1904. Lydia Nsefera was the first and only woman to be elected and hold voting rights on FIFA's Executive Board, and that was in 2013.

The organization was more than 109 years old at the time of her election.

Researcher Johanna Adriaanse from the University of Technology in Sydney, Australia, conducted research examining female leaders in sport throughout the world and discovered that a mere 7 percent (five out of 70) of sports institutions are led by women. Contrasting 2012 to 2016, she observed only minimal change. In 2012 and again in 2016, women occupied only 7 percent (five of 70) of the top positions in these organizations. A bit of good news, nevertheless, is that the percentage of female CEOs in sports rose from 8 percent to 19 percent (from 12 to 64 women) during the course of those same four years; however, the percentage of female directors only rose from 4.2 percent to 16.3 percent, and many sports organizations with female chairs have smaller participation bases and include many nontraditional sports, for example, curling, sled-dog racing, and underwater sports. Both the IOC and FIFA, viewed as two of the most powerful and influential sports organizations in the world, have never had a woman at the top.[15]

It's also important to note how many sports are not readily available for nonwhite female athletes. The "traditional sports" of basketball and track and field are regarded as acceptable for African American women. An example, nontraditional sports are swimming and gymnastics. The first African American rhythmic gymnast of note to represent the United States was Wendy Hilliard, who was also the first African American female to become president of the Women's Sports Foundation in New York City. Hilliard established her own organization, the Wendy Hilliard Gymnastics Foundation (WHGF), with the specific purpose of helping underserved youth in New York City and Detroit, the latter her hometown, learn about and participate in gymnastics.

Gymnastics requires a fair amount of funds to participate, which often restricts the participation of children in lower socioeconomic brackets, including African Americans. WHGF offers free and lower-cost alternatives for practicing and competing in gymnastics for those who qualify. When I spoke with Hilliard, she said she strives to help engage these girls in sport by encouraging them to be the best athletes they can be. She described her efforts to offer good coaching, establish a positive work ethic, and provide positive black female role models for the gymnasts. They learn to win and lose, instilling a feeling of confidence. Hilliard also mentioned that the foundation's teams are often the only ones featuring black gymnasts at meets, and experiencing this helps the athletes learn to work and compete in the world at large. With more foundations like WHGF, female sports leaders from every race can continue to be fostered in the United States.

Critical mass theory suggests that there's a certain point or critical mass after which a group begins to establish trust and influence with its members. Research has defined a "critical mass" as existing when boards of organizations are 30 percent female. There are a few federations in the United States that have this composition, namely triathlon, hockey, and rowing. The vast majority of U.S. sports federations, conversely, lack 30 percent women's representation, and some have zero female representation.

Despite great pushes to elevate women in sport, sporting bodies of significance (e.g., the IOC and FIFA) still treat women's advancement as a farce. They don't seem to want to include truly powerful and knowledgeable women. For example, in 2017, FIFA touted its advancement on this issue when it changed the rules so that each continent's FIFA governance board would include a woman. Maya Dodd, an Australian leader in the football/soccer movement for females, volunteered for three years in a nonvoting position on FIFA. When it came time to vote for the "most qualified" woman to serve on the executive board in Asia, the board voted 27–15 against Dodd. In her place, they chose a Bangladeshi woman who needed three guesses before she could name the winner of the 2016 Women's World Cup, and who had recently forbidden her national team players from speaking with the press. This vote was significant because it was a vote against a powerful woman who was demonstrably the most qualified and the most interested in the advancement of female athletes. Instead, the vote went for a yes-woman who the committee could use as a token female, knowing she would vote with them every time. She was much more likely to go with the status quo rather than take action to make real changes for women in the sport of football/soccer. [16]

Dodd's defeat was a wake-up call for women in sport everywhere. FIFA's decision not to vote her onto the board is indicative of how far we still have to go when it comes to fighting for qualified female leaders who prioritize women's rights in sport.

WOMEN IN NATIONAL LEADERSHIP ROLES

With the recent rise of the Time's Up and #MeToo movements in the United States, it's become clear that female athletes face a multitude of gender equity problems that need addressing by women in governance and significant leadership roles. Somehow, male athletes are still provided privilege and preference over females, and men in positions of power have failed to take the actions needed to address and protect such female-specific issues as sexual assault and abuse at the local, national, and international levels.

The USOC is a prime example of this failure of action. Where are the female leaders who will protect female athletes? For eight years, the USOC was headed by Scott Blackmun, who, during his time as CEO, acted as if the reports of sexual abuse that were coming out were unimportant. Reports surfaced as early as 2010, in USA Swimming, and 2015, regarding Dr. Larry Nassar in USA Gymnastics. Blackmun, however, focused his attention on money and medals rather than the safety of female athletes. His neglect of their safety borders on criminal. When he heard of complaints against Nassar in 2015, he failed to even notify Michigan State University of the reported abuses.

At the close of Nassar's conviction, public pressure to replace Blackmun and Steve Penny, head of USA Gymnastics, increased. Two female senators, Joni Ernst (R-Iowa) and Jeanne Shaheen (D-New Hampshire), called on Blackmun to step down following a *Wall Street Journal* report about Blackmun's neglect of the claims. Blackmun ultimately resigned. Since he resigned in February 2018, a series of interim presidents have resigned. Sarah Hirshland became the USOC's first female CEO. In March 2019, Christine Walshe was appointed president of the U.S. Olympic and Paralympic Foundation. Team Integrity has taken Hirshland to task about better protection for its athletes, especially the harassment and abuse of women in sport. According to Hogshead-Makar,

> Team Integrity (an offshoot of the Committee to Restore Integrity to the USOC) is saying that the USOC board and senior leadership should resign because they were negligent in performing their due diligence in numerous ways. . . . The policies they adopted required them to knowingly ignore the interests of America's athletes, including their health, their well-being, their sexual safety.

As a major female leader in sport, Hogshead-Makar has taken the USOC to task about their accountability for protecting female athletes. This is an issue that they've shown negligence toward in the past. The issue of inequality for and abuse of women will no doubt be better addressed by USOC with a woman at its helm, but will she seriously consider the demands of Team Integrity? That remains to be seen. We need more leaders like Hogshead-Makar who are willing to stand up for fair treatment for female athletes.

Examples of recommendations of Team Integrity are as follows:

Provide for athletic representation on USOC board.
Give athletes improved whistle-blower and retaliation protections.
Demand that National Governing Bodies (NGBs) are in compliance with the Sports Act and USOC bylaws.
Give athletes the same due process as NGBs.
Protect American athletes' opportunities to compete.
Create an athlete advocate position.[17]

The National Olympic Committee of Zambia (NOCZ) had a long-term female president from 2005 to 2016, Miriam Moyo. She was the first woman to become chair of an international affiliate of the IOC. Often labeled the "iron lady," her credentials were strong. She was a businesswoman and a national team field hockey player. Prior to her presidency, she served as the secretary general of the NOCZ for three years. Zambia, a relatively small African nation, demonstrated how women can lead well. "The National Olympic Committee of Zambia (NOCZ), is proof that women can lead, make a difference, and succeed in a male-dominated, traditional environment," says Nicole LaVoi in her book *Women in Sports Coaching.*[18] During the same period, the NOCZ selected a female secretary general of sports, Hazel Kennedy, who also served as president of the Zambia Hockey Association.

One of the major achievements of Miriam Moyo's time as president of the NOCZ was rallying the IOC, in partnership with Zambia, to build the Olympic Youth Development Centre (OYDC) in Lusaka. Lusaka is the capital of and largest city in Zambia, and this project has become the country's largest center for sport development. It provides "sport and community development opportunities for young people and underserved segments of the population from the surrounding communities." It also focuses on community development services, Olympic education, girls' empowerment, and other health services. The project became operational in May 2010, and continues to enrich the community with sports training, practice, and education. The center is the flagship project for the IOC's Sport for Hope Program.[19]

Examples like these demonstrate that women leaders of sports organizations can be successful. Moyo was more invested in encouraging and supporting the positive qualities and respect female athletes deserve than her male predecessors. When her presidency ended, her parting words were, "My appeal is, let's respect each other knowing that at the end we will need to work together."[20] In comparison to the NOCZ, USOC lags far behind; it did not appoint a permanent female president or CEO until 2018.

On another right note, the Indiana Pacers hired the first female National Basketball Association (NBA) assistant general manager, which was announced on Monday, December 17, 2018. Kelly Krauskopf was a longtime WNBA executive (17 years) as president and GM of the Indiana Fever. She commented, "My past experience has shown me that building winning teams and elite-level culture is not based on gender—it is based on people and processes."[21]

Female leadership in sport sorely lags behind that of the general working world. As more female leaders emerge, the younger generation of women will see more role models in sport leadership. Through the female's natural tendency to connect, we look to the girls in sport to stand up and shout out their right to receive greater equality. As Michele Roberts so aptly put it, "When you get in the room, try to own the room."

ACTION STEPS FOR INCREASING THE NUMBERS OF FEMALE LEADERS IN SPORT

1. Mentor young female athletes.
2. Provide information about assisting young female athletes in becoming leaders.
3. Create new programs for girls and women in sport from every socioeconomic background to learn leadership skills.
4. Teach girls strategic planning skills.

5. Open up new internships and jobs for girls in sport to pursue during and beyond the college years.
6. Create workshops meant to build confidence in girls and women to take on the skills needed for leadership in sport.
7. Create and teach workshops for female athletes to learn collaboration.
8. Teach girls to speak up and shout out for what they believe in.

2

SHOW US THE MONEY

Striving for Pay and Funding Equity

When I joined four teammates in filing a wage-discrimination complaint against U.S. Soccer late last month, it had nothing to do with how much I love to play for my country. It had everything to do with what's right and what's fair and upholding a fundamental American concept: Equal pay for equal play.

—Carli Lloyd, U.S. women's national soccer team[1]

Girls and women in sport have struggled for years to get equal pay for equal play. In no place does society's double standard and the gender bias in the United States play out more than in the underpayment of female athletes playing and women working in sport. Despite the 1972 passage of Title IX, there remain unequal opportunities for funding girls in high school sports. In many parts of the country, high school girls are not given equal funds for all sports. There exists a vast difference in "white schools" versus schools heavily populated with "girls of color." Only within the last few years have women begun to stand up to demand change. Since then, however, numerous examples of women in sport not allowing men to intimidate them have emerged. Despite encountering barrier after barrier, they are fighting back and persevering to make sure these issues of inequity in sport are dealt with.

In March 2016, the U.S. women's national soccer team filed a lawsuit against USA Soccer. A focus of the suit was the significantly lower pay the women were receiving in comparison to the men's national team. Despite winning the World Cup in 2015, the team as a whole received only $2 million that year. In 2014, by contrast, the men's team received $9 million despite having only reached round 16.

The major excuse given for not paying equally is that women's sports teams are unable to draw a crowd and acquire major advertising sponsors; however, FIFA did manage to pick up 20 major sponsors for the 2015 Women's World Cup, including Nationwide Insurance, Coca-Cola, Fiat, and Chevrolet, to name just a few. They also promoted the World Cup games through extensive advertising. The Women's World Cup games also drew an audience of more than 24 million—as many watchers as garnered by the NBA Finals. In other words, the sponsors who took a chance on these games were rewarded. This was the largest audience for any soccer game (women's or men's) ever televised in the United States. Clearly, these female athletes had no trouble drawing a crowd.

Nancy Hogshead-Makar and Trina Bolton, U.S. Department of State's Diplomacy Division of the Bureau of Educational and Cultural Affairs—managing sports programs. *Nancy Hogshead-Makar, JD*

Despite the success of the U.S. women's national soccer team, FIFA continues to show distinct misogynistic attitudes toward women's soccer throughout the world. In 2018, the (men's) World Cup was won by France, with the team receiving $38 million. In July 2019, the Women's World Cup winner received only $4 million, with plenty of excuses for not paying the women more. In addition, FIFA scheduled two major men's games on the same day as the final of the Women's World Cup. After researching and interviewing women from different cultures and countries, it appears that FIFA is one of the worst organizations in support of the development of female athletes in the world. The minimal amount they are proposing does not seem to represent an interest in developing a larger future for women's pay and numerous other issues. They are unwilling to pay women anything close to their worth.

Pay for women is slowly increasing in general, but it is also decreasing in subtle ways in women's sport. In tennis, for example, the Grand Slam tournaments and a few second-tier tournaments pay equal prize money to both women and men. There are, however, major third- and fourth-tier tournaments that pay women only 68 percent or less of what men receive. At Ohio's 2016 Western and Southern Open, they paid Roger Federer $731,000 for winning the men's overall title, while Serena Williams received only $495,000 (68 percent) for the women's overall title. In 2018, the situation was shockingly worse in the same tournament: The women's singles winner, Kiki Bertens, a Dutch woman, received only $501,976, just 49 percent to Novak Djokovic's winnings of $1,020,425. Making this all the more infuriating, runner-up Roger Federer earned $500,340, close to the prize money of the first-place woman.[2] As was suggested, maybe the promoters of this event talked themselves into thinking this dramatic decrease would go unnoticed. This is especially outrageous given the efforts of women in sport to improve prize money for females.

In basketball, the average WNBA salary is $75,000, while the average NBA salary is $5 million. WNBA TV viewership, meanwhile, has increased. NBA players receive from 70 to 90 times more pay than WNBA players, although the women continue to fight for additional pay and benefits.

One bright spot for women's pay in professional sport is in surfing: The newly restructured World Surf League plans to pay women and men equally. In 2017, a woman with a heavy resume in sports marketing, Sophie Goldschmidt, became the league's first female CEO. With Goldschmidt at the helm, women surfers have benefited. But these kinds of gains are too few and far between. The time has arrived for more sports to get onboard with valuing women equally to men.

IMPACT OF UNEQUAL FUNDS FOR GIRLS AND BOYS IN HIGH SCHOOL ATHLETICS

In September 2018, the Oakland School District in Oakland, California, was jolted by the district's announcement that 10 sports were being eliminated. "Oakland Unified School District recently offered an extreme example when it eliminated sports' programs to save money, ignoring a disproportionate impact on girls, according to civil rights attorneys," reported the *San Francisco Chronicle*.[3] As is often the case, girls were more heavily impacted by these "eliminations"; half the girls' sports in the school district were cut, including golf, tennis, lacrosse, and badminton. Twice as many girls (347) were affected as boys (183), without a thought given to Title IX's requirement that girls and boys remain equal in their educational endeavors and money distributions. Many of the young women were minorities. Luckily, an anonymous donor contributed enough money to cover the cost of fall tennis and golf.[4]

Next, a major sport franchise, the Oakland Raiders, came to the rescue with a $250,000 donation; however, the fact that Title IX was not even considered in this high school reorganization of sports is deeply concerning, as is the fact that the female high school athletes in this district counting on college sports scholarships were completely ignored when the initial decision was made to cut these programs.

A National Women's Law Center analysis of Department of Education data from 2012 revealed that girls in almost 4,500 public high schools in the United States still face huge inequalities in sport. This accounts for a fourth of all public high schools. There are six states where large gender gaps exist in half of all public schools, with Georgia, where two-thirds of high schools show significant gaps between girls' and boys' sports when it comes to money, facilities, and equipment access, ranking as the worst state for gender inequities. A host of other Southern states, including South Carolina, Tennessee, Alabama, Mississippi, and Louisiana, are doing little better than Georgia. Most of these schools have large populations of lower-income and minority students—students who especially need sports.[5] Without money budgeted for girls' sports, girls encounter dramatically fewer opportunities for access to sports.

Inner-city girls struggle the most to gain equal access to sport, unless they happen to show strong abilities and are noticed by a coach or other sporting official. This is partly a result of poor funding for sports in inner-city schools. In the African American community, one of the easiest sports to participate in, due to low cost and access, is basketball. I interviewed Kisha Ford-Torres, a former WNBA player, who grew up in inner-city Baltimore. She spoke of her mother, a supportive and hard-working woman, who encouraged her in sports and everything else throughout her life, as being her biggest inspiration.

Kisha's journey began at age eight, when she began learning the game of basketball from her brother. She eventually went on to play basketball with her brother and his friends, an activity that became an important respite from the violence and crime that were a part of her environment as a child growing up in a tough neighborhood.

In high school, a coach recognized and nurtured Kisha's talent on the court. In describing her high school coach, who was a white woman, Kisha remarked, "She loved me like a daughter." Kisha was lucky to encounter solid, nonprejudiced, and nonabusive coaches. Due to the low cost of playing basketball—a "traditional" African American sport— and the special interest of a coach, Kisha was able to play her sport at the highest level. Not all female athletes of color are so fortunate.

In yet another analysis of girls' high school sports, the National Women's Law Center joined partners with the Poverty and Race Research Action Council. They came to the conclusion that "schools with high concentrations of minority and low-income students . . . tend to have much larger gender disparities in sports participation than do schools serving majority-white populations."[6]

Even in nonmetropolitan areas, girls are often frustrated by the lack of access to sports in high school due to poor funding or money meant for girls' sports being misdirected, especially to the benefit of boys' sports. One such high school girl, Emma Hastie, wrote an article in the *Buffalo News* in 2017, describing her own experiences being denied access to sports. She spoke of inequality in her area's high schools, writing, "Many girls (still) feel as if they're not being respected or treat-ed like their male counterparts in an environment in which everyone, male or female, should feel as though they have been given an equal opportunity."[7] Issues Emma heard about from other girls included lack of acknowledgment, second-rate uniforms and equipment, more advan-tages for boys than girls, and the belief that girls are the weaker sex, among others. One of the most unsettling examples of neglect of girls' sports and abuse in terms of monetary issues came when two Orchard Park high school rugby players noted that their team received no recog-nition from the school for their accomplishments, but the school re-ceived money as a result of the team's endeavors, benefitting the school. At the same time, the female rugby team saw none of the mon-ey. Moreover, the girls stated, "We cannot promote or ask girls from the school to join our team because our principal told us we couldn't be-cause our team isn't a school sport. With that in mind, our trophies are housed in the front foyer for all to see."[8] This misappropriation of message and money repeatedly rears its ugly head.

In looking at high school girls in sport, the statistics tell part of the story. For example, the number of female high school students partici-pating in sport went from 32 out of 100 girls in the 1999–2000 school year to 41 out of 100 girls in the 2009–2010 school year, as compared to boys, who went from 43 out of 100 to 53 out of 100, respectively. Girls still receive significantly fewer opportunities in sport within the context of urban, town, and rural settings due to lack of funding.

In the 2012 High School Athletics Participation Survey, the author concluded that there is

> absolutely no evidence that boys somehow lost athletic opportunities as a result of girls' gains in sport. . . . Schools with fewer resources or disproportionately higher female populations (with females compris-ing at least 55 percent of the student body) were more likely to drop sports during that time frame.[9]

The Oakland Unified School District's choice of sports to cut from the budget is a perfect example of this type of situation.

Looking at a 2015 report cowritten by the National Women's Law Center and Poverty and Race Research Action Council entitled "Girls Finishing Last: Girls of Color and School Sports Opportunities," we see huge differences when we compare primarily white high schools with primarily minority (African American, Latino, Asian, etc.) high schools. In the predominantly white schools (with *significantly* better funding), girls have a 50 percent chance to play sports. In contrast, minority high schools offer only a 20 percent chance for girls to play sports. And minority girls are penalized even further: In white high schools, girls receive 82 percent of the sport-related opportunities that boys do. In poorly funded minority schools, girls receive only 67 percent of the sport-related opportunities boys do. Minority girls are given only 39 percent of the opportunities to play sports as girls at heavily white schools. The authors conclude, "Girls of color are finishing last when it comes to opportunities to play sports in (high) school and missing out on the lifelong benefits that accompany athletic participation."[10] This is primarily caused by the unequal distribution of funds for sports, which is in direct violation of Title IX.

LACK OF MONEY IN SCHOLARSHIPS AND COLLEGES

Pay inequity does not affect only female coaches and pros. College athletic scholarships for boys and girls are dramatically different. Economics professor Dave Berri of the University of Southern Utah, for example, talks about how college basketball continues to favor male students in both exposure and scholarship dollars. At NCAA institutions, male athletes receive 36 percent more in scholarships than female athletes. Translated into actual scholarship dollars, male athletes receive 65,000 more scholarships than females, the monetary equivalent of $190 million more per year. This imbalance often hampers girls from applying for or even dreaming about receiving college scholarships. According to *HawkHeadlines* reporter Julia Swiatek, "Girls receive less sports opportunities because society treats women's sports as less important. They don't even receive similar donation rates as their male counterparts."[11] Kristi Dosh of the Business of College Sports website further writes, "Women's basketball in Southeastern Conference schools receives $1 for every $6.02 donated to men's basketball and $1 for every $67.03 donated to football."[12] This also gives the distinct impression that girls playing sports is not considered as valuable as boys playing sports.

In African American and Latino communities, girls' exposure to sports participation is restricted. In these communities, girls may be expected to work to supplement family income or take care of younger siblings, or their parents may be opposed to their daughters participating in sports. Years ago, I worked with the City College of San Francisco's women's cross-country team. This team consisted mostly of young women of color groups. One particularly talented young female Latina runner described how since high school she had faced opposition to her participation in running by her father; however; her mother and brothers were always supportive. In the end, this accomplished young athlete's talent landed her a full scholarship to Cal Berkeley, where she went on to become captain of the girls' cross-country team. It was only then that her father began to see the financial and practical value of her participation in sports.

Oftentimes the money donated to college football teams allows other university sports programs, notably a number of men's sports, to continue. As Nicole LaVoi, codirector of the Tucker Center for Research on Girls and Women in Sport, said in an interview, "Most schools have lower budgets for women college athletes." Women's basketball and volleyball programs tend to receive decent funds, but other women's sports do not. This vastly unequal funding impacts such areas as team facilities, uniforms and equipment, travel, female coaching salaries, and much more.

Once again, the stats tell the story. According to the Women's Sports Foundation, 57 percent of college students are female. Yet, these young women receive only 43 percent of athletic participation opportunities at NCAA schools, probably due to limited funding. Furthermore, only 45 percent of NCAA funds are allocated to female athletes. Specifically, college women's teams are given only 40 percent of the available operating money and a mere 36 percent of available funding for recruiting.[13] Those wishing to continue participating in sports and/or working with sports will discover that these opportunities are limited, although there have been increases in hiring females in sport.

PROFESSIONAL SPORTS

When you look at the primary sports in which female athletes have made significant progress in pay—basketball, tennis, soccer, and ice hockey—you still see great disparities in pay between female and male athletes. In 2013, Megan Rapinoe, a member of the U.S women's national soccer team, took a year off from playing in the United States to play for a French team, partially due to the much higher pay she received, at $150,000 for the year. This is a common occurrence for pro female athletes. In golf, the Professional Golfers' Association (PGA) Tour prize money is much more than the prize money for the Ladies Professional Golf Association (LPGA). The winner of the 2018 Masters, Patrick Reed, won $1.98 million, while 76th ranked Angela Stanford received $577,500 when she won the Evian Championship that same year. This amounted to a negligible differential of "only" $1,402,500 between the two players—amounting to almost three and a half times as much money for Reed.

In the WNBA, there have been ongoing issues regarding players' salaries. The estimate that NBA salaries are 50 to 70 times higher than WNBA salaries allows for an incredible margin.

David Berri is a sports economist from Southern Utah University who specializes in the WNBA and National Pro Fastpitch sports. He believes that the economics of women's sport are never explained thoroughly enough and therefore are misunderstood by many. He makes two important points about establishing sports: Building a fan base takes decades, and creating an emotional attachment to a sport takes equally long. There is a clear double standard in the sports world. Women's worth is heavily devalued. Girls and women athletes are often viewed as less-than.

Berri asserts that the NBA administration doesn't appear to care about improving the WNBA's financial situation. From his perspective, the NBA could easily address the matter by contributing an additional $12 million to the budget. Consider the situation: The starting salary of many NBA players is well higher than $12 million. NBA players earn 50 percent of revenues, whereas WNBA players (even the most talented of them) earn only 22 percent, according to Berri.[14]

One complicating factor is the fact that the public tends to focus on the most negative, rather than the most positive, aspects of women's sports. Men frequently make "negative statements" about female athletes without any real evidence to back up those statements. Still, despite the criticism it receives, the WNBA is increasing its viewership. Indeed, the 21-year-old league hit a new high in 2018, with its 12 teams reaching 1,574,078 viewers, for an average attendance of 7,716. In 2018, the situation improved even further with an increased viewership of 35 percent between the ESPN and NBATV channels, and merchandise sales increasing by 50 percent.[15] In fact, the league has increased its social activism since the election of Donald Trump as president, which is thought to have contributed to these increases. The NBA didn't draw crowds of this size until its 26th season, when the league averaged 8,061 fans per game.

The WNBA's average salary is about $75,000, topping out at $113,500 for veteran players. WNBA players deserve respect, admiration, and vastly improved salaries for the hard work they put in—hard work that equals that of their male counterparts.[16]

There is a myth that in tennis, tournaments offer equal pay to women and men. While it is true that the four Grand Slam tournaments offer equal prize money to both women and men, there's a vast differentiation according to tournaments. Equal compensation is the exception rather than the rule. What's quietly ignored is that many tennis tournaments do not offer equal (or even comparable) prize money for women. In actuality, women receive equal prize money *only* at the Grand Slams and a few other tournaments. Wimbledon became the last Grand Slam to agree to equal purses for women and men in 2007, and that was largely due to the efforts of Venus Williams. The 2013 documentary *Venus Vs.* tells the little-known story of how Williams took on the All England Club and basically shamed the old boys into awarding the female tennis players the same payout as their male counterparts.[17]

Prize money is not the only area in which tennis suffers from gender discrepancies. Sponsorships can also make up a significant amount of the financial difference. In 2015, Serena Williams, with a strong, muscled body and plenty of curves, brought in $13 million in endorsements as opposed to Maria Sharapova, a white, thin, blond player, who brought in $23 million. Racial/body discrimination likely played a role in this striking difference. Despite this, Williams has consistently had the backing of Nike and was the most marketable female in 2018. This keeps her in the top 100 pro athletes in terms of money earned—with the exception of 2017, when she took time off to have a baby. That year, there were zero women on the list. [18]

Pay inequity permeates every women's pro sport (except surfing), including prizes and sponsorships, as we've seen in U.S. professional soccer. A good comparison to make is Sydney Leroux, a 2015 U.S. women's national soccer team striker versus Jozy Altidore, a 2015 striker for the U.S. men's national soccer team. When you compare stats, Leroux scored 35 goals in only 12 international games, whereas Altidore scored 21 goals in 80 international games. Given these stats alone, one might assume that Leroux earned a greater income; however, Leroux, as a member of the team that won the 2015 Women's World Cup, earned $92,000, with sponsorships, while Altidore, who was not part of a winning World Cup team, had an income of $6 million, not including sponsorships. In fact, that same year, he returned to the North American market and was offered a $30 million, five-year contract with Toronto FC.

In 2017, after an extended and difficult negotiation, the U.S. women's national soccer team came to terms with U.S. Soccer in a new collective bargaining agreement extending through 2021. "We want to play in top-notch, grass-only facilities like the U.S. men's national team," said player Alex Morgan after the agreement was made. "We want to have equitable and comfortable travel accommodations, and we simply want equal treatment." [19] The agreement addressed the pay issue by increasing the base pay by more than 30 percent and giving players back pay for two years' worth of unequal per-diem payments. Match bonuses were also increased, with additional funds to be paid based on World Cup or Olympic participation; however, the women's national team players had hoped to reach pay equity with the men's national team, and even with this new agreement, they have yet to achieve anything close to that goal. [20]

Five remaining players—Hope Solo, Carli Lloyd, Alex Morgan, Megan Rapinoe, and Becky Sauerbrunn—have an outstanding wage-discrimination action filed against the U.S. Soccer Federation with the Equal Employment Opportunity Commission on the issue of equal pay for equal play. When Solo's contract with the national team was not renewed, she filed another suit in U.S. District Court in August 2018, for only herself, against the federation, focused on the lack of equality in pay for the women's and men's national teams for "similar work." [21]

The U.S. women's national soccer team, although they now have a much-improved contract with the U.S. Soccer Federation, will need to fight for equal pay and for the federation to keep up their end of the contract in the years to come, despite the fact that there is a noticeable distinction between the abilities of the U.S. men's national team, which didn't even qualify for the 2018 World Cup, and the U.S. women's national team, which won the 2019 Women's World Cup. As the Equal Employment Opportunity Commission (EEOC) looks on, we continue to see them delay their decisions regarding the lawsuit brought about by the five women's national team players. Even though the 2015 Women's World Cup was watched by more than 25 million viewers and was the most-watched soccer game (women's or men's) in U.S. history, the gender discrimination and bias in pay for women still controls the outcome. Even more shocking was the amount the women's team was paid for winning the 2015 World Cup. Their reward was a mere $2 million, whereas in 2014, the winning men's team took home $38 million. FIFA is now—apparently due to outside pressure—promising to "significantly" raise more money for prizes in the upcoming Women's World Cup. The men in the 2022 World Cup in Qatar, meanwhile, will be sharing $440 million—a $40 million increase—in prize money. Maya Dodd, a former FIFA council member, commented, "FIFA should increase the women's prize fund by at least the same $40 million raise in men's total prize money from 2018 to 2022."[22] But this is an organization with an extremely poor record of including women on their boards who vote and/or truly care about taking any real action to promote women's soccer. As mentioned earlier, for the 2019 Women's World Cup, they paid only $4 million to the winner. Thus, their stance remains the same, showing no real progress.

When you think the situation can't get any worse, you need only look at the struggles the U.S. women's national ice hockey team has experienced in its efforts to get sufficient and improved investment in their team. In addition to winning the Olympic gold medal in Pyeongchang and the inaugural game in 1998, the team has also won three silver medals and one bronze since women's ice hockey became part of the Olympic Games in 1998. The team has also won the last four world championships. Despite these wins and their powerhouse status, however, the team's members were paid a pittance—only $6,000 every four years—until April 2017, when the team told the Ice Hockey Federation they were planning to boycott the world championships. These brave young women put their careers on the line. The federation tried to get replacement players, but dozens of college players and even some high school players turned down their recruitment efforts, in some cases in a public format. About half of the team members had to hold down second and third jobs or obtain monetary support from their families to cover their basic needs.

The differences between the travel expenses, food, equipment, and publicity they received and what the men's team was provided with were startling. The men's national team also threatened to boycott their world championships. Soon thereafter, the National Hockey League Players' Association and the Major League Baseball Players' Association released statements supporting the women's national hockey team. In addition, 16 senators, both women and men, sent a letter to the executive director of USA Hockey expressing their concerns about paying the team members a mere $6,000 every four years. Billie Jean King also contacted the team's captain, Megan Duggan, and offered to provide even more assistance.[23] Finally, after the public outcry and support, USA Hockey finally promised to provide reasonable movement on the major issues.

As a result of the support the women's national ice hockey team received, USA Hockey and the national team arrived at an acceptable deal. The landmark four-year deal included the creation of a women's high-performance advisory group made up of current and former players to make recommendations on marketing, scheduling, public relations, and further promotion of the women's game. Further details of the plan include the following:

A monthly stipend of $4,000 per player paid for by the USOC and USA Hockey

Bonuses paid for by USA Hockey for Olympic medals, including $20,000 per player for gold and $15,000 per player for silver, in addition to USOC monetary rewards

Travel and insurance coverage to match the coverage provided to the men's team

A foundation to support girls' developmental teams[24]

In the 2018 Winter Olympics, the U.S. women's team showed their strength by winning the gold medal after a 20-year drought. The fighting spirit displayed by these sports teams serves as a model for girls and women in sport that strides can be made in achieving pay equity when teams implement strong strategies in pursuit of improvement. Both the women's national soccer and ice hockey teams have led the way in standing up to their federations, which are primarily run by men. Hopefully, the light these teams are shining on inequity in sport, as well as the hard-fought results they've gotten, will inspire others to take further action. Pushing for better pay in women's sport must be a continuous battle, and it requires patience and perseverance. It wasn't until their backs were pushed into a corner that the women's national ice hockey team was able to exert enough influence to create change. Still, they have shown that female athletes will support and respect one another's efforts to gain greater equality.

Our discussion would not be complete without mentioning the lawsuit filed by senior associate athletic director Jane Meyer against the University of Iowa in 2014, in a landmark case that brought attention to the drastic differences in pay between female and male administrators. Jane Meyer happened to be the highest-ranking woman in the University of Iowa's athletic department at the time. Meyer is the partner of Tracey Griesbaum, the university's former assistant coach and later head coach of field hockey. Griesbaum was fired without cause in 2014. According to Meyer, she directly asked, "Why did we fire our best coach?"

During this time, the athletic director, Gary Barta, was hiring to fill a newly created position for a deputy athletic director. Meyer was told not to apply. She had some of her duties taken away before ultimately finding out that Barta was paying the man in this parallel position $70,000 more than she was making. In addition, her relationship with Griesbaum was questioned. Barta had parents of female student athletes questioning him about the relationship between the two women, implying that they had an "improper relationship." They had been partners for more than 10 years, and up until this point no issues had been raised.

In addition to pay inequity, gender and sexual orientation bias clearly came into play here. Because of this and speaking the truth, Meyer was transferred out of the athletics department and eventually fired. In a discussion with Griesbaum and Meyer's attorney, Thomas Newkirk, his observation was that, in this case, as is typical, women are devalued, while men are overvalued, by both men and women in the world of sport, by administrators, coaches, and players. In Meyer's case, the complaints were related to gender and sexual orientation issues. Meyer received $4 million after a lengthy court battle. Discrimination on the basis of gender or sexual orientation should have no role in decisions to hire and fire female coaches, whether at the high school, college, pro, or Olympic levels.

During a discussion of the case with Newkirk, he commented, "This case provides progress in the areas of equal pay and gender bias." But, he said this is just a start, adding, "We continue to devalue women's participation in sport and overvalue men's." Oftentimes, even if a woman works harder as an administrator, she is not given the credit she is due, particularly when it comes to pay. Too many people continue to believe, whether consciously or not, that women are not equal to men in sport and should not receive equal pay. This is particularly unjust given that female American athletes began getting more medals than male American athletes in the Olympics starting in 2008, and continuing into 2012, 2016, and 2018. In 2018, the current president of the Women's Sports Foundation, bobsledder Elana Meyers Taylor, commented about her silver medal, saying, "To win our medal on the same day as some of these incredible women, it was, yes, girl power, women roar, it was such a magical day."[25]

A shining example of someone fighting for pay equity in sport is cyclocross and mountain bike champion Georgia Gould, who captured a bronze medal for the United States in the women's cross-country mountain bike race in the 2012 Summer Olympics. She has always been conscious of the importance of supporting other young female mountain bike riders in both words and action. During her active years racing, her goal was to be a positive role model for other young women mountain bike and cyclocross racers. She made a focused effort to speak to other young females before and after races.

After one race in Colorado, Gould was speaking to the male winner of a cyclocross race, and he mentioned in passing that they had both won good money. Gould was confused, since she had only won $250. When she inquired about his prize money, he shared that he had been awarded $2,500. Her shock at this discovery motivated her to circulate a petition about this vast discrepancy in prize money. A number of people were unaware of this inequality in pay, and the petition got almost 3,000 signatures—a high number considering that the sport was relatively small at the time. Amazingly, the cyclocross promoters took note and agreed to pay women equal prize money. This was first implemented in Europe thanks to the initiative of Georgia Gould.

Proceeding several steps further, Gould was voted to be a rep for the general athletes committee of UCI Mountain Bikes Worldwide. During her tenure on this committee, however, she believed little was accomplished. A few years later, the head of the UCI committee asked her to join his collegial committee, which until then had included only men. As the only woman on the committee, Gould stepped up and raised the issue of the wide gap between prize money awarded to men versus women. Gould felt listened to and heard by the rest of the men on the committee, and the group unanimously agreed to recommend to UCI that award money be given equally to women and men. "I just chipped away," Gould later explained. "Hopefully, other bike disciplines can use mountain bike prize money as an example." Through the use of her voice and notoriety, Gould raised awareness for fair pay and equality. A mentor and role model, this female athlete represents what elite and pro female athletes can do to improve the gender bias in pay.

SPORTS MATTER

Despite the passage of Title IX, girls' high school sport throughout the country continues to lack sufficient funding without any real enforcement of Title IX. The benefit of sports participation can last a lifetime. Through sports, girls learn to value themselves more highly—but only if they're treated fairly. The earlier example of the female rugby team whose funds were being diverted elsewhere is illustrative of the often-dismissive stance taken toward girls' sport. Oftentimes, girls' sport in low-income areas suffers the most, especially in the Southern states. Work needs to continue at the local and regional levels to educate coaches, parents, teachers, and other personnel about the value of girls to sport and the value of sport to girls. This is especially true with minority girls and women.

In college, the stakes get much higher, with scholarships and careers at stake. Young women, particularly minorities, have fewer opportunities than young men to get college scholarships by a total of $190 million. Furthermore, the many young women who play college sports and want to stay in sports beyond college as athletes, coaches, administrators, researchers, and other actors in the sport world often don't realize just how limited their opportunities still are.

There has been visible progress in gender equity in sport in both professional and Olympic sports. Through challenging the status quo, professional teams and courageous individuals are pledging to directly challenge inequality in pay. Thanks to the World Surfing League, the U.S. women's national soccer team, the U.S. women's national hockey team, Venus Williams, Tracey Griesbaum, Jane Meyer, Georgia Gould, and others, we're starting to see women stand up for themselves and demand equal pay. This is only the beginning of the journey toward equal pay, but it's a start.

ACTION STEPS FOR INCREASING GENDER EQUITY IN SPORT

1. Demand greater transparency. In each sport, ask for the salaries of female versus male athletes. If there is resistance, push harder.
2. Challenge the pay of female athletes with the EEOC.
3. Educate the public about the unequal treatment of women in the sport world.
4. Write articles and op-eds about inequities in pay in the sporting world.
5. Push for recognition of the hard work of high school, collegiate, pro, and Olympic female athletes.

3

HONORING OUR WOMEN ATHLETES

Where's the Media Coverage?

Sports are a great place to show that equality can happen.
—Venus Williams, American tennis player and
winner of multiple Grand Slams[1]

Media coverage of female sports is abysmal. It's almost as if they don't exist. And even when female athletes do receive media coverage, it is not always focused on the athletes themselves. This was evident in the coverage of the 2016 Rio Olympics, where, although there was a marked increase in coverage of women's sports, women were frequently mentioned primarily in relationship to the men in their lives. And rarely do you see much coverage of any girls' and women's sport beyond the Olympics, although if you search the cable networks, you will find that the coverage is slightly improving.

Lack of reporting on female Olympians in prime time continued in the 2018 Pyeongchang Olympics, where the women representing the U.S. team once again won more medals than the men, received the first gold medal in the team sprint in a cross-country skiing event and the first medal since 1976, and won the gold in ice hockey. In the cross-country skiing competition, women won two medals (both gold) but received only one hour and 37 minutes of coverage, in contrast to the men, who received five hours and 31 minutes of coverage.

Despite these incredible successes by women at the 2018 Games, the prime time coverage on television was still more focused on men.

Overall, women received only 32 percent of the coverage through the first 10 days.[2] And following the Olympics, coverage of most women's sports, except tennis, the LPGA, and the WNBA, dropped to virtually nothing. According to Lebel and Danlchuk (2009), women's sports are often regarded as "less exciting and slower" than men's sports.[3] When the relatively new start-up sports media website the Athletic was confronted about their lack of coverage of women's sports by Cheryl Reeves, coach of the Minnesota Lynx, the owners, Alex Maher and Adam Hansmann, simply responded that they would add coverage of the Lynx when the season started. These owners are not offering "full access to all sports," as their advertising suggests. Instead, they are leaving out a huge segment of our culture. They are missing half of the story by omitting women's sports and not truly giving "full access to all sports."

We need to pressure sites like the Athletic that act as if women's sports are not important and do not exist into including women's sports, making it clear that failure to do so will result in a boycott. Women make up 43 percent of sports participants, and 49 percent of women identify as sports fans; this is an audience that deserves serious attention.

The Tucker Center's research on coverage of girls and women in sport has concluded that there is only about 4 percent coverage of female athletes by sports media and estimated that television coverage is as low as 1 percent. In a 2010 study focused on ESPN's SportsCenter and three Los Angeles networks, Scheadler and Wagstaff analyzed the coverage of women's sports. Researchers concluded that a mere 1.4 percent of SportsCenter's coverage was focused on women's sports. On the local stations, the outcome was not much better, coming in at 1.6 percent of the coverage on women's sports. The final observation was that this was the lowest rate in more than 20 years. Unfortunately, this pathetic coverage contributes to the public's waning interest in women's sports and becomes a self-fulfilling prophecy.[4] The lack of promotion of women's sport partly contributes to poor coverage in the media.

"As of 2014, 90 percent of editorial roles, 90 percent of assistant editorial roles, 88 percent of columnists, 87 percent of reporters, and 95 percent of anchors are men. Of the 183 sport talk shows, there are only two female hosts."[5] These stark statistics from Washington State University demonstrate what minimal power women hold in contributing to the reporting of girls' and women's sports. With these stats in mind, the lack of reporting on women's sports is not surprising. Our power of persuasion is extremely limited. More women need to step into positions of leadership to further promote women's sports.

According to the 2017 annual report by the Women's Media Center, women are slowly creeping up in sports story bylines. In 2015, women had 10 percent of sports bylines. This increased to 11.5 in 2016. On the downside, the number of female assistant sports editors working for newspapers and websites has greatly declined, from 17.2 percent to 9.8 percent in the United States and Canada, according to the Associated Press Sports Editor Racial and Gender Report Card, partially facilitated by Richard Lapchick, director of the Institute for Diversity and Ethics in Sports at the University of Central Florida. This report card "analyzed 1,726 sports editors, columnists, reporters, copy editors, and designers at those publications. . . . The decline in female assistant sports editors was one of the most stark [sic] reminders of the gender gap among sports journalists."[6] There are those in the media striving to change these imbalances. In the United States, the Association for Women in Sports Media (AWSM) is a nonprofit advocacy volunteer organization working to mentor women to enter the sports reporting field by gaining visibility through publishing, editing, broadcast and production, and public and media relations. Their members are both female and male, and support women's greater participation in sports media.

In 2018, despite the lack of coverage, Nielsen sports analysts who surveyed women and men sports fans from eight countries—the United States, United Kingdom, New Zealand, Australia, France, Spain, Germany, and Italy—noted more enthusiasm for women's sport than the media recognizes or acknowledges. The study surveyed 1,000 people from each country. Surprisingly, the report discovered that as many as 84 percent of sports fans expressed interest in women's sport. The breakdown showed that 49 percent of females and 51 percent of males were intrigued by women's sport. When looking at women's sport, they noted that 50 percent of women and 44 percent of men thought of women's sport as being "competitive." In viewing inspiration by female athletes, only 41 percent of women and 31 percent of men viewed women's sport in this manner.[7] This study illustrates that the amount of interest in women's sport is much greater than the male-dominated sport world is willing to acknowledge, accept, or even address. Even in New Zealand, the media reports on women's sport 10 percent of the time for all sport reporting.

LACK OF COVERAGE OF GIRLS AND WOMEN'S SPORTS

The inconsistent and infrequent coverage of girls' and women's sport on television and in newspapers and magazines adds to the lack of information about and interest in women's sport. Even at ESPNW, the articles on women's sport highlight special interest stories but don't necessarily follow teams in an ongoing manner during their seasons. Dave Berri, sports economist, compared the top eight most popular online sports websites: Yahoo! Sports, ESPN, BleacherReport, CBSSports, Sports Illustrated, NBC Sports, SBNation, and FoxSports. His conclusion was that female athletes and leagues are consistently getting ignored. He even discovered that horses, dogs, and fish get more coverage than women's sport. Only three of the sites—BleacherReport, Yahoo! Sports, and ESPN—have a page dedicated to women's sport. Berri further notes that only 3 percent of the coverage on all eight sites is dedicated to women's sport.[8] In fact, in the latter half of 2018, ESPN covered the Cornhole Championships (throwing bean bags into holes cut into wood) rather than a woman's sport. This is not a sport, but rather a game. This lack of coverage is nowhere near enough to meet the amount of interest indicated in the Nielsen studies.

In a University of Southern California study, researchers found that there was actually less coverage of girls' and women's sport in 2014 than in 1989. One of the researchers, Michael Messner, commented,

> We've had this incredible explosion of girls and women going into sports in the last 40 years, and we've seen some improvement in the last 10 years in live TV coverage of some women's sports, like college basketball. . . . What's puzzling to us is the increased interest and participation in women's sports has not at all been reflected in the news and highlight shows.[9]

When confronted with this information, the networks use old excuses, insisting there is a lack of interest in watching women's sport. Women are not as strong, they say, and are still regarded as the weaker sex.

Dr. Dave Berri and Sylvia Fowles. *Dr. Dave Berri*

The appreciation for strong women athletes is growing. Yet, the media is still unwilling to even partially respond to it. As Cheryl Reeve, head coach of the WNBA's Minnesota Lynx, tweeted about the Athletic, "Why would a subscriber-based sports medium that claims 'full access to all sports' limit its earning potential by not covering women's sports? The Athletic does just that . . . and it's bad business."[10] This lack of coverage/acknowledgment prevents us from validating the quality and quantity of women's sports, which only serves to perpetuate the ignorance about women's real and existing interest in sport. In restricting its coverage primarily to men, the Athletic is ignoring 43 percent of participants in sport.

Reeve believes that women need to recognize and use their leverage in society. An excellent example of this came in 2017 and 2018, when the USA women's national ice hockey and soccer teams, respectively, used their muscle to garner support and demand better treatment and pay. Both teams ultimately succeeded in getting most of their demands met.[11]

The 2018 landmark Nielsen global study proves that the notion of a lack of interest in women's sports is false. The professionalism of women's sports is increasing exponentially. Yet, many male stakeholders in the sports world keep holding on to the old idea that sport is solely a men's purview. Mike Woitalia, executive editor of *Soccer America*, commented in an interview that the increased skills and professionalism that professional female soccer players demonstrate has dramatically increased in the last five to 10 years. People who take the time to watch women's professional soccer learn to appreciate the high caliber of play the U.S. women's national soccer team shows in games. This was made evident when 24 million viewers tuned in to watch the squad win the Women's World Cup in 2015.

It's baffling that the sports media, still dominated by white men, could broaden their market by featuring more women's sports, but the majority continue to provide little to no coverage in this area. These men have daughters, wives, and sisters who play sports; why aren't they listening to them? When queried about the sports media promoting women's sports, Joan Ryan, a longtime sports journalist who is now the media specialist for the San Francisco Giants, said she believes the role of journalists is to report rather than champion causes, which is the traditional stance. Yet, she is author of a revised edition of her famous *Little Girls in Pretty Boxes*, the first book to address the extensive abuses of gymnasts by their coaches and the system. I would like to challenge other members of the media—both online and print—to, at a minimum, consider writing more op-ed pieces challenging the status quo when it comes to the reporting of women's sports. An example of this is the *Huffington Post*'s 2018 op-ed article "The More Women Sports Are Covered, the More Popular They Will Be." In it, author Jessica Luther suggests that the public, men in particular, is "missing out" on the thrill of watching and cheering on female athletes whether they are girls or women. She suggests sports editors need to make room for women's sports. If more sports editors were willing to be forward thinking in this way and make room to highlight women's sport, she says, it would allow readers to develop an interest in women's performance in sport.[12]

During the last several Olympic Games, an interest was clearly demonstrated by the large numbers of fans who attended women's competitions. When looking at viewership of the Olympics, there is a dearth of information about who viewed which sports, so who is to say both women and men don't watch women's sports when given the time? The one widely watched game during the 2018 Pyeongchang Olympics, with 3.6 million viewers, was the women's ice hockey playoff between the United States and Canada.

MEDIA IMAGES

Although women make up 43 percent of sports participants, they are far more likely than male athletes to be shown in sexually provocative poses. According to a recent Nielsen report, more and more research shows that women and men prefer images of females playing competitive sport to images of them in provocative clothing. In May 2018, ESPNW put out a list of the 25 most "famous" female athletes, based primarily on their performances. This list contained such sports greats as Serena and Venus Williams in tennis, Alex Morgan in soccer, Michelle Wie in golf, and Simone Biles in gymnastics.[13] Despite a recent shift in emphasis, there are still too many websites focused on the appearances of these top women athletes as opposed to their actual performances. And, of course, the factor of whether a woman athlete is white, black, or brown impacts the coverage, sponsorships, and commentary she receives. Black women's bodies especially tend to get intensive scrutiny, with critics commenting on their "different" frames.

Body shaming frequently occurs in women's sport. We frequently see greater muscle definition and physical power in certain groups of female athletes, especially in African American women, and this frequently results in negative commentary. An example from the 2012 London Olympics is when female British heptathlete Jessica Enis, who happens to be mixed race, was criticized by a senior male British official as being "fat" due to her muscled physique. To her credit, she ended up winning the gold medal in the heptathlon. In addition, Serena Williams faces bigotry and racism each time she plays, with spectators calling her the N-word, among numerous other derogative terms. Others often diminish her body as well. According to well-known blogger (A Black Girl's Guide to Weight Loss) Erika Nicole Kendall, "As far back as 2009, a sports columnist (Jason Whitlock) wrote a scathing editorial about Williams's body, likening her derriere to food and complaining that she wasn't attractive to him because of her size."[14] Williams represents the ideal of a big, strong female athlete. Actually, many of her unique features contribute to her strength as an athlete. Unfortunately, the sports columnist's insults simply demonstrate his/her ignorance about Williams—as a player and a human being.

Body shaming in our general culture further contributes to its frequent occurrence in sports. This emphasis on appearance goes back decades. A considerable campaign has been waged to label sports as unfeminine and unsuitable for girls' and women's participation. In the 1950s, there were public campaigns to remove women from the Olympics. One writer for the New York Times even wrote, "There's just nothing feminine or enchanting about a girl with beads of perspiration on her alabaster brow, the result of grotesque contortions in events totally unsuited to female architecture."[15]

Unfortunately, femininity in the more modern day has, for far too long, focused on "good" looks and a certain type of appearance. When we look back in history, even earning two Olympic gold medals in the 1964 Toyoko Olympics and "appearing feminine" was not enough to land Donna de Varona a college scholarship as a young woman in a pre–Title IX world. She would, however, go on to become the first female sports reporter on the Wild World of Sports in the 1960s.

I, too, experienced this type of stigma as a young woman. In 1969, I tried out for the first women's cross-country team at my high school. I was wildly ecstatic when I made the team. Not long thereafter, however, my hopes were dashed; I was not allowed to participate because my parents thought running wasn't "ladylike."

All too often, female athletes' style and bodies are depicted as "male." The *Guardian* did a piece that describes various sportswriters' comments showing sexist, racist, and body bias in reference to women athletes. Such athletes as former tennis players Amelie Mauresmo and Martina Navratilova were criticized more for their sexual preferences and physiques than their actual tennis skills. Meanwhile, WNBA player Brittney Griner, who is famous for her dunking skills, was labeled a "man" for her 6-foot-9 frame. Her response? "Hey, that's my body, and I look the way I look."[16]

A University of Cambridge study found that women in sports are still viewed with a lack of seriousness when compared to men. "The . . . language around women in sport focuses on the appearance, clothes, and personal lives of women, highlighting a greater emphasis on aesthetics over athletics."[17] One of the largest dilemmas for female athletes is this continued focus on appearance over performance in the media. The study reviewed a cumulative 160 million words about sports in newspapers, academic papers, tweets, and blogs. Words frequently used to describe women are "aged, older, pregnant, married, or unmarried." Men, in contrast, are described as "fast, strong, big, real, and great." Men are three times more likely to be mentioned in a sporting context in a positive way. Women are disproportionately described in relation to their marital status, age, or appearance, as mentioned earlier. Additionally, when looking at the concept of performance, women's associative words, including "compete, participate, and strive," are softer and not as strong as those associated with men athletes, which typically include "mastermind, beat, win, dominate, and battle."[18]

A little more than two years ago, an eight-year-old girl, Mili Hernandez, was kicked out of the Springfield Invitational in Nebraska, along with her entire soccer team, simply because she had short hair and "looked like a boy." Her team had just advanced to the finals at the invitational. She had accidentally been listed as a boy on the club roster, so the coach warned her father to bring documentation of her sex. At some point during the tournament someone reported that a boy was playing on a girls' team. Mili's father produced her birth certificate and other forms of ID, but to no avail. The tournament president refused to accept any of the documentation that Mili was a female. Mili, the youngest player on her team, began crying when the organizers stated that she looked like a boy; she didn't understand why her entire team had gotten kicked out. Her coach, Mario Torres, believes this incident involved both gender and race discrimination. Nonetheless, Mili received plenty of support following the incident: Her teammates offered to cut their hair short, and former pro soccer players Mia Hamm and Abby Wambach reached out to her as well. Apologies were extended, but little else occurred.[19]

This considerable emphasis on the looks of female athletes continues to pervade our sporting culture. In recent years, there have been some slight changes. Elana Meyers Taylor, a three-time Olympic medalist, pro bobsledder, and president of the Women's Sports Foundation, was featured alongside three U.S. ice hockey players, Hilary Knight and the Lamoureux twins, in Xfinity ads before and throughout the 2018 Olympics. Taylor is big, strong, and fast. Knight and the twins are also bigger and stronger girls. They are all Olympic medalists. In the ads, they appear in bobsled and hockey uniforms. The question, however, remains: Where would these ads have gone without the Olympic sphere of influence? These women are not the traditional skinny-blond-model type; rather, each one shows the strength and power that is an essential part of participating in sports as women. For a moment, while those ads were running, there was a glimmer of hope that the media might start focusing on another type of female athlete and provide a broader view of females who participate in sports. These types of ads need to continue to model and highlight the diversity of females who participate in sport at every level.

Going backward in time to the 2016 Rio Olympics, a number of reporters wrote about the female Olympians as if they didn't exist and were of lesser importance than their male counterparts. One of the first guffaws during these Olympic Games came in response to a tweet by the *Chicago Tribune* that read, "Wife of a Bears lineman wins a bronze medal today in Rio Olympics," with no mention of the actual athlete's name. A woman named Heather Morrow wrote a responding tweet to the *Tribune* saying, "If winning her own Olympic medal doesn't get a woman her own headline, what will?"[20]

In another incident during the Rio Olympics, U.S. swimmers were highlighted in an article in the Texas-based newspaper the *Eagle*, and Michael Phelps drew a bigger headline for tying for a silver medal in the 100m butterfly than Katie Ledecky, who had broken her own world record in the 800m freestyle and received a gold medal. University of Denver law professor Nancy Leong summed it up by saying, "This headline is basically a metaphor for the entire world." Leong went on to say, "This seems like a clear-cut example of a situation where you have two achievements, one by a man and one by a woman, that were given the wrong treatment. . . . Not only that, but the achievement by the woman is objectively more impressive, but it was put in much smaller font."[21] There are numerous other examples of this clear sex discrimination showing up in other articles published during the Rio Olympics. This occurred despite a record number of female athletes (294) versus male athletes (264) on the U.S. team, and the women earning the most medals (61 women versus 55 men). Of these, five were in mixed events (equestrian and mixed doubles tennis). In addition, women athletes won 27 of the 46 gold medals the team brought home.

MAINSTREAM MEDIA: SPORTS MEDIA COVERAGE

Throughout the country, the athletic community is starting to acknowledge the problems with the media's coverage of women's sports. Yet, the people in charge of mainstream publications and shows—with a few exceptions—continue to report on female athletes even less than they did 20 years ago and use only a miniscule number of female sportscasters, reporters, and writers. Just four years ago, ESPN's *SportsCenter* reported on women's sports a mere 2 percent of the time. In 2015, *Fox Sports Live* "devoted less than 1 percent of on-air time to women's sports," according to the *Huffington Post*; however, there are many organizations trying to draw attention to these deficits.[22] The Tucker Center for Research on Girls and Women in Sport's work focuses solely on the role of women in sport. A video produced by the center, entitled *Media Coverage and Female Athletes*, addresses this topic head-on, covering many of the issues related to media and female athletes.[23]

Organizations throughout the United States need to keep up the pressure on mainstream media to make changes in their reporting. Perhaps if 90 percent of senior sports editors weren't male and white, women athletes would make more progress. LPGA coverage was added to ABC last year, and the viewership doubled from 11 to 22 million.

This shows what a huge difference showing women's sports on major TV channels can make.

A major media site that has taken on the women in sport cause is ESPNW. Founded in 2010 by Laura Gentile and others, ESPNW is dedicated to creating content and voices relevant solely to women's sports. Its primary mission is to create engagement and inspiration for women through the vehicle of sports. Their platform stretches across digital, television, radio, film, event, educational, and social media platforms.

When I spoke with Gentile, senior vice president of marketing for ESPN, her gracious and open manner provided helpful background on the development of ESPNW. In its first five years of existence, executives decided not to focus the discussion on women versus men; rather, they chose to highlight stories about only female athletes. As time passed, however, they began noticing discrepancies in language and even jokes between ESPN and ESPNW. Gentile described the task of gradually building a network of resources and sponsorships, and developing a super-relevant brand, as a slow process. The women of ESPNW needed to be moved in the direction of acknowledging the differences between women and then begin to speak about those inequities. Gentile commented that there still is a lack of understanding about the size of the market of women interested in and participating in sports.

Despite the fact that 115 million American women are interested in sports and 49 percent of all sports fans are women, sports media outlets still don't seem to comprehend the significance of women's sports as a stream of revenue. According to former sportswriter Joan Ryan, what women's sport needs is recognizable stars, as is the case with men's pro sports. If more promotional dollars were spent to introduce outstanding female athletes like Maya Moore and Elena Delle Donne in the WNBA, Hilary Knight and the Lamoureux twins in ice hockey, Simone Biles in gymnastics, Sarah Robles in weightlifting, Alex Morgan in soccer, and little-known Lauren Haeger in National Pro Fastpitch softball, we could build more excitement about a variety of women's sports. We've certainly done this with male personalities in the NBA, NFL, and NBL. Unfortunately, there remains an unwillingness to invest in women's sport promotions, despite the fact that, as Gentile expressed so clearly, sport has grown into "a girls' thing as well as a boys'."

THE PLIGHT OF FEMALE SPORTS JOURNALISTS

In the 2017 Women in Media report, only 11.4 percent of sports stories were written by women, an actual increase of 1.4 percent from 2016. With more than 50 percent of women self-identifying as sports fans, it's disappointing that there aren't more women sports journalists. A primary question remains: Why aren't there more female sports journalists?[24] A tweet from a woman named Burton Svetlana Wendt summarizes this issue: "The women that actually get those jobs are clearly passionate about the game and knowledgeable. They are educated in broadcasting and possess the ability to speak clearly on the fly. My guess is the men simply don't like the intrusion into their mainly men's club."[25]

Sexism and gender bias still exist—in a big way. Female sports journalists encounter harassment in a variety of ways. They receive complaints from men that their voices sound screechy or irritating, encounter unwanted sexual advances, receive inappropriate texts, and have their appearance rated by viewers. One example of the kind of sexism women reporters encounter took place during a 2010 World Cup soccer game in South Africa. The Spanish press blamed the defeat of their home country on a female sideline television reporter, Sara Carbonero, for "causing distractions" on the field. Fans blamed Carbonero's beauty for the loss, describing her as "unprofessional" and a distraction for the goalie, Iker Casillas, who was then her boyfriend and is now her husband.[26]

How ironic is this situation? Usually, only the best-looking (according to mainstream criteria) women athletes get highlighted by the media. Yet, here's an example where beauty *interferes* with a woman's ability to succeed in the athletic world. This is illustrative of the dislike of women sports reporters. When veteran reporter Beth Mowins first called a *Monday Night Football* game last year, Twitter comments abounded with complaints about her voice. Andrea Kremer (another veteran) commented, "I have no doubt that 'hating the sound of her voice' is code for 'I hate that there was a women announcing football.'" According to Julie Dicaro, "The primal masculinity of football makes a woman calling a game antithetical to their core ideas about gender."[27]

A young Latina woman, Jessica Mendoza, who is an ESPN baseball analyst, often receives complaints from fans about her voice and Latin heritage. Men are having trouble adjusting to the new roles women are now playing in sports, notably sports reporting—a traditionally male enclave. In each of the sports we've discussed, including soccer, football, and baseball, we hear about numerous nasty remarks and instances of sexual harassment toward female sportswriters who are paving the way for others to enter the sports reporting world.

Interviewing several female sports reporters, I learned about the obstacles and open avenues some have encountered. A common theme for early reporters was that they attempted to "act like one of the guys" to succeed. In her landmark book *Little Girls in Pretty Boxes*, written in 1995, Joan Ryan highlights the harassment and abuse of girls in gymnastics and ice skating. Her career in sports reporting extends all the way back to 1983, when she began working in the sports department for the *Orlando Sentinel* in Florida. She described herself as lucky to work with a "great group of guys." Covering the United States Football League (USFL), she received bundles of hostile mail and encountered some unpleasant situations in locker rooms. She described an early experience in which she entered a locker room wearing a skirt. One of the players took his long-handled razor and ran it down her leg to the edge of her skirt. This occurred in 1988, but these kinds of incidents continue to occur today.

Although their road is rarely easy, the level of intelligence, fortitude, and persistence women in the sports reporting world continue to display gives me hope that one day there will be further acceptance of women in this field.

PROMISE ON THE HORIZON

Despite the continuing lack of attention being paid to women in sport by the media; there are glimmers of hope. One exception to the sea of men in sports who ignore female athletes is Mike Woitalia, executive editor of *Soccer America*, who frequently writes about female soccer players. I first interviewed him in 2013 for my book about female athletes after discovering a number of articles he'd written about girls' and women's soccer. In a more recent interview, he told me about a regular feature he writes entitled "Soccer America Confidential," which frequently provides news about women's soccer. He even pointed to one piece about the formation of Mexico's first professional women's soccer league.

Woitalia is not alone: An ever-increasing number of women and men are speaking out about the importance of women's sport today. There are more leadership academies and training programs, and, generally speaking, there is more encouragement for females to speak out about the importance of covering girls' and women's sports. Even local markets are slowly improving their coverage of female athletes. In the Bay Area there is local CBS sportscaster Vernon Glenn, who is more consistently covering women's sport. (He happens to be African American as well.) When I interviewed Glen, he stated that he's always been invested in highlighting outstanding females in sport. He realizes that the majority of his viewers are women and believes in equal air time for females and males. He described CBS's reporting as mainly focused on human-interest stories, so he strives to write more stories about girls and women in sports. They usually appear on Friday nights.

One of his most recent stories covered Kate Courtney, a local mountain biking hero in Marin County, California, which is considered the home of mountain biking. She had just won the 2018 Elite Cross-Country Championship in Lenzerheide, Switzerland. Courtney was in third for much of the last half of the race, but during the long homestretch, she passed the second-place woman, and then, close to the end, the first-place woman made a mistake and Courtney was able to pull ahead and hold on for the win. Her next goal is to make the U.S. Olympic team.

One Bay Area newspaper, the *Marin IJ*, does cover girls and women on a frequent basis in its sports section. Each week, the paper highlights both the "Girls Prep of the Week" and the "Boys Prep of the Week." It also often publishes features on outstanding girls' teams throughout the county.

An enormous amount of work needs to be done to increase the media presence of girls and women in sports. Although there is now at least reasonable coverage of female athletes every two years during the Olympics, even more women and men in the media need to stand up and speak out about the ongoing existence and accomplishments of girls' and women's sports. The numbers and interest are there to support the need to report on women's sports, which begs the question, What are white, male sports executive editors afraid of? Even the early qualification of the U.S. women's national soccer team for the Women's World Cup in 2019 did not make most news shows that weren't sports-oriented.

To ensure that girls' and women's sports get greater media coverage in the future, sports departments need to open up more slots for female reporters and have reporters cover female stars in the WNBA and other pro women's sports on a more consistent basis. Fans can also contact sports editors about the accomplishments of girls and women in sport. This is a struggle that requires perseverance and persistence. If we keep up the pressure, we will see girls' and women's sports begin to get the media attention they deserve.

ACTION STEPS TOWARD EQUALITY IN THE MEDIA FOR WOMEN

1. Place pressure on the media to provide greater coverage of Olympians and other professional sports.
2. Assess female athletes based on their performances rather than their appearance. Encourage sport sites to publish these types of lists, as ESPNW has done.
3. Encourage the creation of more athlete-based websites—like ESPNW—with solid content and coverage of a variety of sports to inform the public about the strength of women athletes.
4. Push for reporters to write stories about the positive aspects of women's sport rather than focusing on the negatives and struggles.
5. Have conversations with local sportscasters and offer encouragement when they report on women.
6. Work to dispel the myth that women's sports aren't exciting and interesting to watch or read about.
7. Stop complaining about the way female journalists sound when they are reporting a story. Take time to listen to them and realize they might have more knowledge than the average male sports fan since they have earned their place in the broadcasting booth.

4

THE POLITICS OF WOMEN'S SPORT

Becoming an Active Part of the Sports Network

Don't let fear stop you. Don't give up because you are paralyzed by insecurity or overwhelmed by the odds, because in giving up, you give up hope. Understand that failure is a process in life, that only in trying can you enrich yourself and have the possibility of moving forward. The greatest obstacle in life is fear and giving up because of it.

—Sonia Sotomayor, Supreme Court justice[1]

American sport culture is resisting the inclusion of femininity in sports. There are a number of surface changes taking place. Yet, many sport federations do not include females on their boards, in their voting, and/or in positions of power within their organizations. There are constant blockades to women in sport, especially in leadership, pay, and media coverage.

The idea that sport is inherently masculine is embedded in our psyche. Sports fans continue to idealize male athletes. Oftentimes, they don't even pay attention to our many outstanding female athletes. Examples include WNBA players Maya Moore and Candace Parker, who won ESPY Awards for Best NBA Player in 2018 and 2017, respectively; Lexi Thompson, Kelly Korda, or Brittany Lincicome, top-ranked American golfers; or Alex Morgan, Carli Lloyd, or Megan Rapinoe of the U.S. women's national soccer team.

A common excuse for this failure to spotlight female athletes is that women's sports aren't exciting to watch. When I told him about this book, my professor from the University of San Diego, Dr. John Valois, commented that I was "going to have to challenge the conception that women's sports are simply not as exciting as the men's." My response? When our women's national soccer team was in the finals and eventually won the Women's World Cup, more than 24 million viewers (as many as tuned into the NBA Finals) watched the final game. No one said that was unexciting. In fact, that was the largest viewership of any soccer match ever shown on U.S. television. In the 2018 Pyeongchang Olympics, meanwhile, female athletes won more medals and golds than the men, despite more men being on the team. The United States had two female athletes, Kikkan Randall and Jessica Diggins, each walk away with a gold medal in the cross-country skiing relay for the first medal in that event since 1976. Furthermore, the U.S. women's national ice hockey team eliminated Canada for the gold medal. This was their first gold in 20 years. Who says women's sports aren't exciting?

A primary factor blocking women's sports from being in the media is the "good old boys network," with the idea that they own sports and women just don't belong. During an interview I conducted with Donna Lopiano, former president of the Women's Sports Foundation, she quoted Dr. Harry Edwards, an iconic sports sociologist, as saying, "We use women to promote everything. And we can't promote women's sports." She views power centers as exploiting women to preserve the male-dominant culture that has always prevailed. Despite a progression of change for females in sport, the tribalism that still pervades sport is an impediment to women gaining further power in sport. Powerful women's sport threaten the old boys club. Until this club is dismantled, it will continue to be difficult for girls and women to make gains in sport, especially in attaining positions of leadership and gaining more comparable pay and adequate media coverage.

In a conversation I had with Dr. Dave Berri, a sports economist, he talked about how the media seems to take delight in discussing the most negative aspects of women's sports. The complexity of the economics of women's sports cannot be easily explained. As was the case with men's sports, a fan base takes decades to build. The WNBA was building consistently until recently. Part of the building process involves promotion and easy access to women's sports, however, and a lack of marketing and promotion is stifling this process. Laura Gentile, the primary founder of ESPNW and senior vice president of marketing for ESPN, believes people must begin to believe and acknowledge that sport is both a girls' thing and a boys' thing. In addition, Gentile suggests that we need to encourage female athletes to be more colorful and express their honest opinions to the public more consistently. This is a positive and helpful way to draw attention to various women's sports.

Venus and Serena Williams have vastly contributed to gaining more equality for women in sport. Due to Venus's efforts, Wimbledon became the final Grand Slam to agree to pay equal money to women and men. Serena is responsible for helping pregnant players retain their ranking while out for maternity leave. Serena faced serious medical conditions following the birth of her daughter. We often fail to address that female athletes in the United States, both women of color and white, are not always heard, even when they do speak up. Venus and Serena use the strength of their personalities to draw attention to the plight of inequality of female athletes. Outstanding female and male players in a variety of sports need to get the media's attention on behalf

Laura Gentile, senior vice president of Marketing at ESPN. *ESPN-Laura Gentile*

of women's sports. They need to speak out to let people know who they are and emphasize their support for movement toward the equal treatment of female and male athletes.

The most recent challenge to "institutionalized gender discrimination" has been the class-action lawsuit pursued by the 28 members of the U.S. women's national soccer team against the United States Soccer Federation (USSF) in March 2019. As the 2019 World Cup began, this courageous team of professional athletic women was speaking up for female athletes throughout the world. The lawsuit covers the built-in and unfair gender differences in the policies and practices of the USSF. Some of these include minimal promotion and marketing of their games, poor travel conditions, and differences in coaching and medical staff. As U.S. defender Becky Sauerbrunn remarked,

> The bottom line is simple: It is wrong for us to be paid and valued less for our work because of our gender. Every member of this team works incredibly hard to achieve the success that we have had for the USSF. We are standing up now so that our efforts, and those of future USWNT players, will be fairly recognized.[2]

Many of the men heading up sports organizations helped build this gender bias into their organizations years ago. The resistance remains to integrating women more fully into the leadership of their structures.

This is the "good old boys network" that we're up against as female athletes. We think we're making headway, and then major setbacks take place. For instance, FIFA indicated that they would significantly increase the prize money for women in this year's Women's World Cup. In 2018, the men's Cup money amounted to $38 million, while women took home between $2 million and $4 million. This limited action speaks volumes about how the men in charge of FIFA actually regard women's soccer. Like the women of the U.S. women's national soccer team who filed suit against U.S. Soccer, women in sports need to continue fighting the status quo via a variety of avenues.

Athlete Ally, an organization that engages in advocacy for LGBTQ athletes, perfectly describes the situation in their Athletic Equality Index: "A culture of toxic masculinity pervades sport—one that condemns male athletes that don't adhere to it, polices female athletes that challenge it, and excludes anyone beyond or outside of this binary." This pervasive "masculine" influence and attitude continues to interfere with females gaining ground in the sporting world.[3]

THE CONTINUING IMPACT OF THE "GOOD OLD BOYS NETWORK"

The patriarchal nature of sports continues to block and/or sabotage females in sport from attaining truly significant gains in sports leadership, recognition, and pay. As has long been the case, women are still frequently expected to fight their way into leadership positions. They are also expected to achieve more than their male counterparts and often receive significantly less compensation than men in a parallel position, whether they are leaders or players in sport. (As mentioned earlier, women in sports leadership are worse off than women in the corporate world.)

In many endurance sports, for instance, long distance running and road cycling, women received limited organizational support for years. Numerous excuses were given about false physical limitations. Due to these false beliefs, women were held back from participating in competitive running or cycling races. The 1984 Los Angeles Olympics marked the first Games where a women's marathon was held, and women's cycling debuted. And even today, in most cycling events, women are limited to races that are much less demanding, giving the impression that pro women cyclists aren't able to meet the same physical and psychological challenges as men.

This limitation is based on a false premise. When I participated in my second Davis Double Century in 1998, my boyfriend (now-husband) rode up next to me in a paceline I was leading at mile 165, and suggested that I slow down because I was dropping men off the back. He emphasized that they were grumbling. Clearly, women can keep up with men in cycling. Yet, despite the tremendous endurance capabilities of women and research to support them, the UCI keeps these rules limiting the distances of women's races.

In a study carried out by the University of Oregon, the University of Guelph, and the University of British Columbia, researchers commented, "We know from previous research that for events like ultra-trail running, males may complete them faster, but females are considerably less tired by the end."[4] This study suggests that women's endurance abilities are actually much greater than men's. And women are proving this to be true again and again. In December 2016, five different women won ultramarathons throughout the country. Women keep showing a greater degree of stamina. "A growing pattern of race results suggests the longer and more arduous the event, the better chances women have of beating men."[5] I myself have firsthand experience with this: In 1992, for example, when I ran the Vermont 100 in Woodstock, Vermont, I finished in the dark, easily got up for the awards ceremony the following day, and then got up early on Monday to drive to Boston for my flight home to California.

Disproving the claims limiting female athlete ability for cycling in 2016, Lael Wilcox became the first woman to win the Trans Am. This endurance race consists of a 4,300-mile unsupported cycle, starting in Oregon and ending in Virginia, to be completed in only 18 days. Wilcox is now considered one of the top ultracycling cyclists after taking on many more races since that time. Clearly, based on her example, women are capable of competing in long-distance and multiday cycling events. This is further illustrated by the fact that the number of women riding in double centuries is ever-increasing and indicative of the unwillingness to acknowledge women's endurance capabilities.

The Tour de France is a 21-day event for men. Women are not allowed to compete. There were differing stage versions (from four to 15 stages) for a Women's Tour de France between 1984 and 2009. The last version consisted of a multiple-day stage race known as "La Grande Boucle Feminine Internationale." This event received little to no support through sponsorship, operated on a shoestring budget, had difficulty maintaining sponsorship, and ended up folding in 2009. The race, in its current form, established in 2012 (La Course), in stark contrast, consists of only one stage: seven times around the Champs-Élysées, a route that covers only 89 kilometers. Robin Farina, a former pro cyclist and cofounder of the Women's Cycling Association, pointed out, "Just like with most things, men feel threatened when change is on the table, but that's a mindset we need to change. Opening cycling more to women just creates more opportunity."[6]

The attitudes of organizations like the International Cycling Union (UCI) and FIFA contradict what the growing body of research illustrates regarding women's endurance abilities. The "good old boys network" just isn't able to face the truth: Girls and women in sport are capable of greater participation in endurance sports. What we are facing is the reality of girls and women in sport versus traditional and outdated ways of thinking that are being disproven again and again.

The more powerful girls and women in sport become, the greater degree of threat they pose. Perhaps the most blatant example of gender discrimination in sports today is being perpetrated by FIFA (in English, the International Federation of Association Football). As mentioned earlier, FIFA paid the winning men's World Cup team $38 million and the runner-up $28 million in 2018, and the organization increased the overall budget by $40 million. In stark contrast, the winning team in the 2019 Women's World Cup received only $4 million. This was not even a serious attempt by the FIFA Council to increase the prize money to any reasonable amount; the winning women's team received just 10 percent of what France's men's team received for winning the 2018 World Cup.

Players unions from the United States, Australia, Sweden, and Norway have voiced concerns regarding this disparity. They have rightfully questioned and cited FIFA statutes that claim a "commitment to 'gender equality.'"[7] FIFA's lack of action regarding increasing the Women's World Cup winnings in a substantial manner demonstrates the absence of any real "commitment." They are merely giving lip service and hoping they can pull the wool over people's eyes, as they have in the past. Despite this, FIFA continues to make big promises and take no concrete actions to increase the footprint of women's soccer in the world.

In a December 6, 2018, ESPNW article by Julie Foudy, a member of the 1999 gold medal–winning U.S. women's national soccer team, Foudy clearly expresses her years-long frustration and dissatisfaction with FIFA, writing, "The organization's incessant failure to fulfill its mission to support the women's game is mind-numbing."[8] The pervasive insult continues with their "women's football strategy." This plan has no action items; it only offers more "promises" with zero substance and broadly stated goals with no clear or concise objectives. There are no actual plans for a marketing push that will help broaden the interest in and fan base of women's soccer. The question remains, when will FIFA care enough to make real changes? Individuals like Foudy have fought long and hard to improve the status of women's soccer in the world, only to have the door shut in their faces again and again. With women comprising 49 percent of sports fandom, when will this tunnel vision of men be cracked open?

Even though the "good old boys network" continues to block us, we must persevere. We cannot quit working toward the acknowledgment, recognition, and respect we desire and deserve. And make no mistake, female athletes do face higher expectations than male athletes, who are frequently given the benefit of the doubt. As female college and WNBA sports reporter Christy Winters-Scott has commented, "If you do your homework and do your research, and be incredibly prepared, but also have a passion for what you're doing, you can get respect."[9]

Gaining respect is bound to be a long and arduous process. The strides women are making in various sports are a great help when it comes to achieving this goal. In 2002, for example, Pam Reed became the first woman to win the overall title of the Badwater Ultramarathon, a 135-mile race. She repeated her impressive feat two more times, setting a women's course record by more than two and a half hours.

Female athletes need to press forward, collaborate with one another, and eventually form an "all-athletes club," regardless of gender. When we hit a wall, we need to look at other options to get beyond it, whether it be working our way around it, going over it, or finding ways to smash it to the ground. We must call out those who treat us unjustly, even if through lawsuits. Our work now is to further increase female participation at every level of sport, protect our female athletes from abuse, and keep on working for recognition of the importance of females in sport as positive role models for younger generations.

PROGRESS AND REGRESS: SHIFTING BACK AND FORTH

The small gains women have made in terms of holding positions of power within the sports world directly highlight the politics of sport. Looking at those who were hired as NCAA Division I athletic directors in 2017, out of 52, only eight were women—quite a parallel to Fortune 500 CEOs. (An equally interesting statistic: Of the female Fortune 500 CEOs in 2017, an amazing 95 percent were athletes.)

In sports journalism, women are keeping up the struggle to gain acceptance. Hiring of female sports reporters has actually declined in the past year. In the 2018 Associated Press Sports Editor Racial and

Gender Report Card, the rating for gender hiring was still an F, with women representing only 10 percent of Associated Press sports editors and a mere 11.5 percent of sports reporters. The one bright light is that 30.1 percent of women are Associated Press assistant sports editors.[10] Clearly, we have far to go in this area.

The difficulty female sports journalists face in garnering respect was highlighted by an interaction between Cam Newton, quarterback for the Carolina Panthers, and experienced sports reporter Jourdan Rodrigue, as described in chapter 1. Rodrigue asked Newton a valid question, "What are the teams' routes?" He paused, then laughed (alone), and said, "It's funny to hear a female talk about routes." Sportswriter Jane McManus, speaking to ABC, later reflected, "Newton's 'offhand' comments reflect a lack of awareness of women in this business and what they deal with—and that attitude is part of what they deal with."[11]

For better or worse, politics is part of what authoritative female sports journalists, experts, and athletes deal with. I myself have come up against this: I recently tweeted about women kicking butt at the Olympics, making the point that the number of females who received medals—including the female ice hockey team, the pursuit speed-skating team, and the cross-country team—outnumbered the males, and although most responses I received were positive, my comments also immediately drew criticism from several men.

Progress is slowly making itself known in sports. Some 2017 stats show the strength of female athletes' participation. They are as follows:

There are 3.3 million girls participating in high school sports, compared to 4.5 million boys.

Approximately 212,000 women played on NCAA sports teams, compared to 275,000 men.

There were 10,449 women's college sports teams in the NCAA, compared to 9,057 men's teams.[12]

We've been most delayed in terms of actual positions of leadership and authority—voting and speaking—but at least more women involved in sport are speaking up about this. Their celebrity status is helpful in drawing attention to important issues in sport.

In 2016, CEO Raymond Moore of the BNP Paribas Open tennis tournament in Indian Wells, California, perfectly illustrated the mindset of the "good old boys club" by making offensive comments about women's tennis. He said players from the Women's Tennis Association "ride on the coattails of the men" and should "go down every night on [their] knees and thank God that Roger Federer and Rafael Nadal were born, because they have carried this sport."[13] Sadly, this "club" just can't seem to accept and/or is threatened by the strength of female tennis players.

Some of the gains we've made in recent years present a false sense of equality throughout sport. I recently heard a man say that women don't have to worry about inequality in tennis, since the issue is resolved; however, this is not actually the case. When we take a look at tennis, we are delighted to know that the major Grand Slams pay equal prize money. But looking beyond these tournaments, we see wide pay gaps between women and men in most other events. In 2018 alone, "71 percent of the world's top 100 men . . . earned more than women of the same ranking, based on prize money per tournament played."[14]

Novak Djokovic and Rafael Nadal are two figures in the tennis world who are known to detract from the fight for women to receive equal pay in the sport. They argue that men should be paid more than women because they play a different amount of sets; however, this is only true in the Grand Slams. The other major tour events only require three sets for both sexes. Another argument is that the men's audiences are always bigger, but this has certainly not always been true. For example, the U.S. Open saw bigger audiences for the women's finals from 2010 to 2014. One highly visible male tennis player who has been supportive of women's tennis is Andy Murray, along with James Blake and Englishman Andy Roddick. We need more professional male athletes like them who support female athletes and are willing to speak up about the positive ways women participate in sport.

In 2017 and 2018, our U.S. women's national ice hockey and soccer teams stood up like never before. Both teams used their power and ability to gain support from others, notably men, and demand more equitable treatment. The #MeToo movement in sports has only just begun to address the abuse women have suffered in sport. The good news is that these abuses are now being talked about publicly and not getting swept under the rug as they have been in the past.

More and more men who sexually harass and abuse women are being called on to answer for their sins. On CBS's *NFL Today* show on December 2, 2018, the commentators—all former NFL players—discussed players, domestic violence, and the consequences players should receive for these abuses. It was a conversation you wouldn't have seen on a show like that even five years ago. The topic of inequality needs to be brought forth in sporting contexts like this on a regular basis.

Despite layoffs at ESPN, there are women leaders still working there, especially in higher-level positions of power. In speaking with Alison Overholt, head of ESPNW and editor of *ESPN The Magazine*, I discovered that she represents the type of fearless and risk-taking woman who isn't afraid to parlay her sports desires into action. As a teen growing up in Hong Kong, Alison played basketball. Unsurprisingly, the girls' basketball team was not allowed to go to the more important tournaments at the time, so Alison and her coach approached the headmaster and board of directors about attending the Far East Basketball Tournament, which the boys team attended every year. In Alison's junior year, they were flatly turned down without a solid reason. They went back in her senior year, arguing that not only were the girls good players, but also every girl on the team had high academic standing. This time, the situation was reconsidered, and the girls were allowed to attend the tournament. Overholt's story is illustrative of the leadership she displayed, even at a young age, which has carried over into her work at ESPNW.

Laura Gentile, senior vice president of marketing for ESPN, earned All-American and All-ACC honors in field hockey, led the Duke team as captain for two years, and went on to obtain a MBA. Gentile has worked at ESPN for nine years, and she talked to me about building her credibility through maintaining good relationships, understanding a sense of culture, and practicing patience for change. Her hard work has paid off, as she played an instrumental role in establishing ESPNW.

The 9th Annual ESPNW Summit, which took place in October 2018, focused on the issues most relevant to women in sport today. This event featured many of the current movers and shakers in women's sport, including Laura Gentile, Julie Foudy (ESPNW analyst, World Cup champion, and Olympic gold medalist), Hilary Knight (pro hockey player and Olympic gold medalist), Candace Parker (WNBA player, Los Angeles Sparks), Sarah Spain (ESPNW columnist, radio host, and *SportsCenter* reporter), and Michele Roberts (executive director, National Basketball Players Association). At the summit, Spain clarified her viewpoint on the current situation, saying, "I never lose sight of the progress we're making. Things have never been better for women in sports. . . . By no means does that mean it's time for women to stop speaking up."[15] Gentile, meanwhile, spoke of the Empower Women and Girls Sports Initiative, the Woman Athlete of the Year award, and the Global Sports Mentoring program, as well as the importance of addressing why women still don't have a seat at the table in the sports world. There are 115 leaders ranging from 25 to 40 years of age who participate in 57 countries and 42 mentor organizations. The goal of this work is to push the ball forward for girls and women in sport.

The time is now for more women in sport to start speaking up about the inequities and challenging the structure of the status quo. Events like the ESPNW Summit are prime examples of how to do this.

FEMALE ATHLETES MAKING THEIR MARK

Professional and Olympic female athletes are learning to speak up and support fellow women who are striving toward greater equality both inside and outside of sports. Current and former athletes are speaking up in a more consistent and passionate manner to fight for equality in a wide variety of ways. In 2017, for example, in a basketball game between the Seattle Storm and Chicago Sky, the teams' owners held a pregame rally to raise funds for Planned Parenthood.

When just one celebrity athlete, male or female, speaks in a public setting and passionately expresses their desire for increased equality for female athletes, the risk is reduced for other players who are willing to speak up.[16] The strides that have been made by the U.S. women's national ice hockey and soccer teams in their negotiations for vastly improved contracts set an important precedent for other women who want to come forward and push harder for equal treatment. Their actions have demonstrated that women do have power, especially when they make use of networking. The women's national ice hockey team, for instance, was willing to risk losing its national team status by boycotting the World Cup. The players' success in this endeavor was made possible by the support of fellow female ice hockey stars (who refused to replace them), the men's team (who threatened to boycott as well), other national men's teams (who spoke out in their favor), and 16 senators (who wrote a letter promoting their cause). These bright, intelligent young women used their networking abilities to the hilt, providing the impetus other female sports can use to rally for the cause of increased equality.

Other examples of women in sport making their mark include Olympic fencer Ibtihaj Muhammad, the first U.S. Muslim citizen to wear a hijab in the Olympics; Misty Copeland, American Ballet Theatre's (ABT) first African American principal dancer; U.S. World Cup soccer star Megan Rapinoe; WNBA player Breanna Stewart; nationally known tennis player Venus Williams; and former WNBA player Kisha Ford.

Muhammad won a bronze medal as part of USA Team Sabre in the 2016 Olympics, leading the way as a role model for other hijab-wearing Muslim female athletes. Misty Copeland, meanwhile, is a shining example of how African American female athletes can fight for equality. In 2015, Copeland was named one of *Time* magazine's 100 most influential people, became a principal dancer with ABT, and was featured on *60 Minutes*. She is ABT's first African American principal in the 75 years of the company's existence. As Alison Overholt said when I interviewed her, race and gender are inextricably linked; the public, she said, views female black athletes as black first and women second. Copeland's primary fight is against racism and to address both diversity and inclusion. As an important contributor to ABT's Project Plié initiative, she works closely with the Boys and Girls Clubs of America to address these and other important issues. As a youth, Copeland regularly attended this institution and even participated in her first ballet class there. Project Plié is designed to "promote diversity, bringing ballet closer to kids from underrepresented communities, who normally wouldn't have the opportunity to take part."[17] In addition, Copeland is an ambassador with the MindLeaps program. This program reaches out to at-risk youth in developing and postconflict countries such as Uganda, Kenya, Rwanda, and Mauritania. The focus is on dance programming and vocational training. Copeland has also been sponsored by Under Armour since 2014, when they made her the first ballet dancer under their sponsorship. Through her efforts, both onstage and off, Copeland has become a role model for young girls everywhere.

Since coming out in 2012, Megan Rapinoe has shown great openness, clarity, and advocacy in her efforts to promote and support LGBTQ athletes, involving herself in remarkable activities to help the LGBTQ athletic community. Two of the organizations she's worked with are the Human Rights Campaign and Streetfootballworld. In June 2018, Rapinoe's purpose turned to encouraging LGBTQ kids to participate, feel safe, and compete in sports. An estimated 42 percent of gay, lesbian, and bisexual youth believe their sporting communities don't accept them. As an ambassador for Streetfootballworld, an international nongovernmental organization, Rapinoe aids the organization in its goal to link nonprofit soccer organizations in a global manner. She is also an ambassador for Streetfootballworld's new Play Proud initiative, designed to create safe and inviting places for youth soccer.[18]

In 2016, Breanna Stewart was the number-one draft pick in the WNBA. She won the Most Valuable Player Award and was an integral part of the Seattle Storm's championship in 2017. Since joining the Seattle Storm, she has become a social justice advocate. In 2016, she won an ESPY for Best Female Athlete, and she used her moment to speak up about the inequality of female athletes in sport. "Now that I'm in the WNBA, playing with other amazing female athletes, I'm trying to understand why we, as professional female athletes, don't receive anywhere near the fame," she said in her speech. "This has to change. I know that everyone in this room loves and supports women and girls in sports, and wants to be part of that change, right?"[19] In addition, Stewart has publicly spoken out about a number of other areas of inequality and injustice. Her main focus on equality for female athletes is in media coverage, but she has also voiced her support of Planned Parenthood, gay rights, and the #MeToo and Black Lives Matter movements. She even flew to Los Angeles International Airport in protest of President Trump's travel ban in January 2017.[20]

Stewart is representative of the social justice action the WNBA has taken in recent years. Prior to the start of the 2019 season, for instance, the WNBA released a video on Facebook highlighting the Women's March in Washington, DC, interspersed with basketball scenes and finishing with the messages, "We Stand for Change" and "We Stand for Equality." For the "Take a Seat, Take a Stand" campaign, launched during the 2018 season, they pledged to donate five dollars to one of six selected charities and a ticket to a young girl from each paid WNBA ticket. These donations went to a variety of women's charities. This magnanimous action represented just one of the many efforts made to support the following six social causes: It's On Us, Planned Parenthood, United State of Women, Bright Pink, MENTOR, and GLSEN—organizations that benefit girls and women.[21] The WNBA's involvement in social justice action has occurred as a result of the efforts of women of color who are not only elite athletes, but also well educated, aware of the political landscape, and sensitive to social issues exerting pressure on the league they play in to support these causes.

In 2016, two black men were killed by police officers in Minnesota and Louisiana; when this happened, players from teams throughout the WNBA wore black T-shirts in support of the Black Lives Matter movement. Initially, the league fined the women for not dressing in regulation attire. After further protest, however, the league revoked the fines. Stewart spoke out clearly during this time, expressing the WNBA's stance: "As the WNBA, we need to have a unified front. . . . Obviously, there will be times where we don't agree, but compared to the NFL— the disparity between players, front offices, and management—it's huge. We know change is only going to happen if we're together."[22]

The social justice platform of many in the WNBA and the players' actions have significantly impacted the league. There have been three primary benefits: 1) The fan base has increased by 31 percent between the NBATV and ESPN channels, 2) digital subscriptions have increased by 39 percent, and 3) product sales have increased a whopping 66 percent.[23] With their strong social consciousness and positive marketing efforts, the WNBA appears to be on an upward trajectory, serving as a shining example of the kind of positive change female sports teams can create. If more female athletes can replicate these actions, more and more women's sports will draw increased attention and interest.

Men both inside and outside the sports world struggle with giving women the respect and credit they deserve. The stronger women get, the more threatened they seem to become, and they think, mistakenly, that we will not notice. FIFA is a prime example of this mentality. In 2001, Mariah Burton wrote *The Stronger Women Get, the More Men Love Football*. This book was ahead of its time, and the message it expresses remains true today in many ways; however, the determination of female athletes like those who play for the U.S. women's national ice hockey team and Breanna Stewart and her fellow WNBA players makes it clear that female athletes have the power to continue moving toward more equitable terms in sport.

There is growing support for female athletes by top pro male athletes. Increased actions by men are helping to slowly give validation and attention to the value of women in sport. According to "The She Network" sponsored by the Women's Sports Foundation, there are many male athletes from a variety of pro sports who support the movement for equal pay and treatment for female athletes. In basketball, two primary supporters are Steph Curry and LeBron James. Curry previously stated, "I'm feeling more driven than ever—to help out women who are working toward progress, in any way I can," and James commented, "I think you give respect where respect is due. No matter if you're a male or female."[24] Kelly Slater, 11-time world champion surfer, is a long-term supporter of equality for women. He endorsed equity for women surfers and agreed with the female president of the World Surfing League, Sophie Goldschmidt, to create pay equity.

In tennis, Andy Murray, Andy Roddick, and James Blake have often spoken out in support of women players. Murray has frequently defended women in sport, as evidenced by his 2014 hire of coach Amelie Mauresmo. He was the first top men's player to employ a female coach. In a column for the French newspaper *L'Equippe*, Andy stated, "Have I become a feminist? Well, if being a feminist is about fighting so that a woman is treated like a man, then yes, I suppose I have."[25] Both Roddick and Blake often voice their support of Serena and Venus Williams, as well as other female players. The most recent situation occurred during the 2018 U.S. Open women's single final, in which gender and race were an issue. Roddick admitted to saying even harsher words and never getting a penalty.[26] Moreover, the U.S. men's national ice hockey team threatening to boycott the world championships in support of the U.S. women's team was a major factor in USA Hockey finally negotiating reasonable terms for pay and other benefits for the women in 2017. More men speaking up for women will make a difference in helping female athletes gain further recognition in sports.

The youth and teens of today are looking to us for positive leadership and guidance. We need to persist, no matter what falsehoods and obstacles are thrown our way. As ESPN reporter Sarah Spain stated, "If you're a male in the sports world, you'll be given the benefit of the doubt until you prove otherwise. If you're a woman, it's the opposite."[27] Somehow, women are expected to do more to be treated as equals, both as athletes and leaders, in the sport world. We need additional support from female and male athletes, coaches, trainers, newscasters, administrators, and others. As support grows, our progress will vastly improve.

Change may seem slow, but through determination and persistence, bit by bit, we will work our value into the system, create our own "club," and create political change that goes well beyond lip service.

ACTION STEPS TOWARD GREATER EQUALITY IN THE POLITICS OF SPORTS

1. Continue to push to have a say at the table. As Michelle Roberts suggests, "When you enter a room, own the room."
2. Engage more pro male athletes in endorsing the value of women's sports, for example, Andy Roddick, James Blake, LeBron James, and Stephan Curry.
3. Write op-eds about significant issues, for example, the controversy surrounding Caster Semenya, that come up in women's sports and publish them on highly visible websites and in such important newspapers as the *New York Times*.
4. Strive to increase the number of female sports journalists. Look to programs like those created by Melodie Robinson in New Zealand.
5. Be bold and continue to challenge the status quo. Speak up at meetings. Call out such injustices as the horrific abuse of young girls by coaches. Most of all, be persistent and never give up.

5

SPEAKING UP AND PROMOTING WOMEN COACHES

COACH

Your dedication and direction has put fire in our souls.
You have inspired us to do the best to reach our goals.
Your lessons will be remembered long after the game is won.
For the lessons you have taught us have only just begun.
You've taught us about commitment, perseverance, and hope.
And as we go through life, We'll be better able to cope.
To cope with all our struggles, our failures, and success.
Because we had you for our Coach!!!
One of the Best!
Thanks, Coach!

—Anonymous[1]

The Time's Up movement sought to encourage women to speak up about their oppression in many arenas. This is certainly true for female coaches. When Title IX was first enacted into law, more than 90 percent of girls' and women's sports were coached by women; today, that number has dropped to 41.8 percent, according to the Tucker Center for Research on Girls and Women in Sport—a record low. Just 20 percent of college coaches are female, and the hiring and recruiting personnel in charge of filling these positions are primarily men who also make the final decisions for athletic director positions. Dr. Nicole La-Voi recently commented, "Women coaches or women in any workplace, need *opportunity to develop*. In college sport, men get 75 percent of all coaching opportunities. We can't blame women for lack of competence, interest, or confidence when they are denied opportunity." And for women of color, the percentages are even lower, according to the 2017 College Sport Racial and Gender Report Card on female coaches in Division I schools.[2] This report showed that only 7.5 percent of female head coaches are African American, and mixed race, Latina, and Asian/ Pacific Islander women make up even smaller percentages. White female coaches, on the other hand, are a much more common occurrence, at 45 percent.

Here's an even more startling figure: Only 3 percent of male athletes are coached by women.[3] The lack of female coaches in youth sports is an even grimmer situation. In a 2015 survey, the Sports and Fitness Industry Association found that just 27 percent of coaches working with youth were female. Coaches in Minnesota discovered a similar trend in 2015: Only 21 percent of high school coaches were female, and 28 percent of those were assistant coaches. The same study found that 42 percent of those female high school coaches led girls' teams, only 2 percent led men's squads, and 21 percent led co-ed teams.

This lack of female coaches prevents both girls and boys from witnessing strong women in positions of power. Girls are robbed of exposure to significant role models in sport, and boys aren't given a chance to learn to respect and experience powerful women in leadership positions in athletics. We expect and hope for our younger female athletes to step into the spotlight and play crucial roles in furthering women's equality in sport in the future, but that's a tall order when there are so few female coaches to look up to. When there are limited "inspirational" female role models, both sexes lose.

Dr. Nicole LaVoi is one of the leading experts in women's coaching in sport. In a recent interview, LaVoi described the decline as a complicated matter. Her explanation for the complicity contained the struggles of power, access, and opportunity. Barriers in the system, for example, gender, motherhood, race, and sexual identity, work against female coaches. When women are coached by women, they're more likely to go into coaching, according to LaVoi. In fact, the Tucker Center has established a ranking system for college schools based on the number of female coaches they have. When examining the Final (Women's) Four, the 2019 women's champion, Baylor, received a grade of F. At Baylor, 78% of the women's teams are coached by men. When the defending

Wendy Hillard's the Wendy Hillard Gymnastics Foundation in Detroit, in addition to her New York City location. *Courtesy of the Wendy Hillard Gymnastics Foundation*

team's coach, Muffet McGraw, defended the importance of women coaches, she was met by either strong support or, in contrast, immense disdain. Somehow the men and some women have trouble understanding why women can show leadership and strength as coaches.

COACHING AS A WOMAN: AN UPHILL BATTLE

Since the implementation of Title IX, the coaching situation for female coaches has worsened for a number of reasons. In response to the new laws, colleges and high schools rearranged their structures, combining male and female sports programs under one athletic director—most frequently, a white male—as opposed to separate athletic directors for girls and boys. Meanwhile, the supposed pay parity Title IX brought to the table made coaching women's teams more appealing to male coaches; the pay issue constituted a major change, and instead of creating positive change, it ultimately led to reducing the number of women coaching roles for girls' and women's sports. In youth sports, this is particularly evident with the preponderance of male coaches we see today.

For one study, Penelope Lockwood, a University of Toronto social psychologist, researched the impact of gender on role modeling in boys and girls. Lockwood concluded that same-sex role models are even more significant for girls than boys. Female coaches provide inspirational models of success for young athletes.[4] This speaks to what we know to be true: Girls in sport need strong, positive, and self-confident role models who understand them and how they actually think to help them build their self-confidence through sport. This is why it is so important to increase the number of female coaches as role models and mentors.

In March 2017, Geno Auriemma, the long-standing head coach of the University of Connecticut's (UConn) winning women's basketball team, was asked why there aren't more women coaches. "Not as many women want to coach," Auriemma commented. His daughter, a professor at UConn, immediately tweeted, "Walk it back, Dad!" This is a man who has worked with strong, powerful, and smart women as basketball players for years. Yet, he still has this unconscious bias about women and sport. Auriemma even actively supports women becoming coaches. As Sally Jenkins so succinctly put it, this "makes him no different, really, from the other 80 gazillion nice, wonderful, and utterly blind men who deny the employment numbers—and the accompanying female stresses, insecurities, and resentments—staring them in the face." Jenkins went on to say this: "If you want simple, here it is: Eighty-eight percent of NCAA Division I athletic directors, the people doing the hiring, are white."[5] These white men hire coaches who look like them, which perpetuates a homogenous coach profile in sport.

During the 2019 NCAA women's basketball playoffs, UConn faced off against Notre Dame. Auriemma and Notre Dame's coach, Muffet McGraw, are bitter rivals. McGraw expressed her frustration about the poor numbers of female coaches when a reporter asked about her decision to never again hire a male coach. For the past seven years, McGraw's staff had been made up of women coaches, as has Auriemma's. She went on an understandable tirade about the lack of women in power inside and outside of basketball, declaring,

All these millions of girls across the country. . . . Right now, less than 5 percent of women are CEOs of Fortune 500 companies. So, yes, when you look at men's basketball, and 99 percent of jobs go to men, why shouldn't 99 percent of jobs in women's basketball go to women? Maybe it's because we only have 10 percent women athletic directors in Division I. People hire people who look like them, and that's the problem.[6]

In response to McGraw's comments, Kim Mulkey, Baylor's head coach, said they need to hire the "best person" for the job. Nicole LaVoi tweeted that we need to lose the old mantra of "hiring the best man for the job."

Part of the gap in coaching equality exists because society does not always consider the interest or ability of women to coach. They assume a lack of interest in coaching in women due to their own deep cultural biases. Their ignorance and/or lack of awareness of the desire of women to coach interferes with their judgment. Coach Auriemma's unconscious biases seem to have slipped out.

Even in track and field—a sport in which girls and women have been competing for 50 years—the top U.S. women's runners are still coached by men. Despite its 46 years of existence, USA Track and Field has only 10 women coaches versus 83 men at Division I schools. As Nancy Hogshead-Makar remarked, "Somebody dropped the ball . . . [track and field] is one of the most popular sports in the country. There's no shortage of people with interest and expertise that should enable them to get into coaching."[7] Despite the many qualified women's running coaches out there, USA Track and Field has essentially created a lock on hiring them; the organization appears to have no interest in engaging more women as coaches. This is especially ironic given that the majority of runners in U.S. road racing (across all distances)—59 percent—are women.[8]

In 2018, the Tucker Center and the Alliance of Women Coaches released an annual report entitled "2017–2018 Head Coaches of Women's Collegiate Teams: A Report on Seven Select NCAA Division I Conferences." Despite female participation in sport having reached all-time highs and coaching opportunities ever-widening, the report concluded that "only 20 percent of all college coaching positions" are held by women for women's and men's teams. Other key findings the authors highlighted included the following:

There was an increase in the number of female coaches for women's
   teams for the fifth year in a row, at 41.5 percent.
Fourteen percent of head female coaches have been replaced by
   men.
A male was hired 60 percent of the time for head coaching positions.
Of the seven NCAA Division I conferences, none received higher
   than a C grade for hiring women as coaches.
F grades for hiring women as coaches were earned by nine institutions.[9]

This was the sixth year this report was produced. The center's goal is to
follow the progress of women's coaches in collegiate sport to provide an
ongoing and active measure of the realities for female coaches. Their
hopes are to increase the number of women coaches; develop an awareness of the inequity in this area; open discussions about this topic; and
work toward improved and increased recruitment, assistance, and retention of female coaches at collegiate levels. They hope this will impact
youth and pro sport female coaches.[10] They recognize that these two
actions—increasing awareness and pushing for discussion—are particularly crucial actions when it comes to getting more women into coaching positions.

   The numbers of female coaches are slowly increasing overall; when
it comes to women of color occupying coaching positions, however, the
numbers are still woefully low. One sport in which there are now more
female than male coaches is basketball. Yet, African American coaches
make up a nominal 10.9 percent of coaches in the WNBA. (For
contrast, note that 45 percent of the *players* in the WNBA are African
American.) At the collegiate level, Dawn Staley, head coach of South
Carolina, became just the second female African American coach to win
a national championship in 2018—not because African American female coaches don't have strong performance records, but because so
few have been given the chance to begin with.

   In a 2018 study, Morgan State University researchers found the
major problem holding African American women back is that "black
women's athletic abilities are severely undervalued in favor of their
physical appearance, whether they are attacked for 'mannish' appearances or overly praised for their femininity."[11] In 2017, the Institute for
Diversity and Ethics in Sport created a report card that surprisingly and
discouragingly rated the colleges studied the "lowest combined grade

for gender and racial hiring since the study has been conducted in more than a decade."[12] There exists an entire host of roadblocks surrounding African American women and women in general that prevents them from becoming coaches at every level of sport.

The LGBTQ community also faces a greater degree of difficulty than their straight female counterparts when it comes to hiring, pay, and promotions in the coaching world. A pronounced level of prejudice against female LGBTQ coaches still exists. A report by the Women's Sports Foundation describes the plight of Pat Griffin, author of *Strong Women, Deep Closets*, who was a Division II basketball coach. She describes the intrusive experience of her athletic director "following her home to see if she went to her house or her girlfriend's after work when he suspected her of being gay."[13] The fear continues to this day for LGBTQ coaches and administrators, so many keep their sexual orientation quiet until they get "outed." Unfortunately, when this "outing" occurs, both coaches and administrators may pay a price.

As mentioned previously, Tracey Griesbaum was fired from her position at the University of Iowa without cause after working for the university for 22 years—first as an assistant field hockey coach for seven years and then as the head coach for 14, with a career record of 169 wins and 107 losses. Griesbaum's attorney, Thomas Newkirk, believes this case was 80 percent a gender bias complaint, with an underlying bias against his client's sexual orientation. With this in mind, the lawsuit he filed on Griesbaum's behalf was intended to draw attention to the plight of female coaches, who are always fighting gender bias, sometimes in a subtle manner and sometimes in a not-so-subtle manner, as this case demonstrates. Oftentimes, female coaches are expected to be better than the worst male coach. Newkirk noted that the female coaches he encountered while working on this case were highly competent. Griesbaum has said that her motivation to follow through with the lawsuit was to fight for the rights of all female coaches.

Newkirk's strategy for changing this mindset is to educate universities throughout the country about gender stereotyping and bias. He has already gone to such schools as the University of California, Berkeley and the University of Pennsylvania to educate these institutions about the significance of gender bias and the direct significance it has on their programs. He uses an interesting analogy in which he has them imagine having a sick family member who needs a risky operation. You look around for the best surgeon and hospital that specializes in the type of surgery needed. You find the surgeon and a hospital that offers a viewing room where family members can watch the surgery. Everything seems fine, but you suddenly realize that not one person in the room has washed their hands, yet the surgery is moving forward. In this scenario, the unwashed hands represent the gender bias in your own organization.

The deep-rooted belief that sport culture is inherently masculine prevents many smart and capable female athletes from advancing in their careers and joining the ranks of men in leadership. If they run into problems or get fired, they are also far more likely to be immediately blackballed in the coaching community, unlike their male counterparts. For change to take place, female coaches must continue to fight for their right to lead. Their athletes must follow suit, and sponsors need to step up to support women leaders in sport.

EXPECTATIONS OF PERFECTION FOR FEMALE COACHES

How can coaches promote the rights and strengths of female athletes so they are not afraid to speak up and become leaders in their field? Women have entered into this tacit agreement to not speak up, to not rock the boat. Female coaches are often held to a much higher standard of skill than males, even as they're expected to be happy with less pay, recognition, and media coverage. As women such as field hockey coach Tracey Griesbaum and her partner, Jane Meyer, an associate athletic director, speak up about the different treatment between female and male coaches, there seem to be retaliatory actions that often occur. A discrimination lawsuit was filed by Jane Meyer for firing without cause for gender and sexual discrimination. A verdict was given in her favor against the University of Iowa, and she was awarded $4 million. The most disappointing part of this situation is that it effectively ended Meyer's career and possibly Griesbaum's as well, especially now that their lesbian status is public.

Female coaches deal with the same biases that all women in sport do, notably whether women are truly capable of being leaders in sport. In an interview with *SportsLetter*, Sheila Robertson—author, writer, and editor of the *Canadian Journal for Women in Coaching*—explained that there are "common misperceptions" regarding female coaches:

> There's a suspicion of women's ability to coach, and the particular skills that women coaches bring beyond technical knowledge—like empathy or listening skills—are not necessarily recognized or understood. They've also had difficulty being taken seriously. Even in some traditional female sports, they haven't fared that well.[14]

Women coaches are often expected to coach like men rather than recognizing they have different strengths than men as coaches. Two highly valuable skills they bring to the table are those that set them apart from men: empathy and listening skills. When I interviewed Lindsay Gottlieb (former coach of the University of California, Berkeley's women's basketball team and the new assistant coach for the Cleveland Cavaliers) for my book *Sisterhood in Sports: How Female Athletes Collaborate and Compete*, she explained her practice of speaking individually to every member of her women's team to get to know each player better. In the latter part of this interview, she shared her philosophy on the business of basketball, emphasizing that when she was making play decisions, they weren't personal, but rather based on who was the best player(s) for what was needed at a certain time.

In February 2019, highly successful Georgia Tech women's basketball coach MaChelle Joseph was abruptly put on leave for no defined reason. The university's explanation was that Coach Jo had been suspended for a "pending personnel matter." Yet, at the same time, Georgia Tech was being investigated by the NCAA and discovered that the men's basketball coaching staff had committed "multiple-level recruiting violations," but no one was put on leave. "Joseph was in her 16th season as Tech's head (women's) coach," with the "longest and most successful tenure of any coach in team history."[15] Georgia Tech eventually fired her in late March 2019, due to supposed mental and physical abuse of her players. Coach Jo's perspective focused on the fact that she was pushing the administration to increase their actions in addressing gender equity issues. In direct contrast, in April 2019, a Middle Tennessee State head male volleyball coach, Chuck Crawford, was accused of similar mistreatment of players; although the complaints against him included borderline physical abuse, the athletic director instead set up a last-chance agreement and a "self-improvement program."[16] The un-equal treatment of these two coaches is glaring.

Some important and unique qualities of women that add to their skills as coaches are often questioned. In *Sisterhood in Sport*, I discuss how certain common female characteristics are important to consider when working with female athletes, including talking about relation-ships, empathy, listening, and the desire to collaborate with teammates and other sports personnel. In the coaching world, these qualities are often misunderstood and certainly not appreciated.

Female coaches don't always receive adequate verbal support from male coaches. Men need to take a stand and support their female counterparts' right and ability to work with both female and male teams. In a 2018 study of women's soccer in France, Germany, and Norway, researchers addressed the question, "Does performance justify underrepresentation of women coaches in pro soccer?" The authors reached two important conclusions: 1) A coach's gender does not make a noticeable impact on a team's performance, and 2) a coach's prior experience as a player does not impact team performance.[17]

Nicole LaVoi, a leading authority on female coaches, commented in January 2019 on one key finding: "Gender of coach doesn't matter, so hiring men should not be preferred or the norm!"[18] We should be hiring the best person for the job. It's time for the public to stand up and take notice of the truth—that women are just as qualified and capable of coaching any sport as men. White men, we're giving you notice: Women of every color will be standing up and shouting out their desire to coach, starting now.

A LENS ON WOMEN OF COLOR COACHES

Colleges don't hire women coaches very often, let alone women of color. African American women get limited chances at coaching jobs, especially head coaching jobs. They face the double whammy of being black and female. The Institute for Diversity and Ethics in Sport's an-nual Racial and Gender Report Card: College Sport indicated that the combination of the gender and racial hiring practices in sport received the lowest combined grade in the history of the report for the second consecutive year. As mentioned earlier, Richard Lapchick's "Diversity and Ethics in Sports" report found that in Division I, only 11.4 percent of women's basketball head coaches were African American, compared to 43.4 percent of the players being African American. To put it more directly, only 37 out of 315 basketball head coaches are African American women.[19] In explaining the report's overall findings, Lapchick commented that the improvements in the numbers of white female coaches and athletic administrators were "negatively balanced by the fact that in the 46th year after the passage of Title IX, more than 60 percent of all women's teams are still coached by men." He added, "Opportunities for coaches of color continued to be a significant area of concern in all divisions. . . . Thus, it is even more important for us to create expanded opportunities in college sport for women and people of color."[20] As always, the party-line colleges claim that they plan to establish initiatives for racial and ethnic diversity, but they never seem to get around to taking any substantial action or making any real gains in this area.

The outlook for African American and other women of color *is* improving in the WNBA, albeit slowly. The annual report card from Lapchick's organization asserts that the improvement originates from the league's more recent establishment that there was an emphasis on diversity from the beginning. According to the same report card, 11 women and nine people of color hold ownership in the WNBA, and six WNBA head coaches are women—but only one is African American. Where the league does shine with African American women is in the hiring of assistant coaches: A total of 53.6 percent of the leagues' assistant coaches are people of color, and 61.5 percent of them are women. In professional-level staffing, the percentage of people of color hired rose from 26.1 to 51.2 in 2017.[21] As Delise S. O'Meally, executive director of the Institute for Sport and Social Justice, stated, "It's not by happenstance that the WNBA is the most socially conscious league. . . . Strong leadership and a commitment to diversity and inclusion create an environment where people feel valued, respected, and supported."[22] The WNBA is the leading league by far when it comes to the hiring of African American women; however, there is still a long way to go, both in the WNBA and especially other professional women's and men's sport leagues, before true gender parity can be achieved.

Only 9.8 percent of coaches of NCAA Division I women's teams are female. The majority of these are white women; a total of 8.3 percent of

coaches are white women, while African American women make up a
mere 0.6 percent. In addition, Latina coaches make up only 0.6 percent
and Asian/Pacific Islanders just 0.3 percent. These figures demonstrate
how limited the coaching opportunities are for African American wom-
en and other women of color.

The figures on the hiring of black female coaches are grim; furthermore, once they are hired, they are often pressured to produce results
in unrealistic time frames that would never be imposed on men. And
rarely are African American women or female coaches in general given
a second chance if their first chance doesn't work out.

Felisha Legette-Jack is one of those few African American women
coaches who did get a second chance. In 2012, when she was fired from
her basketball coaching job at Indiana University, she felt defeated, and
her confidence was shot. When, in June of that year, the University of
Buffalo reached out to her, she was thrilled to take the head coaching
position for their women's basketball team. Buffalo believed Legette-
Jack had the characteristics they were looking for in a coach, including a
willingness to support their location, hold players accountable, generate
enthusiasm and energy, and strengthen and fully shape players—both
physically and mentally.[23] Legette-Jack has embraced these coaching
principles and exceeded the University of Buffalo's expectations: In the
2018 season she led her team to a 29–5 record and an entry into the
Sweet Sixteen. Buffalo ultimately lost to Dawn Staley and the University of South Carolina, but just gaining entry to the event was an accom-
plishment greater than the Bulls had ever imagined. When Legette-
Jack was asked after the game about diversity and leadership opportunities for women of color in basketball, she first replied, "Wow." She
then proclaimed, "The fight isn't easy, but it is necessary." She further
stated that female African American players need "role models that look
like them." Her advice: "Stay in the race and keep fighting."[24]

Another strong female force working toward change among African
American head coaches in basketball is Dawn Staley. Staley is one of
only two African American women to win a NCAA women's basketball
championship. Staley feels the discomfort as an African American female basketball player and coach. Even as a winning coach, she feels
extra pressure as an African American female coach and often faces
racial prejudices. Staley, who grew up in the Raymond Rosen housing
projects of North Philadelphia, has an insider's view and understanding

of the background of many of her players. Like former WNBA player Kisha Ford-Torres, she grew up in a neighborhood full of drugs, gangs, and violence but also had both her parents, who closely watched their kids and had strict rules they enforced. Despite growing up in these circumstances, both women have succeeded in their lives—primarily, they say, thanks to their focus on and commitment to basketball. The discipline Ford-Torres learned helped her to become a police officer. As former head coach of Temple University's women's basketball team and current coach of the University of South Carolina, Staley has come a long way since her early years.

The situation for women of color in many sports, especially the ones that aren't "traditional black women's sports," is discouraging. There are success stories of African American women coaches in nontraditional sports that are worth sharing, however—stories that the younger generation needs to know and hear about. Tina Sloan Green's successful coaching of all-white female lacrosse teams is a prime example.

Fencing legend Nikki Franke (now retired), for instance, is a prime example of an African American athlete in a nontraditional sport. Raised in Harlem, she is an Olympian, an internationally known fencing coach, and cofounder—along with Tina Sloan Green, Dr. Alpha Alexander, and Linda Brown, Esq.—of the Black Women in Sport Foundation, located in Philadelphia. In discussing her background, Franke described herself as always being an athlete, playing such sports as basketball and tennis as a girl. She didn't begin fencing until her senior year of high school. At Brooklyn College, she entered the sport full force, being coached by one of her mentors, Denise O'Connor, and almost instantly excelling. Franke found fencing to be primarily a white sport, but she received free lessons and support, which helped her improve her skills, and she eventually became an Olympian in 1976 and 1980. She attended a master's program at Temple University, became a teaching assistant, and transformed the school's women's fencing club into a successful and award-winning team. After coaching at Temple for 46 years, she left with an incredibly successful 807–242–1 record. Despite her success and role modeling, she remains the only African American woman to have coached a Division I fencing team.

GLIMMERS OF HOPE?

There are but glimmers of hope for improvement in this area at the moment. The names of the studies and articles on the subject—"Sports Coaching Is Still a Male-Dominated Field," "Why Has the Number of Women Coaches Fallen since Title IX?," "Lack of Presence for Female Coaches Extends to Kids' Games"—alone demonstrate the high levels of inequality for female coaches.

A revision of the current values in sport is needed to make room for more female coaches. Young girls, teens, and collegiate athletes need to experience female role models and mentors who stand for success in leadership, especially in sports. We need to reverse the takeover of girls' and women's teams coaching jobs by men that stemmed from the increase in salary and value of those jobs after Title IX took effect.

The picture is not hopeful, with a few exceptions, regarding the promotion of women, especially women of color, in coaching. This has never been more evidenced than in 2017, by Coach Auriemma's flippant comment that "women don't want to coach." This unconscious bias exists with many white men who don't understand how many women do want to coach but are not given the opportunity to do so. Even men like Auriemma who are supportive of female coaches and players don't fully appreciate or understand the depth of the problem. His blurted-out comment to McGraw after she vowed not to hire any more male coaches was, "I hope she sends a thank you to all those guys that used to be on her staff that got her all those good players that won a championship."[25] This was not an accurate statement, since she had an all-female staff for six years previous to Notre Dame's championship win in 2018.

What the sports world needs more of is education about and action in increasing the number of women coaches—not only white women, but also African American women, other women of color, and lesbians and transgender women. Girls, women, and even boys need and deserve female role models who can also become their mentors. The following are a couple of examples of support for increasing the number of female coaches is sports.

As an advocate for female coaches, Thomas Newkirk—the attorney for Tracey Griesbaum and Jane Meyer in the lawsuits against the University of Iowa—recognizes the need for greater awareness of the value of female coaches in sport. As Newkirk extensively explained to me about gender bias in coaching,

> One of the largest and most poorly understood challenges facing women in athletics is the impact of implicit gender bias. It affects hiring and pay of female coaches and administrators, resulting in women being paid less and fewer women being hired. It affects women's quality of life by creating workplace hostility and pressure. And it makes female coaches more vulnerable to unwarranted complaints from student athletes and parents. Few, if any, universities presently appreciate how gender bias creates and exacerbates those complaints. The result is that female coaches often receive more of those complaints, they are undermined by them, and then investigated and fired because of them. We have identified over 80 female coaches taken down by these complaints and counting. These complaints are not because women are bad coaches or are doing anything wrong. They are generated simply because the coaches are women. To address this problem, I reach out to universities, not just as a lawyer, but as an educator. I travel to universities to carefully explain how gender bias affects decision-making and what actions each university can take to reduce bias. My presentations focus is on student-athlete complaints because most administrators recognize that complaints are a problem in college athletics. My hope is that, by raising awareness, we can save the jobs of potentially hundreds of great female coaches, leaders, and mentors of young women. Some universities are very open to learning about this bias and are supportive of my efforts. Others are less open, but we are making slow progress.

Newkirk's goal is to offer extensive educational training to major universities about the topic of gender bias to build a better understanding of how this affects the recruiting, hiring, and retention of female coaches.

Meanwhile, in January 2019, Volkswagen of America signed a four-year sponsorship deal worth eight figures with USA Soccer (#VWOne-Goal), part of which stipulates extensive funding for programs for the development of more female coaches. Jill Ellis, coach for the U.S. women's national soccer team, expressed her excitement about the deal and its potential assistance, saying, "Female athletes can relate to female coaches and provide them the aspiration to get into coaching themselves. I'm looking forward to seeing results of this partnership and seeing the impact it will have on providing more opportunities to develop female coaches in the near future."[26] The fact that Volkswagen has budgeted funds for developing female coaches is also an example of the slow, yet hopeful, progress.

It's exciting to hear that funds for the further development of female coaches are starting to trickle in and more men are stepping forward to support women in coaching; perhaps things really are moving in the right direction. As Nicole LaVoi said,

> Having women in athletic leadership and sport coaching matters. Women coaches matter because they provide diversity in the workplace. Women coaches matter because they provide a visible career pathway for young women to enter the coaching profession. Women coaches matter because they can relate differently to young women than men because they are a same-sex role model. Women coaches also provide role models for boys, as well as girls. I think young men and women should have the opportunity to have a variety of role models, and gender is one component of that.[27]

ACTION STEPS TOWARD PROMOTING WOMEN COACHES

1. Rally for increasing numbers of female coaches, especially culturally diverse ones. As alumni of various universities, our role is to put pressure on our alma maters to hire more female coaches through phone calls and letter writing.
2. Encourage more female coaches to be courageous by speaking up about the inequities of women coaches, as Muffet McGraw has.
3. Put pressure on colleges and universities to act on their "policies" to hire greater numbers of culturally diverse coaches, including African Americans, other women of color, and LGBTQ. It's time for action.
4. Work toward creating opportunities for young black athletes to enter nontraditional "black sports," as the Black Women in Sport Foundation has done in its work with youth. It's important for black youth to see coaches who look like them.
5. Educate high schools, colleges, and universities about gender, racial, and sexual bias, as Thomas Newkirk is doing.

6

THE #METOO MOVEMENT IN SPORTS

Speaking Up about Sexual Assault and Abuse

> In order to escape accountability for his crimes, the perpetrator does everything in his power to promote forgetting. If secrecy fails, the perpetrator attacks the credibility of his victim. If he cannot silence her absolutely, he tries to make sure no one listens.
> —Judith Lewis Herman, *Trauma and Recovery: The Aftermath of Violence—from Domestic Abuse to Political Terror*[1]

#MeToo is a movement that encourages and supports victims to speak up to expose sexually predatory men and women; in the sports world, this means calling out people in positions of authority who abuse athletes, especially female athletes. As the Larry Nassar case illustrates, sexual assault and abuse are rampant in U.S. sport today. Dr. Nassar's accusers numbered 256, and there are likely hundreds more who suffered at his hands that we don't know about.

The first complaints about Nassar date back to 1992. Despite the fact that an abuse report was filed with the USOC in 2015, no real action was taken until September 2016. Unfortunately, the USOC has played a strong role in ignoring and covering up abuse complaints. That year, however, 156 brave female gymnasts stood up and told their stories at Nassar's sentencing hearing, and the USOC and the rest of the world were forced to pay attention. "Nassar's trial has shone a light on a mentality in the sports world that values performance over protection, medals over morals," wrote Hadley Freeman in a January 2018 *Guardian* piece.[2]

Where was the protection to prevent the abuse of female athletes in this situation? Where were the USOC and Michigan State University? Can we trust coaches, trainers, doctors, or any other sporting authority to watch out for female athletes? One estimate places sexual abuse of younger athletic children at between 2 percent and 8 percent, with the majority consisting of girls. This report also says, "Elite young athletes were more likely to be sexually assaulted than their lower-level counter-

S-by-SW-at the Heart of Gold: Inside USA Gymnastics Scandal. *Nancy Hogshead-Makar, JD*

parts."[3] The focus of this examination will be solely on the female athletes who have struggled with sexual harassment and abuse.

The shocking case of Dr. Nassar is just one example of this type of abuse. As far back as 1995, Joan Ryan wrote *Little Girls in Pretty Boxes*, a groundbreaking book that was meant to unveil the abuse of female gymnasts and figure skaters. Sadly, what she wrote is still relevant today, and the book was rereleased in 2018.

People working with athletes who have experienced sexual assault and abuse are beginning to recognize three basic premises that clinicians like myself have known for years: Athletes need to find people they can trust to share this information with; they must recognize that they have experienced inappropriate and abusive sexual behaviors by an authority figure; and they need to receive support for, acknowledgment of, and validation of their experiences and the emotional pain they're feeling. The people in sport who they speak to, meanwhile, need to believe their reporting and help them find professional assistance—preferably, both a therapist and legal counsel. Hopefully, the guilty verdict handed down in the Nassar case will help others to be brave and speak up when abuses occur.

Sexual abuse—for some context regarding how far behind the sporting community is in this area—first came to the public's attention in the late 1960s and early 1970s. In 1979, when I was working in a low-income, predominantly black high school as a counselor from an outside agency in San Diego, one of my first referrals was a young African American girl who had a secret that she shared with me: Her four brothers were passing her around for sex. This was the year California had passed a series of laws mandating reporting about child abuse and neglect—the Child Abuse and Reporting Act (AB 1775).

My initial instinct was that this case needed to be reported and the young teen taken from her home immediately. I came to discover that this abused young girl had also told my supervisor and the school nurse what was happening to her at home, but they were unaware of the new reporting laws and had done nothing. When I informed them about this mandatory reporting, they were still resistant to taking action. Only through persistence and sheer determination was I eventually able to convince my supervisor to file a report with Child Protective Services, and I convinced the school nurse to report as well.

As a clinician in 1981, I encountered another case of sexual abuse. This time, the victim was a 15-year-old girl who was being sexually abused by her stepfather. He would sneak into her room at night and crawl into her bed for intercourse, threatening the girl each time to keep her quiet. Unfortunately, despite being presented with physical evidence of the abuse, the girl's mother ultimately chose her stepfather over her daughter. The deep pain that this girl was experiencing was evident the first time I met her. Her trust was so shattered it took her a long time to warm up to me and speak about the terrible sexual abuse she'd suffered at the hands of her stepdad. Thankfully, her best friend, whom she had confided in, had encouraged her to report the abuse. During the time of our sessions, she was living with that friend.

Nancy Hogshead-Makar, a three-time Olympic gold medalist, an expert on Title IX, and an attorney, is a leading advocate for women in sports, now particularly harassed, assaulted, and abused female athletes. She says she only started receiving calls for legal advice regarding sexual abuse in the sporting community in 2010, despite the fact that such abuses had been ongoing for years. Unfortunately, Hogshead-Makar could relate all too well, having been raped herself as a college student at Duke University.

Hogshead-Makar met with USOC officials, one of whom was CEO Scott Blackmun, in 2012, to articulate her concerns about the abuse of female athletes. When she realized her concerns were not being taken seriously enough and no real action was taking place, she went back to the USOC board and convinced them to "pass a resolution that requires all national sports governing bodies to outlaw romantic and sexual relationships between coaches and athletes."[4] On October 28, 2014, she founded Champion Women, a nonprofit organization dedicated to legal advocacy to open the discussion about sexual abuse in sports and encourage action to prevent it. The organization also works for equal sports access and equality for girls and to end discrimatory practices directed at women in sport.

In 2018, the Equality League, with the support of Champion Women, succeeded in getting the Safe Sports Act passed. The act requires youth sports organizations to report sexual abuse within 24 hours of its discovery, extends the statute of limitations, and enforces a mandatory minimal payment of $150,000 to victims of sexual abuse in sports. According to Hogshead-Makar, the Nassar case let the dirty secret of

Nancy Hogshead-Makar. *Nancy Hogshead-Makar, JD*

sports out of the bag and vastly increased awareness about sexual abuse with athletes. This marked the beginning of the #MeToo Sports movement. Male authority sport coaches, doctors, and trainers have long exerted their power and dominance over female athletes; Hogshead-Makar is leading the way to protect these athletes.

VICTIMS SPEAK OUT

So often, the focus of sexual abuse is on the predators themselves rather than the victims. The beauty of the #MeToo Sports movement is the acknowledgment, recognition, and sharing of survivors' stories. So many abused voices were heard and validated in the landmark Nassar case. The 150 gymnasts who stood up and spoke, for example, Olympians Aly Raisman, Simone Biles, McKayla Mahoney, Jordyn Wieber, and Jamie Dantzscher, were listened to and validated after sharing their experiences. Dantzscher, a member of the 2000 U.S. Olympics gymnastics team, described the climate of abuse she experienced in elite-level gymnastics even before the sexual abuse, often being called fat and directed to take off weight any way that she could by coaches; even Bela and Martha Karolyi, legendary gymnastics coaches who denied having any knowledge of Larry Nassar's abuses, she said, were verbally abusive. It wasn't until she heard the story of another gymnast abused by her coach, Keith Willete, while working at a gymnastics camp that she realized Nassar had abused her. Initially, Dantzscher was criticized and ostracized for speaking up about the abuse, which had started in 1994.[5]

Shortly, however, the tide began to change as story after story of Nassar's abuses emerged. Thanks to the reporting of these stories by Chris Chavez in *Sports Illustrated* and a thorough timeline of the Nassar case created by James Dator for SBNation, we are better able to understand the betrayal, pain, and seriously damaging behavior that was inflicted on Nassar's numerous victims.

Kyle Stephens's abuse began at the tender age of six. She was the daughter of one of Nassar's friends. He first exposed himself to her in an isolated boiler room, where he then pleasured himself, rubbed his penis on her naked feet, and stuck his ungloved finger into her vagina.[6] When she shared her story, Stephens detailed the abuse, which had occurred for years. Even when she went to her parents, Nassar persuaded them that her description of her experiences was false.[7]

Rebecca Mark encountered Nassar as a high school freshman soccer player. She only realized that Nassar's "treatment" was sexual abuse after reading an article about him in the *Indy Star*.

Danielle Moore's abuse occurred as a teen. After her inappropriate treatment by Nassar, she felt suicidal and "worthless." Despite earning a PhD, Moore refused to attend graduation because she felt she "didn't deserve the praise."[8]

One of the most damning testimonies against Nassar came from a victim's mother, Donna Markham, mother of Chelsea Markham. At 10 years old, her adopted daughter, Chelsea, hurt her back on the high beam. In 2012, Donna took her daughter to Nassar, who was highly recommended to her. "He put his fingers inside me, and they weren't even gloved," Chelsea told her mother. "Mom, he hurt me," she said.[9] In 2009, Chelsea committed suicide. The majority of his victims have seriously suffered in their lives and survive with major wounds.

The much earlier story of long-distance swimmer Diana Nyad is a powerful example reminding us that sexual abuse by coaches has gone on for decades. Now 69, Nyad wrote an opinion piece for the *New York Times* in 2017, describing her ordeal. In 1964, at age 14, she was naïve and adored her swim coach like a father. One day after a swim meet, the coach invited the team to his home, which was common practice at the time. Nyad woke from a dead sleep in the master bedroom to find her coach on top of her. "He yanked my suit down," she wrote.

> He grabbed at and drooled onto my breasts. He hyperventilated and moaned. I didn't breathe for perhaps two full minutes, my body locked in an impenetrable flex. My arms trembled, pinned to my sides. He pleaded with me to open my legs, but they were pressed hard together. If breath gives us force, that day I could feel the strength in my body from the polar opposite—from not breathing. He ejaculated on my stomach, my athletic torso I was so proud of now suddenly violated with this strange and foul stuff.[10]

Former Olympic and pro female athletes Nancy Hogshead-Makar and Breanna Stewart have also come forward with their nonsport stories of rape. Stewart came forth in October 2017 to share her story of surviving childhood sexual abuse in the Player's Tribune, a media platform where first-person stories from athletes are shared, along with videos and podcasts.[11] She is using her celebrity status in a positive manner to share her experience and support for the #MeToo movement in sports.

The victims in these situations are mostly female athletes who trusted their coaches and other authority figures to protect them and keep their best interests in mind. These abuses are betrayals that cause deep wounds not easily healed. Female athletes at every level have experienced sexual abuse; elite female athletes, however, tend to experience abuse to a greater degree. We are learning about the stories of abuse of athletes in numerous sports by not only sporting personnel, but also other authority figures connected to female athletes.

In 2018, the culture slowly began changing in sports regarding the sexual abuse of female athletes. Now, when athletes report abuse, there are many avenues for them to take where they are more likely to encounter those who will believe them and take action. Survivors are given permission and even encouraged to step forward.

Despite the revelations Ryan's book brought to light in 1995, little or nothing was done to deal with the abuses she reported in gymnastics for 20 years until the ugliness of the Nassar case came into public view. Then, what Ryan had written about many years earlier was revealed by the survivors themselves in court. Julie Foudy commented, "There's finally a feeling among women that it's okay to talk about it. . . . Watching the movement, the bravery of women coming forward, it emboldens others. The whole point is that the new generations shouldn't have to deal with this."[12]

Owning their power, women in sport are speaking up and shouting out to the public that they won't suffer this abuse any longer in silence. The new generation of girls and young women are claiming their voices and demanding to be heard.

PREDATORS

What we're realizing from recent events is that the problem of sexual assault and abuse of female athletes runs rampant in the sports world. From the revelations of the Nassar case to Diana Nyad's story, we're beginning to see the extent of abuse by coaches, doctors, trainers, physical therapists, and others in positions of power in sport. Unfortunately, many sporting organizations have played a major role in covering up these crimes. In a recent tweet, Nancy Hogshead-Makar took to task the USOC for its culpability in all this, writing, "The U.S. Olympic Committee deployed systems by powerful, wealthy people that protected power, not athletes. Scott Blackmun and his law firm, Bryan Cave, convinced even the head of ethics and SafeSport that the USOC 'couldn't' help athletes.'" Her response: "That was never true."[13]

The USOC's negligence in following up on sexual abuse complaints has significantly contributed to the lack of action in addressing these issues. Their protection of predators, not the victims, has allowed sexual abuse to flourish in Olympic sports. This abuse has occurred for decades, with minimal action. As additional revelations occur, the USOC and other sports organizations are being forced to start taking action.

USOC CEO Scott Blackmun resigned in February 2018, shortly after the Pyeongchang Games, amid accusations of neglecting to effectively deal with the sexual abuse allegations made by athletes in USA Gymnastics, USA Swimming, USA Taekwondo, and USA Volleyball. USA Swimming and USA Taekwondo still have outstanding investigations. Blackmum's failure to adequately deal with the complaints in 2015 led to Nassar continuing his abusive and harmful practices for another 15 months. Even more damning, according to court documents, the USOC knew about sexual abuse allegations going back to the 1990s in USA Gymnastics. This accusation has been backed up by statements made by Kathy Scanlan, head of USA Gymnastics from 1994 to 1998. Her portrayal of the situation has been that when she did report the problem, little, if anything, was done. In addition, Scanlan was discouraged from following up, and no consequences were exacted for the professionals involved.[14]

The next head of USA Gymnastics, Bob Colarossi, expressed the same uneasiness about the way female gymnasts had been treated and voiced his feelings that the USOC appeared to hold an "apparent indifference to the welfare of young children."[15] These early reports show us a pattern of concealment that occurred for years without consequences for the predator coaches, doctors, and trainers, amongst others.

Steve Penny, another former head of USA Gymnastics, stayed silent for 15-plus months after receiving complaints about Nassar, allowing the doctor to continue his destructive and abusive behavior. He was fired in March 2017 for his obvious concealment of sexual abuse complaints, and arrested in October 2018 for tampering with evidence in the Nassar case. He was subsequently added to the "permanently ineligible" Olympics list for breaching the SafeSport Conduct Code for the U.S. Olympic and Paralympic Movement. Angela Povilaitis, the Michigan assistant district attorney who prosecuted Nassar, stated, "Steve Penny put money and medals over child protection. . . . When he had the opportunity, he did not do the right thing."[16]

In early 2018, Congress ordered a bipartisan House Energy and Commerce subcommittee investigation into sexual abuse in USA gymnastics, USA Swimming, and USA Taekwondo, as well as at Michigan

State. As committee chair Greg Walden (R-Oregon) stated in December 2018, "The abhorrent abuses associated with Dr. Nassar's case and the allegations by US Taekwondo (athletes) and U.S. swimmers are disgusting and outrageous, and raise serious concerns about protecting athletes from abuse and mistreatment in organized sports." The culpability of the USOC and Michigan State University in the Nassar case will be discovered even further in this investigation.[17]

The Nassar case is illustrative of the pattern of a sexual predator. As one article in the *Guardian* asked, "How was Larry Nassar able to abuse so many gymnasts for so long?"[18] For 20 years, Nassar was the doctor for USA Gymnastics and Michigan State University. His first-known assault occurred in 1992, when he violated a 12-year-old girl while he was a medical student. This action was a big red flag. Yet no one did anything about his behavior. According to Nassar, his intent in that case was to conduct medical research. He went on to repeatedly assault Kyle Stephens when she was only six years old, and then, in 1994, he assaulted Jamie Dantzscher. Nassar accumulated many more victims along the way, leaving the wreckage of human lives in his wake.

Perpetrators work hard to create feelings of powerlessness in their victims. Through the process of grooming, they slowly use manipulative behaviors to insert themselves into their victim's lives. Meanwhile, they are also working hard to cover up the abuse. Kimberlee Norris, an attorney who works on these types of cases, notes, "Across the board, one in four girls and one in six boys under the age of 18 will be a victim. . . . The highest-risk areas are those that allow for one-on-one adult–child interaction, often at the elite level."[19] These abuses often occur in locker rooms and bathrooms, and during travel. One strategy predators employ is to create a sense of intimacy and/or "specialness," or through a power dynamic in which verbal threats and/or lies are perpetuated, including such phrases as "you will be humiliated," "don't tell anyone or I will say bad things about you," or "this is our special, secret time." These manipulations make victims experience such negative feelings as fear, doubt, shame, guilt, self-blame, worthlessness, anger, hopelessness, and depression. According to one report on sexual abuse of athletes, "The intrinsic power dynamics within the coach–athlete relationship inevitably opens that relationship to abuse and enables coercion strategies to be used."[20]

There are three main types of coaches who sexually abuse female athletes, according to one group of European sports researchers. The first type, the "flirting-charming coach," expresses charming behavior by teasing and joking, before slowly moving on to make physical contact with the athlete. The "seductive coach" often applies suggestive terminology and then puts his hands on the athlete. Finally, the "authoritarian coach" uses an actively controlling and domineering style, with the goal of creating obedient and passive behavior on the part of the female athlete.[21] The goal of these three types of coaches is to get the athlete to submit to their sexual abuse by holding power over them. Oftentimes, these coaches play the role of the "father" for youth and teen athletes, making it even more difficult for their victims to say no to them.

Today, USA Swimming's banned list includes 150 coaches, but a New Jersey swim coach estimates that the actual number should be more than 1,000. At the higher levels of swimming, the majority of coaches are males, as they are in many sports. "I think the consequences of having an overwhelming male coaching staff and leadership is a reason for a lot of sexual abuse," Nancy Hogshead-Makar stated.[22]

Predators often hide in plain sight. Nassar is a perfect example of a predator who was able to hide behind his reputation—which, we now know, was not deserved. In the media, we are finally seeing many men of power and prestige with long histories of abuse being exposed. There is a strong body of research showing that in the recent past, there has been reluctance to follow up on complaints, as well as a tendency to quash accusations of star athletes and leading coaches.[23] The ignorance and number of uninformed administrators, even in women-led organizations, is profound.

TAKING ACTION: ENACTING LEGISLATION AND CREATING ORGANIZATIONS FOR THE REPORTING OF SEXUAL HARASSMENT AND ABUSE IN SPORTS

As previously mentioned, due to the work of Nancy Hogshead-Makar and many others, in 2012 a USOC bylaw was created making sexual and romantic relationships between athletes and coaches impermissible. This bylaw was just the start of creating more concrete boundaries to protect female youth and women athletes. Then came the creation of

Hogshead-Makar's organization, Champion Women, in 2014. The S.534 Protecting Young Victims from Sexual Abuse and Safe Sport Authorization Act of 2017, signed into law on February 14, 2018, expanded on the Victims of Child Abuse Act of 1990 and the Amateur Sports Act of 1978.[24] This important act covers stipulations for sexual abuse prevention training, policies, and mandatory reporting. The mandatory reporting has broadened to include any adult working with a minor or amateur athlete in their organization and requires that amateur sporting organizations report any sexual abuse suspicions to police and/or Child Protective Services in California. For certain organizations, there is also a requirement that they report any concerns they might have about the abuse of athletes to the U.S. Center for Safe Sport and the appropriate law enforcement agencies. In addition, sports organizations are now required to provide ongoing child abuse reporting and prevention training, and establish child abuse prevention strategies and policies.

As these new laws were going into effect, the U.S. Center for Safe-Sport opened in March 2018. As an independent, nonprofit organization, the center strives to stop all forms of abuse in sports, including bullying, harassment, hazing, physical abuse, emotional abuse, and sexual misconduct and abuse. It's a confidential organization set up to provide a safe place for athletes in the Olympic and Paralympic movements—roughly 8 million children and a total of 16 million athletes, according to Hogshead-Makar. The goal of SafeSport is to "make athlete well-being the centerpiece of our nation's sports culture."[25]

Prevention/Advocacy in Organizations

What specific actions can sport leaders take to improve the protection of girls and women in sport? An information, education, and action approach can be quite effective. It is essential that concrete actions be taken in preventing abuse in youth sports. Until now, this kind of action has been sorely lacking within the USOC structure and other athletic organizations that work with youth.

Sports can provide youths with positive character and team-building skills. Sports teach young people constructive life skills—when the conditions of their training and competing are healthy. Abuse takes all that away. Because of this, abuse prevention programs are vital. Organizations need to take responsibility for the protection of their athletes. To address this need, additional organizations have popped up, offering tips and suggestions on how athletes can protect themselves. Safe to Compete: Protecting Child Athletes from Sexual Abuse (www.safetocompete.org), an organization sponsored by the National Center for Missing and Exploited Children, was created in 2013 to provide resources for protecting young athletes from sexual abuse. They have developed a series of written resources to help other organizations develop child sexual abuse prevention training programs, one of them being "An Introduction of Sound Practices for Keeping Children Safer in Youth-Serving Organizations." In "Tips for Protecting Child Athletes from Sexual Abuse," there is a section entitled "Make a Game Plan," which includes the following questions:

> Are background checks performed on staff with access to youth?
> Does staff receive training on recognizing and reporting child sexual abuse? How often?
> Is there a staff code of conduct/ethics? Does it address inappropriate behaviors?
> What is your organization's reporting procedure?[26]

As they suggest, there are four things in particular that organizations that work with youth should keep in mind: They should check on who a potential team member really is; provide regular sexual abuse training; create appropriate guidelines for team member behaviors, set up ethical codes of conduct; and establish a consistent reporting procedure. This site also includes discussion guides and age-appropriate parameters, and it is a wonderful resource for organizations interested in improving their sexual abuse prevention infrastructure.

Sexual Abuse Prevention Models for Sports Organizations

A number of models have been developed for child athlete abuse prevention. Taking action to increase the implementation of these frameworks is essential for reducing and preventing further abuse. The Foundation for Global Sports website highlights preventing sexual abuse in sport. According to the site, 35 million children in the United States take part in sport each year, and if only 2 percent suffered abuse annually, that would add up to 700,000 sexual abuse victims in just one year.

Actually, the estimated range of abuse is 2 percent to 20 percent, so even in the middle of that range, that number is 3.5 million. They go on to illustrate a model developed for preventing sexual abuse in sports by Parent and Demers.[27] As the model indicates, there are three main areas to start with, including training and providing supplies to those in charge, providing leadership, and giving further support to sports. These are the main areas that filter into preventive measures and case management issues. The preventive measures are broken down into external and internal blockades, and even list more specific actions to take.

Sadly, about 90 percent of abused children are familiar with their abuser. Given the current climate, the time has arrived to take more strides toward prevention than ever before. Sexual abuse in sports has finally been revealed for the monster that it is. Dozens of reports are emerging in the Olympic movement and elsewhere. The U.S. Center for SafeSport is being inundated by reports as well. The #MeToo Sports movement is spotlighting the "dirty little secrets" that have been kept by coaches, trainers, and sports authority figures for far too long. These powerful male predators and those who have hidden them are at last being called on the carpet thanks to the courage, work, and openness of current and former athletes—athletes like Jamie Dantzscher, Simone Biles, and Aly Raisman, who experienced sexual abuse by Dr. Nassar. What we need to remember is that the USOC should be leading as an example. If the committee doesn't fully address the issue, it will set a precedent for how authorities in sport treat female—and some male— athletes who are sexually harassed and abused. The trauma these young female athletes experience can leave a mark on them that can last a lifetime.

The Committee to Restore Integrity to the USOC, now called Team Integrity, is working to demand better treatment of and safety for elite female athletes who have been sexually harassed and abused, as well as protection from abuse for all Olympic athletes. On January 16, 2019, the team met with Sarah Hirshland, the new CEO of the USOC, who wanted to better understand their frustration.[28] According to Hogshead-Makar, Team Integrity's mission is to "get changes in the Sport Act so that athletes are not dependent on the benevolence of the USOC board and executives, that athletes' seat at the table—their authority— is part of the architecture of the Olympic movement." Team Integrity created a list of 12 recommendations for the USOC to remake it into an "athletes-first" organization. We look to the actions of Team Integrity and others to keep pressure on the sporting community for greater acknowledgment of sexual harassment and abuse within the community and more confidential programs for the treatment of victims.

This is just the beginning. The work has only begun.

ACTION STEPS FOR INCREASING GENDER EQUITY IN SPORTS

1. Believe those athletes who report sexual abuse.
2. Report abuse immediately and/or within a week.
3. Recognize coaches who continually receive complaints about abusive behavior.
4. Support the abused athlete by getting them the help they require.
5. Support legislation that protects athletes from harassment and sexual abuse.
6. Report banned coaches who are coaching illegally.
7. Provide athletic staff with annual training on this topic.
8. Create more organizations that work to help victims of sexual abuse in athletics.

7

DOUBLE STANDARDS

Prejudice and Unequal Treatment of
Women of Color under Title IX

We live in a world where sports have the potential to bridge the gap
between racism, sexism, and discrimination. The 2012 Olympics was
a great start, but hopefully what these Games taught us is that if
women are given an opportunity on an equal playing field, the pos-
sibilities for women are endless.

—Jackie Joyner-Kersee, former Olympian, heptathlon and long
jump, and winner of three gold, one silver, and two bronze
medals in four different Olympics[1]

Double standards prevail for African American women and other
women of color in sports; they constantly face antiblack misogyny. In an
exploratory 2017 study, University of Missouri journalism professor Dr.
Cynthia Frisby reviewed 643 articles written about two top tennis
players: Serena Williams, an African American woman, and Angelique
Kerber, a German woman. She was looking for microaggressions—subtle biases (verbal, nonverbal, and/or visual) directed toward female athletes, especially African Americans and other women of color—aimed
at each woman by the authors of these articles. What Frisby discovered
was remarkable, albeit not entirely surprising: Williams received a massive number of microaggressions, at 723, while Kerber received only
18.[2]

The amount and level of hostility and racism directed toward girls and women of color athletes remains a huge problem in this country and throughout the world. In the 2012 London Summer Olympics, a high-ranking British Olympic official called fellow Brit Jessica Ennis (mentioned previously), a muscled, curvy, petite heptathlon competitor at the peak of her fitness, "fat," adding that she "weighed too much."[3] Ennis ended up winning the gold in 2012, followed by silver in 2016, in the Olympic heptathlon; she is also a three-peat world champion (2009, 2011, and 2015), as well as a 2010 European champion.

Ennis, who is a mixed-race athlete (she has a Jamaican father and a British mother), entered the world of sports in response to getting bullied as a young girl. Despite her incredible athletic accomplishments, many in the sports world persist on focusing on her appearance.

Sports institutions throughout the world still can't seem to accept the variety of body types and skin colors female athletes possess, especially in the case of African American women. Until 2018, it was almost impossible to find a website that listed the top women in sport for reasons not based on their looks. More often than not, the listings were for the "best looking" women (who were usually white and blonde, with nonpronounced muscles), as opposed to the highest-performing women, in sport. Time and again, the media has focused its praise on athletes with the supposedly "more attractive" body type: tall, skinny, and light-skinned. This point needs to be reiterated because this cultural norm directly impacts women of color in sport. Where is the appreciation for the shapely and strong girls? After all, that is the body type many competitive sports require.

The time has arrived to actively promote further discussion about and action against the discrimination women of color still encounter in sports. White women in sport, in particular, must become a part of this process. White women can't possibly know the struggles of women of color athletes, but we can better understand the struggles they face, enabling us to make supportive, helpful, and positive changes in this area.

BLACK AND WHITE NOT EQUAL UNDER TITLE IX

Black and brown female athletes have rarely experienced equal treatment under Title IX. This legislation moved toward improving gender circumstances but not racial equality in women's sports. Dr. Delia Douglas of the University of British Columbia has labeled the biases faced by black women in sport as "antiblack racism in a gender-specific form."[4] Even today, African American female athletes often suffer verbal and written abuse, as indicated by Frisby's study. Specifically, Serena Williams's detractors have called her a variety of offensive terms. She's heard herself described as a "gorilla," "manly," "animalistic," the "n" word, and numerous other derogatory terms. In 2014, a ranking Russian tennis official called Serena and Venus the "Williams brothers." After Serena was given a questionable foul that could have been a warning in the 2018 U.S. Open championship match, several well-known former competitive athletic women, specifically Mary Carillo and Martina Navratilova, spoke in opposition to her. In Carillo's case, she said, "Williams occasionally acts like a bully." Navratilova, meanwhile, gave the benefit of the doubt to Ramos, the official, rather than Serena on a call that commonly merits only a warning, rather than a penalty. Williams, in a moment of obvious frustration, had called the ref a "thief." Following the incident, it was revealed that Billie Jean King tweeted, "When a woman is emotional, she's 'hysterical' and she's penalized for it. When a man does the same, he's 'outspoken' and there are no repercussions."[5] This was an example of gender and racial discrimination.

Because the heart of Title IX, enacted in 1972, has always been gender equality, and not racial equality, the girls and women in sport who have benefited most from it have predominantly been white. In 1989, Professor Kimberle Crenshaw coined the term "intersectionality" to help explain the oppression of African American women in life.[6] When applied to women in sport, this term implies that female athletes and women of color working in sport may experience increased inequality and oppression because of the intersection of various identities that put them at a disadvantage in comparison to their white counterparts.

Intersectionality plays a large role when it comes to women of color in sport. Discussing this concept in terms of African American females in sport, increased discrimination occurs with the crossover of multiple roles, including gender, race, ethnicity, and limited financial resources. "Through the lens of intersectionality," wrote Heather Pressley in a piece published by Girls on the Run's website, "you can see that Title IX has a different impact on poor girls and girls of color."[7] Three primary factors come into play with girls participating in sports: White girls tend to start a year ahead of girls of color, black girls drop out of sport at greater rates than white girls, and poverty and the elimination of sports are especially poignant issues for girls of color.[8]

The schools whose women's sports programs rank lowest for diversity in the United States are found in states in the Deep South and Midwest, for the most part. Georgia, Alabama, Louisiana, Michigan, South Carolina, Tennessee, and Mississippi, where there is 50 percent or less participation in school sports by girls of color, are at the bottom of the pile. This is in addition to six states where 30 to 49 percent of females of color are not given equal opportunities to participate in sports, often due to economic reasons, as well as their being pigeonholed into "traditional" African American female sports, including basketball and track and field. A 2017 Forbes magazine article suggested, "It's tough for low-income kids, especially girls, to participate in sports." The article further pointed out that "half of public-school children are from families poor enough" to prevent them from being involved in sports.[9]

A 2015 study released by the National Women's Law Center and the Poverty and Race Research Action Council looked at opportunities for high school girls in sport at 90 percent white schools versus 90 percent minority schools, specifically examining the states of Alabama, Illinois, Louisiana, Massachusetts, Michigan, Mississippi, North Carolina, New Jersey, New York, Ohio, Pennsylvania, Tennessee, and Texas. They were able to identify a wide gap between the sports opportunities afforded to white girls and those afforded to black girls. There were four main areas of general conclusions and discussion in the report: 1) "Girls of color are not receiving equal opportunities to play sports"; 2) "School-sponsored sports opportunities are particularly important for girls of color, yet schools are failing to provide them with equal chances to reap the many benefits of participation"; 3) "The disparate sports opportunities provided to girls at heavily minority versus heavily white schools raise questions under the civil rights laws prohibiting gender and race discrimination"; and finally, 4) "Policymakers and communities must increase their efforts to ensure that girls of color receive equal opportunities to secure the advantages associated with playing sports."[10]

AFRICAN AMERICAN GIRLS AND WOMEN IN SPORT

Despite the many accomplished African American girls and women who have risen to prominence in the sport world today, African American female athletes still struggle to garner respect and admiration for their strong minds and bodies. Instead, the media persists in using negative and derogatory words to characterize both. They continue to paint a picture of the successes of these remarkable young women— women like the Williams sisters, Simone Biles, Simone Manuel, and Elana Meyers Taylor—as being solely attributable to their naturally strong physiques. According to an ESPNW article, "Several recent socio-metric studies have shown that black adolescent girls test higher in self-esteem than their white counterparts."[11] In other words, these young women are proud of their bodies.

About 10 years ago, I worked with a young African American female boxer with many performance blocks that came from her high-powered and aggressive mom always screaming at her during high school basketball games. She had been pushed into basketball despite her ambivalence about the sport. Eventually the pressure and expectations she felt as a basketball player overwhelmed her, so she quit. When she later became involved in boxing, a sport she had chosen for herself, she blossomed as a truly talented athlete.

While researching this book, I had the privilege and honor of interviewing a number of African American national leaders in sport who work directly with female African American athletes. These leaders are positive role models for the younger generation. One of these leaders was Tina Sloan Green. Sloan Green is a former lacrosse player and the first African American woman on the U.S. women's national lacrosse team; the first black women's lacrosse head collegiate coach, working at Temple University (1973–1992); and a cofounder and former president of the Black Women in Sport Foundation (BWSF). In our conversation, she expressed her belief that to find the best talent, recruiters and coaches need to open their doors to all public schools, even underperforming schools comprised predominantly of young women of color. She also said there is work to be done to achieve greater equality for women of color in sports.

Sloan Green said that she recognizes a gradual change taking place, especially in the younger generation. But as of 2019, only 3 percent of the women playing NCAA Division I lacrosse were African American. Due to lack of access and opportunity, few African American girls and women are playing lacrosse despite girls' lacrosse being the fastest-growing high school sport in the United States. Meanwhile, other sports, for example, tennis, golf, and field hockey, have hardly any women of color participating in them, either. What do these sports have in common? They require greater financial investments and don't fit the traditional expectations for black girls' participation in sports. (All you need to do to confirm this is look at the majority of the opponents Serena and Venus Williams play tennis against.)

Sloan Green started the nonprofit Black Women in Sport Foundation in 1992, along with cofounders Dr. Alpha Alexander, Dr. Nikki Franke, and Linda Greene, Esq., as a means to create opportunities for all African American women in sport, not only athletes, but also those interested in coaching and working in administration. The BWSF represents the voice of the African American girls and women in sport. I briefly mention BWSF in the leadership chapter, but there is much more to convey about this important organization. The founders of BWSF serve as solid role models for up-and-coming African American women in sport.

When I interviewed Sloan Green, she explained that she and her cofounders created the foundation to provide a place for African American girls to see and experience people who look like them and create an atmosphere of inclusion. "Dr. Carole Oglesby would drag us to conferences and seminars focused on sports at the beginning of Title IX," she told me. "From attending these conferences, we got the idea to start such a foundation for African American girl athletes, since we would never see other women (women of color) who looked like us at these conferences." BWSF's programs address both athletic and educational opportunities. As their website explains, the foundation "facilitates the involvement of women of color in every aspect of sport in the United States and around the world, through the 'hands-on' development and management of grassroots-level outreach programs," providing "educational and athletic instruction" to "schools located in disenfranchised neighborhoods in the Philadelphia area." The foundation specializes in such sports as fencing, tennis, lacrosse, field hockey, golf, soccer, and softball, among others.[12] This organization provides a variety of services for girls from the pre-K level through the high school level. These include after-school and summer school programs with staff and volunteer mentors; small scholarships; and the Next Step Mini-Forum, which promotes the increased participation of women of color in coaching and athletic administrative positions at NCAA institutions. By building their self-esteem and confidence, the BWSF encourages African American girls and other girls of color to participate in sports not "traditionally" played by African American female athletes and teaches them leadership skills for the future. As is posted on the foundation's website, "The BWSF Next Step Mini-Forums help women to become empowered, enlightened, and educated about the world of sport."[13]

Sloan Green's daughter, Traci Green, grew up to be an excellent athlete, choosing tennis as her preferred sport. Tennis, as I discuss earlier in this chapter, is still a white woman's domain. As Green stated, "The sad truth is that many people actually believe sports are not for women or girls of color and tennis is not for African Americans."[14] Arthur Ashe, an African American tennis player who won three Grand Slam titles, was "special for her" and actively supported Green in reaching national-level play throughout her career. In 2017, she made her own history by becoming the first African American head women's coach at Harvard and in the entire Ivy League. In 2009, after coaching for three years at Temple University, Green became the first coach at Harvard to win an Ivy League crown; she still holds the career coaching record at Harvard. In 2017, her Harvard team won the Ivy League championship for the second time.

In speaking with Traci Green, I found that she expresses herself in a soft and solid manner. She said the sport world, in general, has a subtle bias that women don't deserve the same attention as men, even when they are training as hard, playing as well, and participating in more exciting matches than men. It's up to women—white, black, or brown— she said, to help and support one another; we all—especially African American women—need to create positive, meaningful relationships with others to build our own network.

In late October 2018, Green and Sloan Green joined up as two of the headline participants in an "Invisible Women in Sports" podcast, sponsored by the Institute for Sport and Social Justice (ISSJ) and partially funded by the University of Central Florida's Office of Diversity and Inclusion (ODI).[15] Both mother and daughter continue to work for the promotion of African American girls in sport.

Dr. Alpha Alexander, who is mentioned in the leadership chapter, played both college basketball and volleyball but still felt alone at mostly white Wooster College while she was still a student. While a doctoral student at Temple, she developed widely and connected with like-minded black women, and together they decided to start the Black Women in Sport Foundation. Alexander led U.S. delegations to Barcelona, Atlanta, and Nagano for Olympic Youth Camps, plus led Citizen Ambassador delegations to China, South Africa, Russia, and Cuba.

When she and I spoke, she also recalled a time when the black male editor of *Black Enterprise* refused to put a photo of Olympic track and field star Jackie Joyner-Kersee on the front cover of the magazine. Historically black colleges, she says, are the optimal places for African American women in sport to reach their potential. Dr. Alexander believes that racism in sport begins in athletic administrative offices and filters downward. In administration, she believes this is where equity for African American women needs to start. Dr. Alexander is forthcoming, generous, and humble, often focusing on the accomplishments of others as opposed to herself. She has received numerous awards, including the Billie Jean King Contribution Award from the Women's Sport Foundation and the Olympic Shield from the USOC, as well as being named one of the 100 Most Influential Student-Athletes of the Century by the NCAA.

Dr. Nikki Franke's interest in helping build the BWSF came from her desire to dispel the myth that African Americans excel in sports due only to their natural athletic talents. She succinctly told me, "Hard work beats talent every time!" Teaching African American girls and other girls of color to train hard and work at their sport prepares them with skills for success in life beyond sport. Although Title IX opened up opportunities for female athletes generally speaking, it had a far less positive impact on African American girls, and they ended up taking a backseat to white girls. Dr. Franke says it's important to remember that racism is institutionalized. Sexism in sport was reduced by Title IX, but racism was not.

As a coach at Temple, Franke went to the female athletic director and inquired about why the men had a fencing team but the women had only a club. The response was, "Should we have a team?" Of course, we all know Dr. Franke's response, and now, 40 years later, she remains the only African American college fencing coach in the country. Through modeling and encouraging hard work, Dr. Franke has made herself into a positive role model for young African American girls.

The other cofounder of BWSF, Linda Greene, Esq., is equally impressive. She was a student at Temple when she helped cofound the foundation. Greene was a middle-distance runner and track and field athlete during college and law school. She has chaired many committees and served on many boards, including, during the 1990s, committee vice chair of the United States Olympic Committee Legislation Committee and vice chair of the Audit Committee, and member of the University of Wisconsin Athletic Board from 1990 to 1995. She also coauthored the USOC's diversity and inclusion policies.

Together with Sloan Green and Franke, Alexander and Greene had the vision of creating a sport foundation for African American female athletes and the will to make it happen—and thousands of girls of color have benefited as a result.

When I spoke with Dr. Margaret Ottley of West Chester University about the importance of diversity, she stated, "Diversity works for all women. We need to present ourselves from all perspectives to truly understand." We need to remember that "one hand can't clap without the other."

LIFTING UP WOMEN OF COLOR

Two important foundations that work with urban children of color in New York City are the Wendy Hilliard Gymnastics Foundation and the Peter Westbrook Foundation, focused on fencing. In interviewing both Hilliard and Westbrook, it was easy to understand the inspiration both provide for children of color to not only pursue sport, but also learn and establish solid life skills.

Wendy Hilliard was the first African American to participate in rhythmic gymnastics as a member of the U.S. national rhythmic gymnastics team and the first African American to serve as president of the Women's Sports Foundation. Throughout her life, she has served on numerous boards and in various significant leadership positions, but her dream was always to start a free program for inner-city children. In 1995, she began her first free program in Harlem. She started with 200 children. The Wendy Hilliard Gymnastics Foundation has grown each year since its founding, and to date it has provided "support and funding" for more than 4,500 local underserved children and children of color who otherwise likely would not have had access to gymnastics. Hilliard has also served as a role model for thousands of girls of color. As most of her compatriots have observed, she believes African

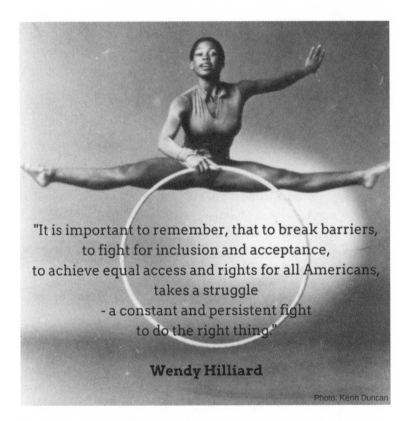

"It is important to remember, that to break barriers,
to fight for inclusion and acceptance,
to achieve equal access and rights for all Americans,
takes a struggle
- a constant and persistent fight
to do the right thing."

Wendy Hilliard

Photo: Kenn Duncan

Young Wendy as a gymnast. *Courtesy of the Wendy Hillard Gymnastics Foundation*

American women are most accepted in basketball and track and field, while they face more obstacles when they want to participate in sports not considered "traditional" for them. Gabby Douglas and Simone Biles have led the way for young African American women in gymnastics. Douglas encountered the struggle of being raised by a single mother, a common occurrence in the black community. Biles, in particular, has led the way for a broader view of an athletic body, with her curves and prominent muscles. But their road to success was not an easy one.

When I asked Hilliard about the issues of inequality in sports, she said her viewpoint is twofold: men versus women and white versus black and brown female athletes. She also views socioeconomics and financial barriers as frequent blocks to access for black and brown athletes, and asserted that a major factor blocking African American women and other women of color from reaching leadership positions in sports is the protectiveness at the top by the "good old boys network," guarding their positions of power. Her current work focuses on helping girls in her program be the best athletes they can be, guided by good coaches who reinforce a strong work ethic, perseverance, staying in the mix at meets, and learning to both lose and win.

The nonprofit Peter Westbrook Foundation, founded in 1991, emerged as a way to empower girls and boys—primarily minorities— and teach them basic life skills through the sport of fencing. Peter Westbrook was an Olympic fencer who competed in the men's sabre. When he won a bronze medal, he became the first African American to win a fencing medal in the history of the Olympics. He won the U.S. National Sabre Championship 13 times between 1974 and 1995, a never-matched record that placed him in the U.S. Fencing Hall of Fame in 1996.

Westbrook's foundation's primarily draws its participants from underserved programs in metropolitan New York City. Many of the children are from single-parent households, and African American and Latino children comprise 85 percent of his total enrollment. Westbrook says U.S. culture still regards people of color and the lower classes as second-class citizens. His viewpoint is that even today our culture dissuades women of color from becoming involved in sports and appears to lack substantial opportunities for African American women in sport. He believes women are far superior to men in certain areas; they have, he says, an ability to withstand more pain, a greater accessibility to their emotions, a tendency to act as a catalyst in the family, and more persistence. These are useful strengths for participating and competing in sport. Clearly, Westbrook works hard to promote girls and women of color in sport.

THE VARIOUS OBSTACLES FACED BY OTHER WOMEN OF COLOR

The estimated 55 million Latinos in the United States make up 17 percent of our population. Yet the participation of Latinas in sport is sorely lacking. According to one *Women's Health* article, "Almost half (47 percent report) of adult Latinas . . . report they never engage in any leisure time physical activity, compared with just 29.2 percent of non-Latina white women."[16] This population is strongly influenced by their culture and values placed on women as caretakers of the family.

In the early 1990s I worked as a sports psychologist with a community college cross-country team that was heavily Latina. During that time I heard a story from a young Latina about her father's vehement opposition to her participating in competitive running. Apparently he believed that sports, especially running, were not appropriate for girls. Luckily for her, both her mother and brothers, who she ran with, were in support of her athletic endeavors and always showed up for her meets when they weren't competing. We discovered in a group meeting that she was holding herself back from passing an older, more accomplished teammate. I gave her permission to pass her teammate. In the next meet, she passed her teammate and never looked back. Ultimately, this athlete's running (and academics) got her a scholarship to the University of California, Berkeley, where she became captain of the women's cross-country and track teams, and an All-American miler.

The lack of Latino representation in sports, according to Richard Lapchick, director of the Institute for Diversity and Ethics in Sports at the University of Central Florida, might be due to the fact that, "Unlike African Americans, Latinos have not been drilled that sports are a way out of poverty."[17] There are some Latinos making headlines in the sports world. Two of the most well-known Latina athletes in the United States today are Sofia Huerta, who plays for the U.S. women's national soccer team, and Laurie Hernandez, a gymnast who won gold and silver at the 2016 Olympic Games. But Latinas in college sport make up just 4 percent of female athletes in the NCAA, and numerous studies illustrate that Latinas represent the lowest sport participation rate in high school. This is due to many factors, notably family demands and economic circumstances; many agree, however, that the enduring bent toward machismo in this culture is one of the biggest factors preventing more Latinas from entering and staying in sport. This negative family view, along with the virtual absence of Latina role models in public view, creates an atmosphere where girls get the message that sports aren't for them.

Asian American female athletes, who are still often stereotyped as being reserved, intelligent, subservient, and excelling at math and science, are basically invisible in sports research, partially due to the stereotypes. Some U.S. journalists continue to label them negatively as not being American, despite the fact that they were born in the United States or arrived in the country as children. Asian American females, according to a piece in the *New Yorker* by Jiayang Fan, are often put into one of five stereotypical categories: evil temptress, obliging mistress, loyal servant, fanatical tiger mom, or ruthless overachiever.[18] The level of negativity and microaggressions faced by Asian American female athletes, then, are high. Then along comes Chloe Kim, a Korean American, who fits none of these stereotypes and makes a strong and solid stand that Asian American female athletes can be much more than the stereotypes they've been assigned and play sports outside the box. The most "traditionally" accepted sport for Asian American girls is ice skating. Kim broke this ideal wide open when she won the gold medal in the snowboarding half-pipe competition in the 2018 Winter Olympics.

Half of the Asian American athletes at the 2018 Olympics were females. The most visible women were Kim and Mirai Nagasu, who won the bronze medal in the team event for figure skating. Mirai Nagasu, a Japanese American, was born in the United States but was labeled an "immigrant" in a tweet about her triple axel (despite the more impressive and true fact that in landing the jump, she became the first American woman to complete a triple axel in competition). In the past, Asian American female athletes have simply blended into the background. Not since Kristi Yamaguchi has an Asian American woman garnered such attention and notoriety as Chloe Kim at the 2018 Winter

Olympics, except, perhaps, for Michelle Wie, who was often put in the spotlight when she first entered golf competition on the pro circuit.

In a 2015 study sponsored by Dick's Sporting Goods for the Women's Law Center, a blunt conclusion was reached regarding girls of color in sport:

> Girls of color are finishing last when it comes to opportunities to play sports in school and missing out on the lifelong benefits that accompany athletic participation. While the playing field is far from level for girls in general, it is particularly uneven for girls in heavily minority schools. Tackling the problem will require policymakers at all levels—federal, state, and local—and communities to work together to increase opportunities for girls of color to play sports and be physically active. Doing so is not only required by law, but is also a critical investment in their future.[19]

THE CURRENT STATE OF WOMEN OF COLOR IN SPORTS

We saw improved coverage of African American and Asian female athletes at the 2018 Pyeongchang Olympics (although not of Latina women). When there was no medal, however, the coverage quickly faded away. This was true for up-and-coming speed skater Maame Biney, who was the first African American short-track speed skater to compete in the Olympics for the United States. Initially, she received a lot of media attention. But when she didn't get past the quarterfinals, the media ceased talking about her altogether.

The Olympics isn't only about medals; it's about simply getting to that level of competition. The media could have focused on Biney's journey to the top and, in doing so, excited young girls of color to aim to participate in the Winter Olympics. But they failed to take advantage of this opportunity to highlight Biney's rise to the top of her sport. Showing more of the U.S. women's bobsled team, which included three-time Olympian Elana Meyers Taylor and brakewoman Lauren Gibbs, who won silver, in prime-time slots also would have boosted the visibility of women of color competing in "nontraditional" sports. But again, these athletes were passed over by the media.

Progress for women of color in the sporting world is painfully slow and limited in many ways. Women of color who receive medals in the

Olympics do receive some media attention; however, once the Olympics is over, the media ceases to pay much attention to female athletes, let alone women of color athletes.

An exception to this rule, of course, is Serena Williams. The media seems to place their negative projections about minority female athletes on her, since she is the most visible woman of color athlete in the world. At the time of this writing, she was the unofficial primary spokeswoman for women of color and the top-earning female athlete in 2018, despite the fact that she didn't play the entire season, only appearing in certain matches. Williams frequently voices important truths about women in sport, especially minority women, that many others are afraid to say. But she can't be the only voice.

An article by Richard Lapchick entitled "The WNBA Leads All Sports Leagues in Diversity and Inclusion" was featured on ESPNW in late 2017, and according to a report produced regularly by Lapchick and fellow researchers at the University of Central Florida's Institute for Diversity and Ethics in Sport, this really is the case.[20] The percentage of black players in the WNBA is quite high, at 69 percent. Yet, the league has only one African American female head coach, Pokey Chatman, with the Indiana Fever. Latinas make up only 3.5 percent of the league.

The responsibility rests with each and every one of us. Yes, more women of color need to find a way to stand up and shout out about the inequalities faced by women of color athletes. So do male athletic figures with a huge platform, like LeBron James and Steph Curry. But the onus also falls on white female athletes to step up and ask women of color how they can support them in gaining further involvement and recognition in sports. With Simone Manuel receiving gold in swimming in the 2016 Olympics, it will be interesting to see if more African America women enter the sport. Furthermore, the concept of "intersectionality," in which gender and race are combined reasons for further bigotry and injustice in the world of sports, applies to every woman of color in sport. Taking the time to unite as women and build relationships is essential if women of color are to make true progress in sports. White women must take the time to work to understand why women of color are not as well represented as they should be in the sport world and increase the participation of girls and women of color in a manner that makes sense to the African American community. Together, through discussion and action, women can come together to build a better network of communication and start addressing the needs of those women in the United States and throughout the world who have limited opportunities in sport.

ACTION STEPS TOWARD EQUALITY FOR WOMEN OF COLOR

1. White women need to take time to listen to and understand the concerns of women of color in sport. White women can never know what it's like to be a woman of color, but they can strive to understand the different experiences.
2. Work to understand and respect the cultural issues of women of color rather than criticize them.
3. Spread the word about famous female leaders in sport, for example, Tina Sloan Green, and the existence of the BWSF, with its many projects that introduce African American and other girls of color to nontraditional black sports.
4. Increase the number of showings of the podcast "Invisible Women in Sports."

8

THE LGBTQ COMMUNITY

Lesbian and Transgender Athletes

We are watching a transition in sports from the culture of the closet to one in which young women athletes embrace openness and activism to not only live their truth, but also to speak out to make sports more inclusive and welcoming for the athletes and coaches who follow them. . . . The challenge is that the old guard holds the power, and their internalized homophobia and fear of change are holding back progress.
—Pat Griffin, "grandmother of the LGBTQ sports movement," and Nevin Caple, director of LGBT SportSafe[1]

Coming out as a lesbian or transgender female athlete is easier than it has been in the past, although the extent to which this is true depends on where you live and your status. In 2017, more LGBTQ people in sports—184 total—came out than in any previous year. Almost half of them were women.[2] The numbers of openly gay and trans athletes have continued to grow during the last couple of years. Yet, there are still many athletes and coaches who don't feel comfortable revealing their LGBTQ identity in collegiate and pro sports. Among athletes and coaches, there is also debate over whether it is important for LGBTQ leaders of and participants in women's sports to be out.[3] Despite the growing number of people in the sporting community who are coming out publicly, there are continued negative consequences for some of those who do.

Social Justice and Exercise in Sport Psychology organizers and keynote speaker (L to R): Vikki Krane, Heather Barbour, Carole Oglesby, Nicole LaVoi, Jennifer Waldron, and Diane Whaley. *Dr. Joan Steidinger*

The moment has arrived to dispel the "myth" of the lesbian athlete. Just a few decades ago, certain sports garnered the reputation for attracting only lesbian players. During my own high school years in the late 1960s and early 1970s, girls who played badminton and tennis, and competed in equestrian sports, were considered feminine, while field hockey and basketball players were regarded as "lesbians." The truth, of course, is that there is a mix of lesbians and straight girls in every sport. Today, as the media has become more accepting of people's differences in sexual and gender identification, the conversation has finally begun to open up. "Research has shown that since the turn of the millennia, matters have rapidly improved . . . for lesbians in sport. Where lesbians were merely tolerated a decade ago, today they are celebrated."[4] Nonetheless, gay and trans athletes still face challenges straight and gender-conforming athletes do not.

Much more action needs to take place in the struggle to gain greater ground in understanding and educating ourselves about LGBTQ individuals in the sport world. More policies that are supportive and inclusive of LGBTQ athletes and coaches need to be established and maintained. Although the NCAA has a strong policy with recommendations for understanding and accepting transgender athletes written by leading LGBTQ activists Pat Griffin and Helen Carroll, many colleges still have not read or recognized these recommendations, let alone implement them. Progress in this area is further hindered by a number of factors, including sexism, homophobia, racism, and the failure to approach the issue from an intersectional perspective.

When I spoke to Pat Griffin, the "grandmother of the LGBTQ sports movement," she described her experience at University of Massachusetts, Amherst, as "lucky." Griffin worked as an academician in the mid-1970s and returned to grad school in 1976. As she gradually came out, she received the full support of her department chair and colleagues, but as time went on many young women started coming to speak to her about their negative experiences, sharing horrible stories of discrimination and abusive treatment.

Griffin started speaking out about this in the early 1980s. In 1982, she gave her first public speech on gay rights at the New Agenda for Women in Sport as part of a three-person panel focused on the question, "How can women deflect threats to femininity?" She decided to attack the question rather than answer it, as did her colleague, Cheryl Coe, who she contacted ahead of time. The third panelist, Janet Guthrie, who was unavailable for Griffin to speak with in advance, was so upset about their approach that she accused Griffin of leading a gay rights rally. Finally in 1987, the Association for Health, Physical Education, Recreation, and Dance held an actual panel on homosexuality, which Griffin contributed to, and it ended up being a standing-room-only event. By this point, Griffin had embraced the idea that she needed to be the person to break the silence. For decades, she has led the way for LGBTQ rights in sports. Her contributions to this battle, along with those of others, are referenced throughout this chapter.

DEFINING COMING OUT

"Coming out" is a lifelong process of becoming aware of, accepting, and sharing your gender/sexual identity as lesbian or transgender with others when and where it feels right for you to do so. Some athletes have found that coming out can be "freeing" (Nefertiti Walker, LGBTQ advocate and former college basketball player), can normalize your lesbian or transgender identity (Sue Bird, WNBA), or simply be a clear acknowledgment of who you are (Megan Rapinoe, soccer). On the other hand, for many, coming out still feels like a risk, depending on their sport and circumstances. LGBTQ athletes or coaches are not embraced everywhere. At the collegiate level, many schools continue to have policies that are explicitly against homosexuality or no policies at all regarding the inclusion or protection of lesbian and transgender women athletes.

Strong Family Alliance, an organization dedicated to helping families understand their LGBTQ youth, has adapted the stages of coming out first established by Dr. Richard Niolon to clarify what this process entails. They are as follows:

Stage 1: "Self-recognition" as lesbian, bisexual, or transgender encompasses realizing they may be homosexual and keeping their identity to themselves.

Stage 2: "Disclosure to others" involves starting with a close friend or family member and then gradually revealing their identity to more people throughout time.

Stage 3: "Socialization" with other lesbian, gay, bisexual, and transgender people tends to reduce any isolation that the person might feel. Role models further help in the transition.

Stage 4: "Positive self-identification" occurs when you feel positive about your identity and recognize that your same-sex interest is healthy and normal.

Stage 5: "Integration and acceptance" consists of an open and accepting attitude regarding your gay identity, although this does not necessarily mean you will choose to announce your homosexuality to the world.[5]

Of course, this may be an ongoing process depending on the circum-stances of each athlete's life. Being a lesbian is especially hard in certain sports.

In an interview with Athlete Ally in December 2018, Mel Reid, a 31-year-old British golfer, shared that she was gay. Her primary rationale was that she wanted to be able to be her true, authentic self, especially in dealing with sponsors. Quite simply, her message is this: "Be proud of who you are!"[6]

THE CONSEQUENCES OF COMING OUT

Coming out can still result in shocking behavior from family and friends. One of the saddest stories that has been reported on occurred in the fall of 2018, involving sophomore cross-country athlete Emily Scheck. After Scheck returned to Canisius College in Buffalo, New York, in August 2018, her mother came across pictures of Emily and her girlfriend on social media. Scheck had not yet come out to her family for fear of their reaction, and their reaction did indeed prove to be cruel and unusual punishment. They insisted that she immediately move home, foregoing her partial athletic scholarship; attend counsel-ing; and enroll in the local community college. Her family only lived 85 miles away. Upon hearing the stipulations, Emily turned them down, which resulted in her family cutting her off completely. Her mother texted her, "Well, I am done with you. As of right now, declare yourself independent. You are on your own. Please don't contact us or your siblings."[7]

The situation escalated when Scheck's father drove to Buffalo from Rochester, bringing her belongings, including her birth certificate, tro-phies, stuffed animals, and the rest of her clothes, with him. He dumped her things in her car, ripped off her license plates, and can-celed her car insurance. After this incident, Emily received no further financial support from her family; she was forced to turn to her girl-friend and friends for help buying whatever food and other necessities she couldn't afford on her own, despite the fact that she was working two jobs to make ends meet while still competing on the cross-country team and attending college.

After three months passed without any contact between Emily and her family, Emily's roommate decided to start a GoFundMe page. The campaign was a huge success; however, another blow came when the NCAA took a hard-line approach and told Emily she had two choices: return the money or lose her eligibility for the cross-country team and her athletic scholarship. News of this development went viral, and the NCAA ultimately reversed its position—seemingly thanks to the vast amount of public support and pressure the case was receiving.

Today, some communication has opened up between Emily and her family, but her relationship with her family will never be what it once was. Emily had to travel a tough road just to be who she is: a LGBTQ athlete.[8]

Throughout the years, a number of professional female athletes have come out. Tennis greats Billie Jean King and Martina Navratilova were both "outed" in 1981. When King's former partner "outed" her in a palimony suit, King suffered a grave consequence, losing every single endorsement she had within 24 hours. She struggled with coming out as a lesbian, since it had transpired in such an unexpected and sudden manner. In a now-famous quote, she described her predicament at the time:

> I wanted to tell the truth, but my parents were homophobic and I was in the closet. As well as that, I had people tell me if I talked about what I was going through, it would be the end of the tour. . . . I ended up with an eating disorder that came from trying to numb myself from my feelings. I needed to surrender far sooner than I did. At the age of 51, I was finally able to talk about it properly with my parents and no longer did I have to measure my words with them. That was a turning point for me, as it meant I didn't have regrets anymore.[9]

Since then, King has become a role model and inspiration for many other lesbian and straight female athletes. As the founder of the Women's Sports Foundation and a longtime activist, King has dedicated her life to fighting gender (sexism) discrimination and supporting lesbian rights issues. She has shown by example that the road is not always smooth for LGBTQ athletes, but with determination and fortitude one can overcome significant obstacles.

Martina Navratilova was "outed" after defecting from Czechoslovakia to the United States in 1981, when she was asked to deny or confirm if she was, in fact, gay. By her own choice, she became the first major athlete to come out publicly. Former Women in Sport president Donna Lopiano told ESPN, "Martina was the first legitimate superstar who literally came out while she was a superstar. She exploded the barrier by putting it on the table. She basically said this part of my life doesn't have anything to do with me as a tennis player. Judge me for who I am."[10] For years afterward she acted as a strong advocate for gay rights. Unfortunately, in December 2018 Navratilova suggested that transgender women participating in women's sport competition was a form of "cheating," taking a transphobic stand. Since that time, she has faced stiff scrutiny and outrage from the LGBTQ community. Rachel McKinnon, who became the first transgender woman to win a world track cycling title in October 2018, challenged Navratilova in a Twitter battle.[11] Athlete Ally, an advocacy group whose mission is to end homophobia and transphobia in sport, ousted her from an ambassador position she held with them in February 2019.

In 2016, Jennifer Azzi, a former WNBA and Olympic team member, came out when she acknowledged her marriage to her University of San Francisco assistant, Blair Hardiek. Azzi did this while providing an introduction to Rick Welts—who had come out as the first openly gay NBA executive in 2011—at the Anti-Defamation League's Torch of Liberty Award Ceremony. "I, too, lived a long time not being 100 percent honest," Azzi told the *San Jose Mercury News* after coming out. She added,

> Kind of the don't-ask-don't-tell kinda thing. And it's so stupid. I don't know why we do that, but we do. I'm a college coach. Is it going to hurt me with recruiting? What are people going to think? And you are constantly worrying about those things. What I realized watching Rick in his path and his journey is that there is nothing more powerful than living the truth. And the best thing I can do for my team is to be authentic and true to myself.[12]

Azzi can now be an "out" sports role model for other gay female coaches and players in basketball.

Coming out of the closet as lesbian or transgender in sports is a powerful step in self-acceptance and self-confidence. Just weeks before the 2012 Olympics, Megan Rapinoe, a member of the U.S. women's national soccer team, came out publicly. Her reason for coming out, she said, was less about sexuality and more about "standing up for what's right and fighting for equality."[13] She now serves as an activist who stands up for different social justice causes, notably gay rights, and acts as spokesperson for Athlete Ally, among other organizations. In 2017, she knelt at a game during the national anthem in support of Colin Kaepernick. In 2018 she lent her support to a group called Play Proud, a global initiative sponsored by Street Football World designed to teach soccer coaches about acceptance and inclusion of LGBTQ kids through the use of a digital toolkit. She is dating Sue Bird, a WNBA player who came out as gay in 2016, when she began dating Rapinoe. In 2018 they became the first openly gay couple to be featured in *ESPN The Magazine*'s "The Body Issue." In describing Rapinoe's influence on her coming out to the public, Bird commented, "She opened my eyes to another way of looking at it, which is that in today's time, in today's society, it's still important to say it to make it the norm."[14]

At the 2018 WNBA All-Star Game in Minneapolis, LGBTQ player Candace Parker elected to publicly come out. Almost one-third of their All-Star Team had already done so. This was an inspiring game to watch for many in the LGBTQ community. The WNBA is one of the few leagues where a number of top players are gay and out. Players and coaches estimate that 33 to 50-plus percent of players in the league are LGBTQ. One of these players, Elena Delle Donne, came out to the public just before the 2016 Olympics. The following year she decided to make her wedding to Amanda Clifton public—partly, she said, to encourage people to regard gay marriage as normal.[15]

Other top players in the WNBA who are out and proud include Brittney Griner and Seimone Augustus. Griner, who attended Baylor University in Texas, says she was cautioned that her college had an antigay policy, which is why she waited until the end of her senior year to come out. Augustus, meanwhile, came out in 2012, before the Olympics. She described her coming out to ESPN as a positive experience, relating, "I was on such a high note, as far as being happy with who I am, it didn't really matter what anybody else thought. . . . It really was a nonissue. Every text, every call, every e-mail, any type of communication I received has been positive."[16]

Kisha Ford-Torres, a former WNBA player, commented about being a lesbian athlete in college, declaring, "As a lesbian, I felt the sharp words and comments about my sexuality. It was unrelenting with my group of girlfriends." It looks like we are indeed making some slow progress, but we still have a long way to go.

HARASSMENT/DISCRIMINATION AGAINST LGBTQ ATHLETES

Lesbian and trans females in sport still struggle daily for acceptance, equal opportunities, and fair treatment. The Campus Pride 2012 LGBTQ National College Athlete Report found that 39 percent of LGBTQ athletes feel discriminated against and have been harassed in sports due to their sexual orientation. The main perpetrators of harassment are coaches and other student-athletes, and the incidents the students cited most often took place during practice (64 percent) or competition (28 percent). They even reported a number of instances (4 percent) where campus security/police harassed them.[17] A further startling statistic from Athlete Ally is that out of approximately 10,000 athletes surveyed in the Athletic Equality Index, only 1 percent believe LGBTQ people are totally "accepted" in sport. Many coaches marginalize their lesbian and transgender athletes in a variety of ways, including requesting that they keep their identities hidden, giving them less playing time, encouraging them to alter their sexual orientation, or not allowing them on a team at all. Given these realities, it is of the utmost importance and urgency that we rally around and support the LGBTQ community in sports.

According to Helen Carroll, subtle discrimination against lesbian coaches and athletes happens throughout the United States. Carroll is a former basketball coach at the University of North Carolina, Asheville, where her team took home the school's only national championship title; athletic director for Mills College in Oakland, California; and a sports project leader (for 15 years) with the National Center for Lesbian Rights (NCLR) in San Francisco. She is considered one of the godmothers of lesbian rights in sport. Throughout her career, she has encouraged her players and others to fight for lesbian rights.

Carroll was the sports project director for NCLR when the organization filed the case that changed the landscape for lesbian coaches—a case against Penn State and women's basketball coach Renee Portland, who had a "no lesbians" policy for her team that had gone unchecked for years. Players who were openly gay or even suspected of being gay faced harassment and discrimination at Penn State. This case drew national media attention and was settled in 2007, with Penn State's president deciding Portland wasn't a good fit and performing a revamp of the athletic department policies concerning their LGBTQ athletes. Portland resigned and never worked as a coach again. The case served as a warning to other colleges that anti-LGBTQ policies would be taken to task, causing many colleges to review and/or create policies protecting LGBTQ athletes, although there are still many that do not have such guidelines. And even those colleges that do have the necessary policies in place are generally set up for reactionary rather than proactive responses related to LGBTQ athletes, so again, there's much progress to be made.

The Human Rights Campaign and the University of Connecticut conducted a vital report on LGBTQ student athletes in 2018 called "Play to Win: Improving the Lives of LGBTQ Youth in Sports." The report analyzed the responses to sports questions by 12,000 youth, ages 13 to 17, from every state in the United States, as well as the District of Columbia.[18] The study discovered that, despite some progress, many LGBTQ athletes remain in the closet due to harassment, discrimination, and fear for their safety. Three key stats found were that 83 percent of LGBTQ teens aren't out to their coaches, 34 percent of transgender girls do not feel safe in the locker room, and only 24 percent of LGBTQ youth report playing a school sport.

A program called the GLSEN Sports Project, launched in 2011 by Pat Griffin and others, strives to remedy the kinds of issues identified in the report by creating safe and affirming schools for everyone, regardless of sexual orientation, gender identity, or gender expression. GLSEN stands for Gay Lesbian and Straight Education Network. In a research brief from the GLSEN Sports Project for a study of 8,584 LGBTQ students from all 50 states and the District of Columbia, researchers highlighted five major findings about LGBTQ youth in their experiences in physical education and sport participation:

1. Physical education classes were unsafe environments for many LGBTQ students.
2. LGBTQ students may be underrepresented on extracurricular sports teams.
3. LGBTQ student athletes (as opposed to nonathletes) reported better academic and mental health outcomes.
4. Many LGBTQ students experienced discrimination and harassment in school sports.
5. LGBTQ student athletes may not feel fully supported by athletics staff and policies. [19]

Sport participation, which can be so valuable to success in life, may be limited for LGBTQ students due to ignorance and fear for their safety.

Although some progress has been made in this area, said Griffin, discrimination against LGBTQ athletes and coaches remains a real problem in the United States; it also manifests itself in different ways when directed toward lesbian coaches and athletes than when directed against men in sports. "Coaches still lose their jobs and players are still kicked off teams for being lesbians, and that doesn't seem to interest the media as much," Griffin said in one interview. "I think it's just related to the general sexism we see in sports anyway." [20]

TRANSGENDER AND INTERSEX ATHLETES

Transgender athletes continue to be misunderstood, as evidenced by Martina Navratilova's uninformed comments about the "cheating" of trans women and that, "Even if they've had hormone treatment," they have an "unfair advantage over other female competitors." [21]

The word "transgender" is meant to describe those whose gender identity is divergent from the sex they were assigned at birth. Trans people may take hormones and have surgical procedures, while others may choose not to.

Pat Griffin and Helen Carroll were responsible for writing the NCAA's original transgender policy, entitled "NCAA Inclusion of Transgender Student-Athletes." This resource was meant to serve as a guide for NCAA athletic programs on "how to ensure transgender student-athletes fair, respectful, and legal access to collegiate sports teams based on current medical and legal knowledge."[22] In the document, the authors define the term "transgender" and further specify the two types of transgender identity, including male-to-female (a person who was assigned male sex at birth but identifies as female) and female-to-male (a person who was assigned female sex at birth but identifies as male). They go on to explain the variety of steps transgender people take to adapt to their actual gender identity.

An important area Griffin and Carroll address in this guide is the difference between transgender and intersex individuals. Intersex individuals ("disorder of sex development") have "physically mixed or atypical bodies with respect to sexual characteristics such as chromosomes, internal reproductive organs and genitalia, and external genitalia."[23] Transgender individuals are those who believe they were born in the wrong body and work to become either a women changing to a man or a man changing to a woman. Men transitioning to women must take appropriate hormones for a minimum of a year before they can compete in sporting events. The authors also address the expanding numbers of high school and college students who are identifying as trans or transgender. After providing a thorough review of the reasons why this type of policy is needed to understand and protect transgender students, Griffin and Carroll present "guiding principles" and "policy recommendations for collegiate athletics," including the following:

Transgender student-athletes should have equal opportunity to participate in sports.

The integrity of women's sports should be preserved.

Policies governing sports should be based on sound medical knowledge and scientific validity.

The medical privacy of transgender students should be preserved.

Athletics administrators, staff, parents of athletes, and student-athletes should have access to sound and effective educational resources and training related to the participation of transgender and gender-variant students in athletics.[24]

Describing this guide as an "emerging endeavor," Griffin and Carroll recommend periodic review and revision as updated research and information come forth.[25]

The most well-known intersex woman in sport is South African Caster Semenya. In response to Semenya's intersex identity coming out, the

International Association of Athletics Federations (IAAF), the international governing body of athletics, proposed a testosterone limit for women—despite the fact that Semenya's levels are not as high as those of most men, not to mention the fact that the IAAF is operating on flawed research and information about the role of testosterone in athletic performance.

"It's a total disgrace how they've treated her," said Carroll. "Intersex should be a nonissue. Competitive advantage should not be based solely on testosterone." Griffin added. "Semenya has lived her entire life as a girl and a woman. Increased testosterone in a person should not be the sole basis for deciding which sex they are."

This notwithstanding, Semenya has been ordered to reduce her testosterone levels prior to competing again. In late February 2019 her case went to arbitration in front of the Court for Arbitration for Sport in Switzerland. She is challenging the IAAF ruling based on flawed research/lack of research by the IAAF. The obvious conflict of interest with the IAAF sponsoring and helping conduct the research that supports their new regulation should weigh in her favor. Other scientists who attempted to replicate the results found by the IAAF were unable to do so. Furthermore, those scientists found that IAAF's research was flawed and that the federation had misinterpreted data. In early February 2019, scientists Roger Peike, Ross Tucker, and Erik Boye put out a paper entitled "Scientific Integrity and the IAAF Testosterone Regulations," disputing claims that testosterone gives individuals a competitive advantage. The paper refers to the testosterone rule change as "discriminatory, irrational, and unjustifiable."[26]

In the wake of this controversy, Caster Semenya has become a hero among South Africans. They even voted her "Most Influential Young South African" for 2018 through the ranking company Avance Media. She was nominated in the sports category for her achievements in track and field, notably her gold medal in the 2016 Rio Olympics. One hundred South Africans in 10 categories were nominated. What makes this an even more remarkable and historic achievement is that Semenya is the first woman to win the prize.[27]

LGBTQ ADVOCACY EFFORTS IN SPORT

Throughout the years, a number of different organizations have worked for the rights of lesbian and transgender athletes. Today there are a number of organizations rallying in support of the acceptance and rights of LGBTQ athletes. Three of the top advocacy groups are Athlete Ally, the You Can Play Project, and LGBT SportSafe.

Athlete Ally has three major goals: 1) educate, 2) change sport policy, and 3) advocate for LGBTQ rights. Education is done to reach out to communities about the inclusion of LGBTQ athletes in colleges and such sports leagues and institutions as the WNBA and NCAA. Athlete Ally views changing sport policy as a vital component of their work. Just last year they introduced the Athletic Equality Index, which monitors inclusion policies and practices in the NCAA's Power Five conferences. They advocate through their Ambassador Program, which uses the talents of athletes to support and speak out for LGBTQ rights.

The You Can Play Project is a "social activism" campaign devoted to reducing homophobia in sports. The motto of the project is, "If you can play, you can play." Their mission statement simply states, "You Can Play works to ensure the safety and inclusion of all in sports—including LGBTQ athletes, coaches, and fans."[28] The project strives to guarantee that athletes are given a fair opportunity to compete and are judged by other athletes and fans only on what they contribute to the sport or their team's success. You Can Play seeks to challenge the culture of locker rooms and spectator areas by focusing on an athlete's skills, work ethic, and competitive spirit. This program encompasses youth sport as well, and its goal is simple: to achieve fairness for the LGBTQ athletic community.

LGBT SportSafe was founded in 2015 by Nevin Caple (a diversity in sport consultant) and Dr. Eric Lueshen (a former Nebraska football player). They started off by recruiting a number of founding member schools, for example, the University of Nebraska, Temple University, and the University of California, Los Angeles, and have since expanded to a number of other schools. Their mission statement reads, "LGBT SportSafe Inclusion Program was developed to create an infrastructure for athletic administrators, coaches, and recreational sports leaders to support LGBTQ inclusion in college, high school, and professional sports."[29] They describe their model as a "3-Peat Model" due to its consideration of three core areas: "programming, policy, and public awareness." A key goal for Caple and Lueshen is the inclusion of LGBTQ athletes in every aspect of sport.

Finally, it's important to give a shout-out to *Outsports* (a subsidiary of SBNation), which has been in existence since 1999, when two gay men took a risk and started writing about LGBTQ athletes in sports. The publication quickly found many interested readers and has since become the major sporting publication for reading about LGBTQ athletes in the United States. *Outsports* has featured hundreds of coming-out stories from athletes and also stays on top of current news involving LGBTQ athletes, coaches, and administrators in sport.

Recently even major sports manufacturers are starting to emerge with campaigns that include lesbian and women of color athletes. The latest campaign by Adidas is "She Breaks Barriers." One of the leaders of this campaign is Layshia Clarendon, a well-known lesbian and woman of color WNBA star. She is a point guard for the Connecticut Sun. Her role is bringing attention for equal media representation for women in sport and to inspire young female athletes. This was the message communicated in one of the short films about women in sport that Adidas released in March 2019. This demonstrates a small step toward inclusion of LGBTQ and women of color athletes in the media.[30]

When Pat Griffin decided to be the "person to break the silence" in the 1980s, she took a gigantic step forward for lesbians and transgender athletes to be acknowledged and at least start to gain acceptance in the sports world. Further advocacy efforts for lesbian and trans women were continued in earnest by Helen Carroll and are now being led by Nevin Caple of LGBT SafeSport. The current situation is a far cry from what things were like in the 1980s, when Griffin was accused of holding a gay rights rally in 1987. Today in the United States, greater numbers of athletes, coaches, and sports administrators are coming out. We anxiously await the outcome of Caster Semenya's case with the Court for Arbitration for Sport as an indication of how far the world's acceptance of women has actually come. Despite this progress, the lesbian, trans, and intersex communities have a long way to go to fully gain acceptance.

ACTION STEPS TOWARD GREATER EQUALITY FOR LESBIAN, TRANSGENDER, AND INTERSEX WOMEN IN SPORTS

1. Provide education and training about lesbian, transgender, and intersex female athletes to athletic staff on an annual basis.
2. For "out" athletes, help provide support for those who are considering coming out.
3. For those who are comfortably out, be a positive role model as a lesbian woman for peers and younger athletes.
4. Change sport policy based on solid "scientific knowledge and medical validity."[31]
5. Put pressure on colleges and universities to enact the guidelines provided by the NCAA.
6. Support advocacy efforts through volunteering for such advocacy groups as Athlete Ally, the You Can Play Project, and LGBT SportSafe.
7. "Be proud of who you are!" as suggested by newly out lesbian golfer Mel Reid.

9

A GLOBAL CHALLENGE
International Women in Sport

Sport has the power to change the world. It has the power to inspire,
it has the power to unite people in a way that little else does. Sport
can create hope, where once there was only despair. It is more powerful than governments in breaking down racial barriers. It laughs in
the face of all types of discrimination.

—Nelson Mandela[1]

Throughout the world, girls and women in sport are afforded fewer
chances and less money, sponsorships, training, and resources than
their male counterparts. Many of the issues female athletes face in the
United States are encountered by their sister athletes in other countries
as well but to an even greater extent. In some countries, especially the
Middle East, women struggle to be allowed to play at all. When they do
manage to participate, they often find limited facilities, dress restrictions, and stiff parameters dictating when and how they can compete,
especially at the elite levels. In Iran, for instance, any woman competing—even non-Muslims and foreigners—must wear a hijab.

Female inequality in many cultures, especially in sports, is a problem
worldwide. In India, Deepika Kumari went from a simple life in a rural
Indian village to becoming an elite Olympic archer. Although she did
receive some support from her country, she was never given access to a
sport psychologist or mental coach, despite apparently requesting such
assistance. This conceivably would have helped her cope more effec-

tively with the media at the Rio Olympics. Instead, the experience of the massive media onslaught there, especially when she did not perform her best, proved overwhelming for her. The resources made available to her and other Indian female athletes were sorely lacking compared to what was provided for their male counterparts, particularly since archery is not considered a premier sport in India. Ultimately, she did not medal, as she had hoped, for her country, and it is not a stretch to say that this is at least partially attributable to her having to cope with these issues without extra assistance.

SPORT POWER FOR GIRLS AND WOMEN

"Sport has huge potential to empower women and girls," Lakshmi Puri, United Nations (UN) assistant secretary-general and deputy female executive director, remarked at a UN event discussing the impact of mega sports events. She went on to say that "sport can be a force to amplify women's voices and tear down gender barriers and discrimination. Women in sport defy the misperception that they are weak or incapable."[2] Participation in sports strengthens girls' and women's standing and presence in the world. This engagement increases girls' and women's confidence and self-esteem. Young girls who feel positive about themselves are more likely to occupy leadership roles and positions of power later in life. Ultimately, this will create a brighter and happier world for them in the future.

Attending the Seventh International Working Group (IWG) World Conference on Women and Sport in 2018, it became clear to me that the plight of girls and women in sport is a global concern. This organization, which advocates for girls and women globally, came into existence following the 1994 Brighton Declaration on Women and Sport—created at a conference jointly sponsored by the British Sports Council and the International Olympic Committee (IOC)—which endorsed the idea that the participation of women in every level of sport should be increased.

The female sport leaders at the IWG's 2018 gathering came from a huge and ever-growing array of countries that are advocating globally for girls and women in sport. At the conference were 280 delegates from 82 countries committed to establishing further sport strategies

Dr. Joan Steidinger at the 2018 International Working Group (IWG) World Conference on Women and Sport, presenting on "Sisterhood in Sports" with (on the right) Annamarie Phelps, vice chair of the British Olympics Association, Erica Tibbetts, lecturer at Smith College, and a delegate from the Congo. *Dr. Joan Steidinger*

inclusive of every woman on every continent. They gathered to network, learn, share, and collaborate with those who work with girls' and
women's sports via a multiplicity of strategies according to the needs of
each particular country. The meeting took place in Gaborone, Botswana, and its theme was "Determine the Future. Be Part of the Change."
The main subtopics covered were leadership, health and wellness, safety, media, empowerment, and "cross-cultural collaboration." An important goal of this conference is to bring women in sport together every
four years to discuss and learn about current global issues, notably
similarities and differences between different nations. Those in attendance aim to address timely issues and help with the development of
women through sport, with leadership remaining a crucial and ongoing
theme.

The focus of UN Women is also on improving girls' and women's
roles in the world. The fact that women are generally more collabora-
tive, hold broader viewpoints and ideas, and work in the spirit of cooperation becomes a great asset in global sport initiatives. At the 2016 Rio
Olympics, in which 45 percent of the athletes were women, UN Wom-
en and the IOC launched "One Win Leads to Another," a program
designed to teach leadership abilities, how to "create safe spaces,"
methods for crossing social obstacles, and where to get help when experiencing violence. Violence remains a common problem in African and
Middle Eastern countries. Ironically, in Botswana, where the IWG conference was held, 67 percent of women have encountered gender violence, despite holding 45 percent of the senior level roles in government; however, when you look at the country's political leadership, a
mere 6.6 percent of members of parliament and just 17.4 percent of
cabinet ministers and assistant ministers are women, indicative of the
true limitation of women's power in the country in both sport and life.

In these countries, the same general issues overlap. The prevailing
attitude is that female athletes are inferior to male athletes. But women
are increasingly standing up and shouting out for their rights, as was
evidenced by the 2017 worldwide "Women's March." The number of
women who participated in this march speaks to the desire for women
to be taken seriously in their fight for equality in sports and life in
general.

My experiences as a presenter and attendee at the IWG World Conference on Women and Sport provided me with a broader perspective

of female athletes throughout the world. My interviews of major female sports figures who are taking on a variety of roles to increase women's participation and leadership in sport were especially eye-opening. In this chapter, I will highlight the issues faced by individual countries based on the information I gathered through numerous interviews of key women leaders in sport, with the goal of providing a broader view of women in sport worldwide.

Europe

In Western countries, the hot topics of gender and cultural diversity are gaining even more significance in the sports conversation. When we start looking at countries like Norway and Iceland, we recognize that there are leaders aside from the United States in the pursuit of true gender equity. In many measures of equality ranking, Iceland and Norway are leading the way.

Starting in 2018, the Norwegian Football Association changed the pay for the women's and men's national teams so both would receive equal compensation. Iceland, meanwhile, has been doling out equal base pay to their football (soccer) teams since 2007. According to Iceland's Ministry of Welfare, almost "90 percent of boys and girls at the age of 12 participate in organized sports in Iceland."[3] In late 2017, Iceland also elected its second female prime minister, Katrin Jakobsdottir. In 2018, this led to the next step of requiring companies of 25 employees or more to prove that women weren't being paid less than men or risk being fined, resulting in greater pressure on sports entities to pay sports other than soccer more equitably.

According to Dr. Stiliani "Ani" Chroni, president of Women Sport International, professor of sport psychology and coaching at Inland Norway School of Sport Sciences, and a former alpine ski racer, Norway offers advantages to girls that other countries do not. As a Greek transplant, Dr. Chroni moved to Norway in 2013 to find easier living as a single mom working in academia. While still living in Greece, she collaborated in 2004 with Kari Fasting, a professor in the Department of Social and Cultural Studies at the Norwegian School of Sport Sciences, on a vital project examining sexual harassment data from 300 women in sport. This study revealed that 74 percent of the women surveyed had experienced sexual harassment. Chroni worked in a country where misogyny is prevalent, even today. Upon returning to campus following the publication of the study, staff and students started taunting her with jeers of, "Good morning, Ms. Sexual Harassment." When Chroni cut her hair short, her peers and students also began labeling her a lesbian. Moving to Norway, she says, has allowed her to continue her work on women and sport research with better funding and resources. The country's more egalitarian attitudes allow for equal access to sport for girls and boys, and equal pay for women and men—at least when it comes to the national soccer teams. Democratic values are applied in Norway, creating a more equitable and friendly sport culture for women.

Norway is not perfect, of course. While girls do enter sports coaching at younger ages and in greater numbers than boys, they also tend to drop out during their early 20s due to issues of work–life balance. In the Norwegian Federation of Sports, which covers both Olympic and Paralympic sports, there are almost 6,000 coaches, and only 24 percent are women. In terms of racial issues, one study of race and racism in Norway alluded to the issue of institutionalized racism getting in the way of the success of black athletes—both male and female—there.[4]

Even in countries one would expect to be more equitable, male athletes often still receive the lion's share of the money. In spite of Sweden's "feminist" reputation, for example, Aida Rejzovic plays professional volleyball but has to work a full-time job to survive. The town she lives in, Orebo (population 140,000, located in central Sweden), allocates 35 million kroner ($4.2 million) to sports. Yet, the female national volleyball team only receives $50,000 per year. In contrast, the men's football team is paid $1.8 million annually, and the ice hockey team is paid $1.2 million per year. Rejzovic dreams of working part time, which would give her the time to rest and recuperate between training and games, which her male counterparts are afforded.[5] Interestingly enough, in Sweden volleyball is a dominant sport for women. Twice as many females as males are registered with the Swedish Volleyball Federation. Rejzovic's coach, Matilda Wikander, comments, "In sports, like elsewhere in society, men have been given positions of power due to age-old quota systems, but the sports movement needs to use all its talent, and [they] are missing out on what women can offer."[6]

Dr. Nad'a Knorre, a former national-level gymnast, has held a spot on the official board for gymnastics on the Czechoslovakia National

Olympic Committee for 22 years. Dr. Knorre worked as a teacher of gymnastics at Charles University in Prague from 1986 to 2004. In 1997, she was elected as the first chairperson of the Women and Sport Committee of the Czech National Olympic Committee, and she continues to hold this position today. Knorre's view of the Czech Republic's treatment of women in sport is that women are not placed in decision-making positions often enough to make a difference. The country still operates in a "traditional" male–female manner, with the culture expecting women to stay home with the kids and primarily accepting female athletes only in the sports traditionally associated with women there: track and field, gymnastics, basketball, swimming, and snow skiing.

Oceania

Australia is beginning to stand up for its female athletes. Research demonstrates that women's sports are being followed in greater numbers than had previously been reported; however, the coverage of women is still quite low, at about 8.7 percent.[7] A study conducted by Commonwealth Bank, a sponsor of Australia's women's cricket team, found "surprisingly an observable increase in TV coverage and broader media coverage as rationale for the escalating interest." The authors went on to say, "The money put into the promotion of pro female cricket players has clearly paid dividends." The research revealed a "48 percent increase in interest in women's sport from last year, with 53 percent of Australians now watching broadcasts or attending live women's sporting events."[8]

Three factors contributed to this rise in enthusiasm for women's sport in Australia: more thorough airing on TV (31 percent); positive reporting on women's sport (30 percent); and the visibility and personalities of two women's sport leaders, in particular, Ellyse Perry in cricket and Sam Kerr in soccer. The area in which Australia needs to do the most work is in the inclusion and encouragement of indigenous women in sports. With rare exceptions (e.g., Cathy Freeman, who won gold in the 400m in the Sydney Olympics in 2000), this is a population that has been highly neglected when it comes to opportunities in and exposure to women's sports.[9]

In New Zealand, in contrast, Maori and Pacific Islander women are an essential part of the sporting culture. They have power with the Caucasian population, and this enables them to act as an integral part of the sporting power structure. "New Zealand women punch far above their weight at the international level," said one *Guardian* article. "Sponsors are increasingly seeking sports women ahead of sportsmen as brand representatives." Media coverage of women's sports in New Zealand may come in at a mere 10 percent, but that's at the top end of coverage for the vast majority of countries in the world.[10]

Melodie Robinson, a Maori, is one of the most well-known, pioneering female sports journalists in rugby, the first female rugby commentator in the world, and a mentor for other women commentators, and she also ranks as one of the top women in sport in New Zealand. When you meet her in person, what most impresses is her personable, likeable, no-nonsense style. In our discussion, her devotion to empowering women quickly became clear. She played rugby for the national team from 1996 to 2002, helping New Zealand win two World Cups. After initially commentating on breakfast radio, she turned her attention to sports journalism, both nationally and internationally. For the past 14 years, as a sportscaster for Sky TV, Robinson's focus has been on the elevation of women in sport. Recently she launched "The Wonderful Group" and "It Takes Two" to further promote women's involvement in sports broadcasting.

When I spoke with her, she described her country's attitude toward women athletes as sometimes proud but often ambivalent, with pockets of antiwomen men. Just as I was finishing the writing of this book, she was appointed as the new general manager of sport and events at TVNZ, where she will lead the sport and event strategy. For Robinson, this is a dream come true. Still, even women's rugby has a large male following, and the participation and power of Maori and Pacific Islander women is respected by New Zealand's Caucasian population. Robinson's focus has now shifted to the upper reaches of sport, where her goal is to make an even bigger impact for women in sport and life.

New Zealand's investment in women in sport is further indicated by their offer to host the next IWG conference in 2022. The representative who will host the conference for the Women in Sport Aotearoa, Kirikaiahi Mahutariki, recognizes that her cultural strengths lie in her New Zealand Maori, New Zealand–born Cook Islands Maori, and Tahitian roots. As an attorney she belonged to the Wellington Rugby League Judiciary for eight years. Raised in a sports-minded family, Mahutariki believes sport has shaped the person she is today.

In our conversation, she described Maori culture as inclusive, saying that it welcomes other people into the household. Growing up, girls weren't allowed to play in sports leagues with other girls, but the situation has changed. In her interview with *Global Women*, she commented,

> Sport has taught me to be disciplined (turn up to training regularly, put in the hard yards) and resilient (overcoming setbacks, getting back up every time and continuing on). It's also taught me to work well in a team, be courageous, and confident, to back myself and have faith in my team to deliver. Determination and constantly pushing to better yourself are also key learnings that have helped me on my leadership journey. [11]

Mahutariki depicts herself as never having been discriminated against and living in a country that believes, "Where there's a will, there's a way!" As a foundation board member of Women in Sport Aotearoa, she is committed to creating change for women and girls in sport through research, leadership, and advocacy. In New Zealand, they need to build a strong network devoted to improving the situation of girls and women in sport.

The Caribbean

In the Caribbean, there are pockets of countries/islands that support and encourage women in sports and are open to developing women's leadership in sports. Probably the most well-known of these are Jamaica and Trinidad and Tobago. In attending and presenting at a conference in Barbados, the patriarchal nature of the island was evident in the structure and presenters. A number of the women involved were in lower-level administrative positions, with only a few presentations focused on women's issues. In fact, the most well educated and involved authority in sport, Marcia Oxley, was not even invited to participate.

Dr. Margaret Ottley, who hails from Trinidad, played field hockey for 13 years, first in high school and then at the national level. In 2004 she traveled with the Trinidad and Tobago teams to the Olympics and helped their track and field team prepare for the 2012 Olympics. While getting her PhD at Temple University and working as an associate professor at West Chester University in metropolitan Philadelphia, Ottley worked with both the 2012 and 2016 U.S. Olympic track and field teams. Additionally, she worked with the Trinidad and Tobago athletes in the Rio Games in 2016. She had led the way for other Trinidadian female athletes.

Barbados is an island, yet many of its occupants don't swim. Such are the dichotomies of an island whose acceptance of female athletes can be a struggle. Marcia Oxley, who also attended graduate school at Temple, has acted as a leader in women's sports in the United States and Barbados for decades. She was an accomplished netball and track and field athlete. While receiving her MS from Temple University as a foreign exchange student, badminton became a mainstay sport for her. Her mentors included such imminent women as Tina Sloan Green; Carole Oglesby; and the first Division I African American athletic director, Dr. Dorothy Richey (Chicago State). In leadership roles, Oxley supervised a joint physical education development program with Canada and the Caribbean, served on the Women's Sports Foundation International Committee, and developed the sport management program at Barbados Community College. Her leadership in sport provides a model for other Barbadian women to look up to. As Oxley observes, the message in her home country remains clear for girls: Don't consider sport as a career. As with many other countries, they have difficulty keeping girls in sport during adolescence.

Despite certain roadblocks, the tide seems to be shifting toward paying more attention to girls in sport. One sign of this is the appointment of Ytannia Wiggins as the first female director of the Women's Committee on Sport of the Barbados Olympic Association. Wiggins was also the first team manager for the Barbados senior national and women's under-20 teams, and she is a former Miss Barbados. Between sport and her role as a model, Wiggins played volleyball and soccer, and began writing a chronological history of women athletes in Barbados. She went on to start the first women's soccer team at the University of the West Indies Cave Hill campus, becoming the manager and captain of the team. Her belief is that the newer generation in Barbados is more aware of the important role women play in sport. The increase in co-ed sports, she says, has helped. Wiggins also thinks that a new initiative to bring girls to sport, called the "Play Like a Girl Workshop," which focuses on such issues as body image and sexual harassment and abuse, led by former national athletes, will help make new strides for female athletes. Her parting words to me were that we must all respect our differences, connect to our tribes, and quit being so angry.

South America

One of the foremost authorities on Latin America and females in sport is Dr. Rosa Lopez D'Amico from Venezuela. Aside from her role in leadership promoting women's sports in South America, Lopez D'Amico serves as president of the International Association of Physical Education and Sports for Girls and Women and is on the executive board of the IWG on Women in Sport. As a young girl and teen, she was a national-level artistic gymnast. Lopez D'Amico reported that the position of women in sport has improved in South America but still requires additional work both now and in the future. She frequently finds herself the only Latina woman in senior positions. The three ways the sporting world has advanced, according to Lopez D'Amico, include improved policies, increased engagement with girls and parents, and more media coverage. In Venezuela, there are even two female sport ministers. Male attitudes are just starting to improve due to outside pressures. Men are beginning to respect some principles and mandates, as well as acknowledge basic human rights for women in sport. The primary area where movement is at a standstill is the overemphasis on appearance over performance. Since their rural areas remain conservative, the schools may not offer physical education for girls or encourage them to participate in sports.

"In most countries, gender inequality and poor access to physical education and school sport continues. . . . A major exception is Cuba, where the status of physical activity across all of society, including in schools, is higher than in most countries of the world."[12] In South America, the culture's machismo attitudes interfere with the ability to understand and appreciate the strength and power of the female athlete.

Football/soccer is a widely popular sport in South America. Yet only Brazil, Argentina, and Uruguay have held women's football championships for more than 20 years. Despite this limitation, the South

American Football Confederation coordinates football concerns throughout South America. Players fall into the three divisions of U-17, U-20, and Copa Libertadores for private clubs for all females and males. In 2016, an 18-year-old Venezuelan was the first woman to be nominated for the Puskas Prize for Best Goal of the Year. Brazil actually holds its male players in higher esteem even though Marta won FIFA World Player of the Year five consecutive years.[13]

The Middle East

In Middle Eastern countries, women face multiple barriers to engaging in sport. Their experience is divergent from that of Western women. This is gender discrimination in its extreme, and it impacts women's health, as well as their social and economic concerns. Women still live under male guardianship in Saudi Arabia and stricter male control in a number of the countries in this area of the world. According to Islamic law, women obtain "full legal capacity once they attain puberty," except with strict Sharia law.[14] In terms of current legal rights, one recent report says that, looking at "countries in the Middle East and Sub-Saharan Africa . . . the typical nation in those regions gives women under half the legal rights of men." These statistics are important when it comes to understanding the cultural context of women and sport in the Middle East. Essentially, women in many of these countries only have access to sports as their husbands and fathers allow it.[15]

Saudi Arabia is by far the most restrictive country for women. Despite these severe limitations, women in the Middle East have forged ahead and found avenues to participate in sport. Saudi women, for example, have taken to the streets to run from Jeddah to Riyadh, the capital. In spite of restrictive cultural norms and oppressive laws against women, women run in groups, sometimes with men, and even do secret races without head covers far outside the city of Jeddah in the Hejaz Mountains.

Nesreen Ghonaim's determination to run came to fruition when she heard about a new women's running club, Jeddah Running Collective (JRC) Women, and joined in. She is now head of JRC Women. With her twinkling eyes and short, curly hair, Ghonaim inspires and mentors, as well as advocates for, women runners. Interestingly enough, JRC was founded by a man, Rod (he gave no last name, due to fear of arrest). He initially set up JRC as a mixed group but quickly became aware that many women preferred not to run with men. That was the birth of JRC Women.

The road for JRC has not been a smooth one. In 2016, two religious police stopped a mixed running group. The officers queried the men, wondering why they were "doing 'such things.' The police rounded up five male runners and took them in for questioning."[16] The questioning was solely focused on why men would encourage women to run. Now, the government allows access once a week for women, men, and children to play sport together, something that previously was banned. One of the first female JRC members has been quoted as saying, "There is no law that says women can't run. It's just not common—it goes against our culture."[17]

The last three Middle Eastern countries to send female athletes to the Olympic Games were Saudi Arabia, Qatar, and Brunei. Saudi Arabia remains the most restrictive for female athletes who wish to become elite athletes since the culture is resistant to allowing women to compete in sports in general. In the majority of Middle Eastern countries, women are still not supported in their work to become involved in competitive and elite sports. In 2012, however, "sixteen Muslim countries from the Middle East sent 158 women to compete in London, with Egypt sending its largest female contingent—37 athletes—since 1912."[18] Clearly, the participation of women in sports in Middle Eastern countries is slowly shifting as female athletes in those countries demonstrate their abilities and strength in sport. Despite this progress, women are often not encouraged or supported to work toward involvement in competitive and elite sport. This recognition allows for more female athletes to have dreams and earn respect as athletes.

In the 2016 Rio Olympics, some Middle Eastern women won medals. For instance, Sara Ahmed from Egypt won bronze in the 69-kilo weight class in taekwondo and became the first Egyptian woman to win an Olympic medal. She was soon followed by countrywoman Hedaya Wahba, who tied with Kimia Alizah (who became Iran's first woman to receive an Olympic medal) for bronze in taekwondo's 57-kilo weight class.[19] Other examples of women who have defied the odds are Wojdan Ali Serjai Raha Moharrak (the first Saudi woman to summit Mt. Everest, in 2013), Tahmina Kohistani (the only Afghani Olympic female runner), and Amna Al Haddad (an Emerati weightlifter).

Fifteen universities in the Middle East now enjoy intercollegiate athletic tournaments for 450 women and 550 men, according to Peter Dice, athletic director and assistant dean of students at New York University Dubai. Dice explained that 90 percent of the women are local and realize sports don't interfere with their academics.

True change always takes time; this is especially true in a place like the Middle East, where restrictions have been placed on female athletes—and females in general—for centuries. Indicators are that the situation is changing in urban areas, but the rural areas continue to maintain traditional ways of thinking. As urban areas develop stronger women's advocacy groups in sport, things will improve, but there's still a long way to go.

Developing Nations

Women in sport in developing countries face such hurdles as misogyny, ignorance of women's value, and the staunch traditional belief that women belong in the home. In many of these countries this unbending view of societal norms often prevents women from receiving adequate, if any, education, and participating in sport.

Primarily due to religious and patriarchal structures, the majority of these countries do not recognize the full value of women, let alone allow them to engage in physical activity and sport. Without education and sport, women are prevented from acquiring the skills they need to feel empowered in their lives; however, there are programs, symposiums/conferences, and initiatives in Africa and Asia that aim to help promote involvement in sport by girls and women.

In Nepal, an organization called Ladies Mountain League was founded in February 2016 to "empower Nepalese women through outdoor sports."[20] In Kenya, there is a program called "Moving the Goalposts," which advocates for the empowerment of girls and young women.[21] This program assists girls and young women in tackling societal barriers in coastal Kenya. In South Africa, Girls and Football SA's mission is simply to "encourage the development of girls and women through sport, media, and education."[22]

However, there are countries that must fight even bigger battles before they can begin to consider getting girls involved in sports. One example is the African country of Zambia. More than 60 percent of the country lives below the poverty level, with 42 percent of the people living in extreme poverty. The practice of child brides and prohibition of girls receiving an education endures. The executive director of NOWSPAR, the National Organization for Women in Sport, Physical Activity, and Recreation, Matilda Mwaba, works for the inclusion of girls and women in sport and physical activity in Zambia through a number of different avenues, notably enlisting volunteers to perform outreach to girls in local tribes that still encourage child brides and purposely prevent their girls from receiving an education.[23] NOWSPAR received praise from the UN in 2012 for the effective way the organization uses "sport as a tool to attain humanitarian, developmental, and peace-building objectives . . . as well as playing a significant role . . . in poverty reduction, attainment of universal education, and gender equality."[24] When we met in Botswana, Mwaba spoke with a twinkle in her eye about two girls they had just convinced to leave their village and seek out education. Another example of progress in Africa happened at the 2016 African Women's Championships, where three African countries, South Africa, Namibia, and the Ivory Coast, had women head coaches, up from one the previous year.[25] Sometimes it's the small yet significant wins that make all the difference.

In Nepal, where women are mostly still treated as second-class citizens, a young Nepali woman, Pratima Sherpa, dreams of becoming the country's first female professional golfer. She was raised in a maintenance shed on the Royal Nepal Golf Club, where she spends three to four hours per day practicing while attending college. In 2017, at age 17, she competed in a tournament against a field of 21 men. This tournament was designed to determine who would become a professional golfer in Nepal. The promoters would only take the top five players after three days of play, with no extra consideration afforded to Pratima for being a woman. Sherpa finished ninth and didn't advance to the professional level. Only when they acknowledge and accept that women play against women—not against men—in most pro sports will Sherpa be allowed to become a pro athlete.

Nepal's heavily patriarchal system has quite a distance to go before it will truly acknowledge, support, value, and respect the intelligence, abilities, and strength of its female athletes. Limiting attitudes, mainly by men, and resistance to women in sport remains entrenched in many developing nations, and years of advocacy work will have to take place before some of these places are able to step up and recognize the strengths of women in sport and life.

English-Speaking Countries

A national survey about attitudes toward women in sport released in the United Kingdom in 2018, reported that both women and men recognize the unequal treatment of women in sport. More than 75 percent of the women and 68 percent of the men surveyed agreed with this statement. Although there is pay equality in the majority of athletics in the United Kingdom (track and field, swimming, tennis, rowing, and volleyball), and "recent research shows that 83 percent of sports now give men and women equal prize money,"[26] there is still a massive inequality in pay for the top four sports in the country: football (soccer), cricket, golf, and cycling. Soccer, of course, is the worst offender; in fact, the poorest paid major sport for women throughout the world is soccer, due to the massive misogyny in FIFA. The figures show that prize money for male soccer players in the United Kingdom is £22,075,000 as compared to £561,230 for women, with men earning 40 times the amount women do. This is a massive gap, especially in a country where women's soccer is popular. In cycling, meanwhile, men receive six times more than women.

Despite more recognition and acceptance of women in sport, many believe that girls don't receive the same opportunities for participation in sport as boys. Lizzie Deignan, an Olympic medalist, said of the survey's findings, "While this survey shows that attitudes towards women's sport are changing, particularly amongst the younger generations, there is obviously still a long way to go to achieve parity in sport."[27] Clearly, even England struggles with adequately addressing gender equity in sports, including in its most visible sports.

England's Annamarie Phelps leads the way in British rowing. Her humble yet solid presentation forcess one to take notice of a quiet authority. She didn't begin to participate in sport until her university years, even though she came from a sporting family. As a lightweight rower, she was encouraged to join the national team and went on to win three silvers and one gold in the world championships in the lightweight coxless four. Her international career in rowing culminated in representing Great Britain at the Olympic Games in Atlanta in 1996. Phelps retired from elite competition after the 1996 Games, although she continued to row for her club team.

When I spoke to Phelps, she mentioned that she chaired the British Women's Rowing Commission in 1997. This was the only aspect of her success that she disclosed to me. In looking deeper into her background, however, I discovered that she was also elected deputy chairman of British Rowing in 2002, subsequently served in such roles as lead safeguarding officer of antidoping issues, and became chairman of the British Rowing Association in 2013.

Phelps's involvement in rowing endures today; it's work she's always loved, she said, and she views doing it as a privilege.[28] One of the few women on the British Olympic Association board, she was most recently appointed vice chair of the association in February 2017. It's a role she occupies to this day.

Attending the IWG conference in 2018, Phelps came to learn more about the state of women in sport throughout the world. She described the attitude about women athletes in Great Britain as rather good, except in the four sports previously mentioned: soccer, cricket, golf, and cycling. In rowing, Phelps happily reported, "Pay for men was decreased a bit and women's brought up to equal in boat races." She believes one of the biggest barriers to women's participation in sport is the fact that girls are almost talked into not doing sport at a young age, whereas boys are expected to participate. There are still societal expectations that are skewed toward women "doing the work of the household," she said. She also added that for some unknown reason, it's a constant battle to get coaches to coach women's rowing. This seems like further proof that women like Phelps need to use their positions of power to help girls and women gain further recognition in sports and appoint more women coaches.

In Canada, there are many of the same issues of inequality in sport for girls and women. Of girls aged 13 to 17, Canada has 59 percent participation in sport. "By 10 years of age, if a girl has yet to participate in sports," according to a study on female sport participation in Canada published in 2016, "there is only a 10 percent chance that she will be physically active as an adult."[29] In adolescence, the dropout rate for girls is significant: Overall participation sits at a mere 22 percent, and school participation in sport declines by 26 percent during this time.

In terms of coaching, the study found women coaches comprise only 0.3 to 0.5 percent of coaches in amateur women's sports. In professional positions and coaching roles, furthermore, women face extensive gender discrimination. Eight themes were listed in the study as blocks to female leadership for women in sport. These themes included the following:

predominant culture of sport (23.1 percent)
financial implications (20.4 percent)
access to sport on their terms (18.1 percent)
alternate demands on time (14.3 percent)
sharing the sport experience (11.6 percent)
public perception (5.9 percent)
peer/parental influence (3.8 percent)
media (2.9 percent)[30]

When I was lucky enough to meet Allison Sandmeyer-Graves, the new CEO of the Canadian Association for the Advancement of Women and Sport and Physical Activity (CAAWS), in Botswana, she provided me with a good overview of female athletes' struggle for equality in Canada. CAAWS, which has operated since 1981, strives to create tangible change for women in sport and achieve respect, inclusion, and equity for girls and women in Canadian sport. Since the election of Justin Trudeau, huge changes have been made that have benefited women, both in general and in high-performance sports. In fact, the minister of sport, Carla Qualtrough, has taken real action to support women in being their best in sport. The motivation behind CAAWS encouraging girls to enter sport is twofold: 1) harnessing sport to advance equality in society, and 2) helping sport to be equitable for women.

As Sandmeyer-Graves points out, Canada ranks poorly on the pay equity scale. One recent study found that more Canadians are taking female athletes' performances more seriously and not focusing only on appearance, so clearly progress is being made, although there's still a long way to go. Sandmeyer-Graves impressed upon me that sports are still designed according to a male model. This alone lends itself to the problem of the higher dropout rate for teenage girls in sports. She also emphasized something I addressed in my last book: the importance of coaches taking the time to understand the qualities and motivation strategies of women, the things that make them unique. Working from this understanding, coaches can better serve the needs of their female athletes.

CONCLUDING REMARKS

From this limited summary of women in sport worldwide, we can recognize the numerous struggles women in sport encounter on an ongoing basis. According to the "Women, Business, and the Law 2019" report, only six countries offer equal rights to women and men in the business world. Women in sport, then, are a long way away from gaining equality in sport, since general business opportunities for women have historically always been well ahead of opportunities for women in sport. In this report, the United States placed outside the top 50, with the United Kingdom, Australia, and Germany ranked well above it.[31] This gender gap in sport actually hurts the global gross domestic product (GDP), as well as discourages the empowerment of women through sport.

The recognition of the value of empowering girls and women in sport throughout the world, including in the Middle East and developing nations, is essential to further overall growth for each and every country. Although many of our issues are the same, the differences faced by girls and women in places like Zambia and Nepal are equally important. It's crucial that we all take the time to reach across country lines and assist our sister athletes. It's women leaders like Lilamani de Soysa, working on a project to establish a gender and sport model as a legacy for Tokyo 2020, through the International Academy for Sports Studies, that make all the difference in opening doors for women. Only through global communication among women's sport networks can we lend our support and strength to girls and women in sport who need it and begin to make a difference.

ACTION STEPS TOWARD GREATER GENDER AND GLOBAL EQUALITY

1. Support women's programs (e.g., ESPN's global mentoring program) and develop and encourage further female sport participa-

tion since it empowers girls and women to be a presence in the world-at-large.

2. Increase the number of U.S. female sports leaders going to international conferences to exchange information.

3. Form more organizations in Second and Third World countries for the participation of girls in specific sports.

4. Work directly with media channels to increase the levels of coverage of women's sports (e.g., women leaders in sport, like Melodie Robinson).

5. In such countries as Zambia and Nepal, and throughout the Middle East, the value of girls and women needs to be recognized first and foremost. Only then will they be allowed to participate in sports. Take action to improve these situations to help better the situations for females in sport.

10

TIME'S UP

Primary Concerns and Action Steps

She who is courageous enough to overcome fear and take risks in
sport will live a full and challenging life.

—Dr. Joan Steidinger

On March 8, 2019, 28 members of our world champion women's
national soccer team filed a "gender discrimination" lawsuit against
USA Soccer concerning pay equality and working conditions. The lawsuit addresses the "institutionalized gender discrimination" that has affected their paychecks, along with "where they play and how often, how
they train, medical treatment and coaching they receive, even how they
travel to matches."[1]

The plight of female athletes remains serious, despite the gains that
have been made throughout the years. The primary areas in need of
attention include leadership, pay inequity, media coverage, prestige,
and respect. In terms of leadership, leading authorities and pioneers
like Carole Oglesby, the "godmother of sports psychology," and Donna
de Varona, the first president and chairman of the Women's Sports
Foundation, have both indicated in my interviews with them that wom-
en in sports leadership positions are of primary concern and a number-
one priority. Although at the advent of Title IX, 92 percent of female
teams were coached by women, that figure now runs at about 41.8
percent. Now that good salaries are being offered, men are playing

dominant roles in coaching women, and they are usually offered significantly higher salaries than female coaches.

Girls and young women in sport need female coaches as role models. They need to see more women in sport leading and being allowed to have more seats at the table, getting paid equitably, having the media actually showing them in a variety of sports and a vast increase in exposure, coaching in larger numbers, speaking up and confronting the massive problem of sexual harassment and abuse, embracing the differences between women of color, supporting and accepting lesbian and transgender athletes, and understanding the world's sexist attitudes toward women in sport.

The question remains, What are the priority issues to address, and what steps and actions are being taken to move the needle farther to the left, toward greater equality for women in sports? This chapter works toward developing an "action model" for establishing greater equality for women in sport—even if it means taking legal action. In our culture, the abuse of female athletes by coaches and others is just beginning to be exposed. It's time for female athletes, as well as women involved in any aspect or level of sport, to join together, stand up, and shout out for our rights. Through researching and interviewing leaders in the field, six major themes emerged: 1) mentoring and building bridges; 2) attitudes of men toward women in sport; 3) legislation; 4) education, information, and training; 5) inclusion of women of color, lesbian women, and transgender women; and 6) actual and consistent enforcement of Title IX.

MENTORING AND BUILDING BRIDGES IN SPORT

Mentoring was the major focus of the 40-plus women and men I interviewed. To get and keep girls in sport we must make sports fun and joyful. Mentors, who are usually older, are guides that help their mentees grow and develop in sport and life. They can be family, coaches, former competitive athletes, and/or other authority figures. The common thought is that only youth and teens need mentors, but so do older women, especially those participating in sport when they're older. Two major advocacy organizations that support female athletes are the Women's Sports Foundation and the Black Women in Sport Foundation (BWSF). Founded by Billie Jean King and several other former elite athletes in 1974, the Women's Sports Foundation is dedicated to creating leaders through advocacy work to bring more opportunities to girls to participate in sport. The foundation has led major initiatives for furthering women in sport, including fostering the ongoing development of girls in sport, recognizing and honoring elite female athletes, creating programs to support girls in sport, and leading the way with research on girls and women in sport.

Leading African American women who were interviewed repeated the same theme: They would attend conferences and compete in sport without seeing other girls and women like themselves. This provided an important motivating factor in the birth of the BWSF in 1992. Tina Sloan Green and her cofounders, Dr. Alpha Alexander, Dr. Nikki Franke, and Linda Greene, Esq., have worked hard in the Philadelphia area to direct their focus on exposing girls of color and girls from poverty to nontraditional sports and provide assistance with academic development. They have provided opportunities in sport and life-development skills. The BWSF has provided numerous mentors throughout the years for girls of color, even when there were far fewer women of color playing sports.

Two examples of women I have interviewed who were mentored by strong women and have become mentors themselves are Marcia Oxley and Vikki Krane. Oxley, a native Barbadian and community college educator in Barbados, lived part of her life and attended school in both the United States and Barbados. As a national athlete for Barbados in track and field, as well as netball, Oxley built a solid interest in sport as a young woman. She received her BS at the University of the West Indies and her MS at Temple University, where she met Tina Sloan Green and Dr. Carole Oglesby.

She described a variety of mentors for her in sport. These included her female physical education teachers; her dad; her male netball coach; Dr. Oglesby; Sloan Green; and Dr. Dorothy Richey, the first black athletic director at Chicago State. Each of her mentors helped her in different ways. In 2010, she served as manager and coach for the netball team at the Commonwealth Games. In addition, she developed a program for black students in physical education and activity at Barbados Community College that continues to this day. Mentors helped her lay a foundation to become an important leader herself.

Dr. Vikki Krane, a lesbian professor at Bowling Green University and a former president of the Association for Applied Sports Psychology (AASP), grew up in a nonsexist, traditional family with a white picket fence. In high school and college she competed in running and soccer. Her mentors spanned the spectrum, beginning with coaches when she was younger and including such notable sport psychology luminaries as Jean Williams and Dan Gould, both past presidents of AASP. Krane learned strong leadership skills and has fought for the rights of LGBTQ leaders and athletes. Although she grew up thinking women and men were equal, she soon realized the numerous inequities between the haves and have-nots. She has fought these battles with great frustration and helped found an annual symposium, "Social Justice in Exercise and Sport Psychology."

There are a few examples of entities that have worked to help female athletes—active and retired—focus on developing leadership skills. An early proponent of leadership training for elite athletes is the accounting firm Ernst and Young, which worked with Olympic swimming gold medalist Donna de Varona. Ernst and Young created a Leadership Academy in which they would match an Olympic athlete with a mentor to further develop the athlete's leadership skills. Many of the girls from this program have blossomed into leaders. In 2013, they collaborated and launched a program to develop the leadership skills of elite and Olympian female athletes following their retirement from sport, establishing the Women Athletes Global Leadership Network. The network was set up to "share lessons learned from career transitions to mentor, open doors, and create opportunities."[2]

ESPN established a worldwide leadership program for women in the sport movement to address these issues more effectively. Laura Gentile assisted with the establishment of the Empower Women and Girls Sports Initiative, which provides for global sports mentoring, reaching out to 57 countries and choosing 115 women to participate in month-long mentoring programs with female business leaders. Their goal is for women to keep pushing the ball forward for women in sport. In addition, Julie Foudy, soccer icon and legend, established the Julie Foudy Leadership Academy (JFSLA), a summer sports camp and leadership academy for girls ages 12 to 18.

Mentoring is a key ingredient in supporting and helping develop young women in sport, especially with the high dropout rate of teens in

2018 ESPNW Summit. *ESPN-Laura Gentile*

sport, which is even higher with girls of color. If those in sport would engage with at least one young female athlete and offer encouragement, it could make a big difference. Developing an increased number of advocacy programs for girls in sport is an action that could be taken in more communities, especially those heavily populated by the poor and girls of color, if only those of us interested in social justice would step up and create more programs. Especially in youth sport, our culture needs to open up more spots for women to coach. As Donna Lopiano stated, "Kids see a powerful woman and think it's great!"

The interviewees repeatedly spoke of the importance of building strong alliances with other women. In February 2019, Nefertiti Walker was appointed associate dean of inclusion at the University of Massachusetts Amherst. In addition, she will become the full-time chief diversity officer for the university at only 35 years of age. The fact that she is both black and lesbian is a great platform for her to build bridges through the lens of her own experience in collegiate sports. She describes the situation at her school as inclusive to a certain extent. All the lesbian women at her school have leadership roles, as they band together to accomplish change in the system, according to Walker.

Former *San Jose Mercury News* reporter Mark Purdy believes that female CEOs in business need to step up and begin supporting women's sports in a variety of ways. In January 2019, the national championship football game, held in the Bay Area, was entirely run by women who worked together collaboratively. His question: Why aren't women like these working in women's sports?

ATTITUDES OF MEN TOWARD WOMEN IN SPORTS

As Heather Barbour, associate professor at the University of New Hampshire, concluded in her interview, "Through more training and teaching, coaches need to realize that people play better when they are themselves, whether they're lesbian, black, or other women of color. Actually, the attitudes and hiring practices of men directly affect female athletes in sport. Repeatedly, I heard about the all-white men's club in positions of authority blocking the advancement of women in sport. One of the major drawbacks of Title IX was that women were significantly pushed out of coaching. As previously mentioned, men hire people who look like them.

In the 2019 women's basketball championship, the coaches for both teams were female: Muffet McGraw, who shouted out for women in coaching, and Kim Mulkey, who suggested that we start looking for the "best person" for the job. What Mulkey didn't realize is that McGraw was shouting out for more female coaching opportunities in a league that's still predominantly male and overflowing with male coaches. On NCAA teams, women in Division I hold only 8.6 percent of the head coaching positions, 10.6 in Division II, and 12.2 in Division III.[3] These statistics are pitiful given that 43 percent of active athletes are women. Female athletic directors account for only 10.5 percent in Division I schools. Women hold only 40.8 percent of all head coaching jobs. The large differential between white and black female coaches leads us to the conclusion that sports clearly has a gender and racial problem. What accompanies this is discrimination against lesbians, transgenders, and intersex women, according to the findings of the 2019 annual report by the Institute for Diversity and Ethic in Sport, which sees little change for women. In fact, 85 percent of those coaching jobs are held by white women.

Richard Lapchick, a lead researcher in diversity and ethics in sport, summed it up nicely: "The biggest takeaway—and unfortunately has been for a number of years—is that white men are overwhelming in the key positions of college sport at the university and college level."[4] Men in power are ignorant of the fact that women can be as smart—and even smarter at times—causing the huge imbalance in sport for players and female leaders. They're just afraid that in sharing power they will lose power in every area of sport. They fear sharing power will lessen their own power. And, of course, there's not enough to go around. In fact, the excuses they've used for years are certainly invalid today.

Several years ago, before I knew about the dynamics at the higher levels for women leaders in sport, I traveled to Barbados for the Caribbean Sports Conference. Despite several higher-level women (myself included) presenting, I noticed a certain level of misogyny in the white men attending the conference, considerably more than in the black men and women. I only submitted to present because I wanted to meet Terry Orlick, who was the keynote speaker, as I figured I'd learn a lot. Orlick, one of the grandfathers of sports psychology, had a white man, a former police officer, assisting him. This man clearly wasn't qualified or trained to do workshops. He made frequent derogatory remarks, even in regard to my book. He had a shtick about some personal trauma. Plus, most of the women putting on the conference were obviously lower-level administrators. In fact, I ended up going to lunch with Marcia Oxley and was shocked to realize that she hadn't even been invited to present at the conference. Watching and feeling the misogyny displayed by the white men and a few of the black men was disappointing, to say the least. Yet, it remains a factor for women in sport.

LAWSUITS AND LEGISLATION

Between lawsuits and legislation, there is increased legal activity taking place fighting for further equality in sports. We've seen over and over again the women who are standing up for their rights. What is most admirable is the perseverance and persistence of the U.S. women's national soccer team. In March 2019 the 28 members of the team filed suit in U.S. District Court in Los Angeles. The suit addresses "institutionalized gender discrimination" and focuses on the Equal Pay Act and

Title VII of the Civil Rights Act. Remember, both Tracey Griesbaum and Jane Meyer won lawsuits for their firing without cause, involving gender and sexual identity discrimination. Although they received solid monetary renumeration, the question remains: Will they ever work again in coaching and administration?

Lesbians and women of color are even more vulnerable than white women. Many of them are never given a second chance. The numerous lawsuits stemming from the Larry Nassar sexual abuse case will continue into the future, even after the publication of this book. The latest victim of an unexpected firing was MaChelle Joseph, "Coach Jo," at Georgia Tech, after she called out the administration for allowing inequities on the girls' teams. Public lawsuits call greater attention to girls and women in sport. Women in sport may need this venue as a way to directly attack the injustices they constantly face. So, when a male athletic director or coach proclaims, "Sue Me!" women coaches will! Girls and women have been given permission to hit the pass-go button and carry on when justified. According to Donna Lopiano, "lawsuits are uncovering the depths of excuses" used for unequal treatment.

At the forefront of developing legislation and policies for women in sport and the need for safety for women in sport is Nancy Hogshead-Makar. She's working dutifully with her organization, Champion Women, to advise girls and young women on any number of gender discrimination issues, especially sexual harassment and abuse. In California, progressive Democratic lawmakers Tasha Boerner Horvath and Lorna Gonzalez are cosponsoring legislation that would require competitions on "state-owned land or property" to provide equal pay for women and men, calling it the "Equal Pay for Equal Play Bill," #AB467, which "requires sports prize gender equity for athletes in all competition held on public lands."[5] If this legislation passes, it will be a big boon for women in sport, but even getting this far is groundbreaking. Lawmakers need to step up their focus on bills like #AB467 that move women toward greater equality in sport.

EDUCATION AND TRAINING

Education and training are two vital aspects of women in sports gaining equality. Relevant training about the importance of supporting issues related to female athletes is a vital topic to cover with staff in athletic departments. A major issue to be discussed in training is the "unconscious gender bias" that is often built into men and institutions as part of their structure of underlying beliefs. Even men who the public believes to be unbiased, for example, Geno Auriemma, slip up with sexist comments. This "institutionalized gender discrimination" blocks the path for equal treatment of female athletes and their coaches. Thomas Newkirk, an attorney who takes on inequality issues for women in sport, leads the way, traveling the country to provide education and training about "institutionalized gender discrimination" to colleges and universities. His work is groundbreaking and stems from his work in Tracey Griesbaum and Jane Meyer's gender and sexual identity lawsuits. Every school with collegiate and high school sports could benefit from developing a broader awareness of the issue of "unconscious gender bias" and the benefits of girls participating in sport, especially during their high school years.

INCLUSION AND ACCEPTANCE OF WOMEN OF COLOR, LESBIANS, AND TRANSGENDERS

Living in the Bay Area, one is lucky enough to encounter more open-mindedness about lesbian and transgender women. Although there are many white women who have tried to "help" women of color, we've failed miserably due to the lens we look through—our own white world. When teaching a sports psychology class, I had a young Jewish woman come up to me and tell me a story. Apparently, the student and a young African American woman were standing in line for some type of mandatory registration on campus. They turned around at the same time, noticing a group of white supremacists gathering for a protest. The black woman immediately told her classmate to hide her Star of David. She commented, "At least you can hide your identity, I can't." This is just one instance of the experiences of women of color that white women will never know.

We do need to take the time to understand what they need for support in sport and quit preaching about what we think they need. We need to stress that the norm to succeed in sport is *not* tall, skinny, blonde women, but rather women with strong, powerful physiques, which many women of color who are elite athletes have. Serena Williams represents the power of mind and body working together, and she is not afraid to speak her mind. Former female athletes who speak out against her don't always understand the need for more assertive actions to draw attention to the inequities of women of color. It's also important not to pigeonhole black women to the traditional sports of basketball and track and field. All this does is block the growth of young women of color who may want to try other sports, as modeled by Simone Manuel's swimming gold at the 2016 Rio Olympics. The goal is to move toward widening the opportunities for all women of color and lesbian and transgender women.

UNDERSTANDING THE GLOBAL ISSUES RELATED TO GIRLS AND WOMEN IN SPORT

On the global stage, we realize the difficulty of sport across nations. There are still places like Saudi Arabia where women need permission from a man (father, husband, etc.) to participate in sports, let alone compete. Then there are numerous nations with metropolitan areas where women can compete in sports, but no outreach for girls in sport is offered in rural areas.

In some countries, for example, Zambia, the major sports organization for young women is also working to prevent child brides and convince these young women to pursue an education. The idolization of male athletes in such countries as Brazil provides the backdrop for regarding female athletes as second rate, with little to no attention paid to them. In the Middle East, the level of women's participation in sport can be quite limited due to the attitudes of countries whose need to control women is vast. "The Global Gender Report 2018" reports on equality for women based on economic opportunities, political empowerment, education, health, and survival. This report is important, as it provides an overview of how equality for women is progressing.[6] The 10 worst countries for women's equality were Yemen, Pakistan, Iraq, Syria, Chad, Democratic Republic of Congo, Mali, Iran, Saudi Arabia, and Lebanon. On the other hand, the 10 best countries (in order) were Iceland, Norway, Sweden, Finland, Nicaragua, Rwanda, New Zealand, the Philippines, Ireland, and Namibia. In particular, high-quality research has been coming from Norway for years. In the early 1990s researchers there were studying the abuse of women in sport. Of note, the United States didn't even make the top 50.

When presenting in May 2018 about "Sisterhood in Sports" at a conference in Botswana, I was surprised at the number of men who coached women's sports wanting to buy my book. Between UN Women, the IWG on Women and Sport, Women in Sport International, ESPN's Global Mentoring Program, Women in Sport Aotearoa (New Zealand), and numerous other advocacy groups throughout the world, support for girls and women in sport is growing, but sometimes at a snail's pace depending on the country.

Action plans for joining forces and helping to promote female athletes, no matter the color of their skin or type of experience, need to be stepped up and established to promote the equal value of women in sport. This is an overview of the interviewees' primary areas of concern. Ytannia Wiggins, chair of the Barbados Olympic Women's Committee, said something significant to me: "I just want everyone to stop being so angry and rebuild our base through strengthening the foundation." She brings girls to sport through "Play Like a Girl Workshops" in Barbados. This is just another example of women throughout the world helping to improve the situation of girls in sport everywhere. We need to be courageous, take risks, have guts, be determined, work hard, take heart, show guts, and practice persistence to move toward greater equality for girls and women in sport. The following are 10 action steps to speak up and shout out to support girls and women and push toward greater equality for them in sport.

ACTION STEPS TO SPEAK UP AND SHOUT OUT

1. Speak up and shout out in support and encouragement of girls and women in sport.
2. Speak up and shout out to your legislators to take legislative action. Contact your senator or congressperson when bills about equality for women in sport come up for vote.
3. Speak up and shout out about the importance of equality in sports for girls and women. Challenge the myths about female athletes whenever you have the opportunity.

4. Speak up and shout out to the media about providing wider coverage of girls' and women's sports.
5. Speak up and shout out for women of color in sports.
6. Speak up and shout out for lesbians, transgenders, and intersex women in sports.
7. Speak up and shout out against "institutionalized gender bias" in organizations in the U.S. sports community.
8. Speak up and shout out about inequality in pay in your sport.
9. Speak up and shout out for female coaches.
10. Speak up and shout out about sexual abuse in sports.

The glory of sport comes from dedication, determination, and desire. Achieving success and personal glory in athletics has less to do with wins and losses than it does with learning how to prepare yourself so that at the end of the day, whether on the track or in the office, you know that there was nothing more you could have done to reach your ultimate goal.—Jackie Joyner-Kersee, multiple Olympic medal-winning track and field athlete[7]

NOTES

ACKNOWLEDGMENTS

1. T. Coles, "Famous Olympic quotes to get inspired about the games," *Huffington Post*, February 7, 2014, https://www.huffingtonpost.ca/2014/02/07/famous-olympic-quotes_n_4745472.html.

INTRODUCTION

1. "Julie Foudy Quotes," *Brainy Quote*, https://www.brainyquote.com/quotes/julie_foudy_910328.

I. LEADING THE CHARGE

1. A. Meah, "35 inspirational Billie Jean King quotes on success," *AwakenTheGreatnessWithin.org*, https://www.awakenthegreatnesswithin.com/35-inspirational-billie-jean-king-quotes-on-success/.
2. K. Kay and C. Shipman, "The confidence gap," *Atlantic*, May 2014, https://www.theatlantic.com/magazine/archive/2014/05/the-confidence-gap/359815/#_blank.
3. S. Fowler, "Cam Newton's sexist comment to Observer reporter wasn't one bit funny," *Charlotte Observer*, October 4, 2017, https://www.charlotteobserver.com/sports/spt-columns-blogs/scott-fowler/article177107336.html.

4. J. Belzer, "The most powerful women in U.S. sports 2018," *Forbes*, March 27, 2018, https://www.forbes.com/sites/jasonbelzer/2018/03/27/the-most-powerful-women-in-u-s-sports-2018/#54443889423f.

5. M. Emmert, "Griesbaum on lawsuit against Iowa: I tried to represent the coaching professional," *Des Moines Register*, May 22, 2017, https://www.hawkcentral.com/story/sports/2017/05/22/tracey-griesbaum-her-lawsuit-vs-iowa-i-tried-represent-coaching-profession/337109001/.

6. M. Lovelin and M. Hanold, "Female sport leaders' perception of leadership and management: Skills and attitudes for success," *Global Sport Business Journal* 2, no. 1 (2014): 14–29, http://www.gsbassn.com/Journal/Vol2-1/14-29.pdf.

7. J. Adriaanse, "Women are missing in sport leadership, and it's time that changed," *Conversation*, December 11, 2016, http://theconversation.com/women-are-missing-in-sport-leadership-and-its-time-that-changed-69979.

8. N. Hogshead-Makar, mission statement for Champion Women, Championwomen.org.

9. Black Women in Sport Foundation, https://www.blackwomeninsport.org/.

10. N. Amuchie, "How black women shaped the law banning sex discrimination in education," *Rewire.News*, February 28, 2018, https://rewire.news/article/2018/02/28/black-women-shaped-law-banning-sex-discrimination-education/.

11. L. Gentile, "Playing a sport can get women to the c-suite," *Fortune*, January 23, 2016, https://fortune.com/2016/01/23/sport-women-c-suite/.

12. J. Doubek, "'We don't have enough women in power': Notre Dame coach Muffet McGraw goes viral," *NPR*, April 6, 2019, https://www.npr.org/2019/04/06/710539614/we-don-t-have-enough-women-in-power-notre-dame-coach-muffet-mcgraw-goes-viral.

13. S. B. Jimbo, "Geno was asked about Muffet not hiring male assistants," *Ndnation.com*, April 4, 2019, https://ndnation.com/boards/showpost.php?b=mcgraw;pid=70019;d=all.

14. L. J. Burton, "Underrepresentation of women in sport leadership: A review of research," *Sport Management Review* 18, no. 2 (March 2014): 155–65, https://daneshyari.com/article/preview/140857.pdf.

15. Adriaanse, "Women are missing in sport leadership."

16. C. Settimi, "Maya Dodd, one of soccer's most powerful women, isn't done playing," *Forbes*, March 27, 2018, https://www.forbes.com/sites/christinasettimi/2018/03/27/moya-dodd-one-of-footballs-most-powerful-women-isnt-done-playing/#310bb3af458c.

17. Committee to Restore Integrity to the USOC, "Our recommendations to create an athletes-first culture at the U.S. Olympic Movement," *Around-*

theRings.com, January 21, 2019, http://aroundtherings.com/site/A__75538/ Title__the-committee-to-restore-integrity-to-the-usoc-our-recommendations-for-an-athletes-first-olympic-committee/292/Articles.

18. N. LaVoi, ed., *Women in Sports Coaching* (New York: Routledge, 2016), 54.

19. Olympic Youth Development Centre, https://www.olympic.org/news/olympic-youth-development-centre-oydc.

20. "Who succeeds NOCZ boss Miriam Moyo?" *Zambia Daily Mail*, December 9, 2017, http://www.daily-mail.co.zm/who-succeeds-nocz-boss-miriam-moyo/.

21. A. Wojnarowski, "Pacers hire Kelly Krauskopf as NBA's first woman assistant GM," *ESPN.com*, December 17, 2018, http://www.espn.com/espnw/story/_/id/25559938/indiana-pacers-hire-kelly-krauskopf-nba-first-female-assistant-general-manager.

2. SHOW US THE MONEY

1. C. Lloyd, "Why I'm fighting for equal pay," *New York Times*, April 10, 2016, https://www.nytimes.com/2016/04/11/sports/soccer/carli-lloyd-why-im-fighting-for-equal-pay.html?action=click&module=RelatedCoverage&pgtype=Article&region=Footer.

2. "Prize money: 2018 Cincinnati Masters 1000," *Tennis Planet.me*, August 13, 2018, https://www.tennisplanet.me/blog/2018/08/prize-money-2018-cincinnati-masters-1000.html.

3. J. Tucker, "Oakland schools' blunder shows larger issue: Girls' sport stuck at second," *San Francisco Chronicle*, September 2, 2018, https://www.sfchronicle.com/education/article/Oakland-schools-blunder-shows-larger-issue-13199449.php#photo-16098893.

4. M. Capper, "Donations help restore funding for school sports, but not bowling," *OaklandNorth*, September 3, 2018, https://oaklandnorth.net/2018/09/03/20180830_sportscuts_capper/.

5. A. Wong, "Where girls are missing out on high school sports," *Atlantic*, June 26, 2015, https://www.theatlantic.com/education/archive/2015/06/girls-high-school-sports-inequality/396782/.

6. Wong, "Where girls are missing out on high school sports."

7. E. Hastie, "Despite progress made under Title IX, gender inequalities still exist in high school sports," *Buffalo News*, November 9, 2017, https://buffalonews.com/2017/11/09/despite-progress-made-under-title-ix-gender-inequalities-still-persist-in-high-school-sports/.

8. E. Hastie, "Gender inequality persists in high school sports," *Athletic Business*, November 2017, https://www.athleticbusiness.com/high-school/gender-inequality-persists-in-high-school-sports.html.

9. B. Toporek, "Gender gap grows in high school sports, report says," *Education Week*, October 10, 2012, http://blogs.edweek.org/edweek/schooled_in_sports/2012/10/gender_gap_grows_in_high_school_sports_over_past_decade_report_says.html.

10. National Women's Law Center, Poverty and Race Research and Action Council, "Finishing last: Girls of color and school sports opportunities," *PRRAC.org*, 2015, https://prrac.org/pdf/GirlsFinishingLast_Report.pdf.

11. J. Swiatek, "Sports scholarships most often received by male gender," *HawkHeadlines*, April 21, 2016, https://hawkheadlines.net/news/2016/04/21/sports-scholarships-most-often-received-by-male-gender/.

12. K. Dosh, "Why women's college basketball might be stuck in the red," *SBNation*, November 12, 2013, https://www.swishappeal.com/2013/11/12/5090384/ncaa-womens-college-basketball-profits-donations.

13. "Beyond x's and o's: Gender bias and coaches of women's college sports," *Women's Sports Foundation*, September 2, 2016, https://files.eric.ed.gov/fulltext/ED570470.pdf.

14. D. Berri, "Some popular sports sites appear to cover more animals than women," *Forbes*, November 29, 2017, https://www.forbes.com/sites/davidberri/2017/11/29/some-popular-sports-sites-appear-to-cover-more-animals-than-women/?curator=SportsREDEF.

15. B. Hershman, "The WNBA is scoring new fans: Merchandise sales up 50 percent, viewership up 35 percent in 2018," *Benzinga.com*, August 9, 2018, https://www.benzinga.com/news/18/08/12177369/the-wnba-is-scoring-new-fans-merchandise-sales-up-50-viewership-up-35-in-2018.

16. N. Lough, "The case for boosting WNBA player salaries," *Conversation*, August 9, 2018, https://theconversation.com/the-case-for-boosting-wnba-player-salaries-100805.

17. Reliable Source, "How Venus Williams got equal pay for women at Wimbledon," *Washington Post*, July 2, 2013, https://www.washingtonpost.com/news/reliable-source/wp/2013/07/02/how-venus-williams-got-equal-pay-for-women-at-wimbledon/?noredirect=on.

18. "U.S. women's team files wage-discrimination action vs. U.S. Soccer," *ESPN.com*, April 1, 2016, http://www.espn.com/espnw/sports/article/15102506/women-national-team-files-wage-discrimination-action-vs-us-soccer-federation.

19. A. Das, "Long days, Google docs, and anonymous surveys: How the U.S. soccer team forged a deal," *New York Times*, April 5, 2017, https://www.

nytimes.com/2017/04/05/sports/soccer/uswnt-us-soccer-labor-deal-contract.
html.

20. Das, "Long days, Google docs, and anonymous surveys."

21. M. Lewis, "Going Solo: U.S. goalkeeper sues U.S. Soccer over pay discrimination," *Front Row Soccer*, August 25, 2018, https://www.frontrowsoccer.
com/2018/08/25/going-solo-ex-u-s-goalkeeper-sues-u-s-soccer-over-pay-
discrimination/.

22. "FIFA to upgrade flights, raise prize money for Women's WCup," *USA
Today*, September 2018. https://www.usatoday.com/story/sports/soccer/2018/
09/20/fifa-to-upgrade-flights-raise-prize-money-for-womens-wcup/37873887/.

23. S. Berkman, "U.S. women's team strikes a deal with U.S.A. Hockey,"
New York Times, March 28, 2017, https://www.nytimes.com/2017/03/28/sports/
hockey/usa-hockey-uswnt-boycott.html.

24. Berkman, "U.S. women's team strikes a deal with U.S.A. Hockey."

25. S. Blum, "American women are winning more medals than men for
Team USA," *Thrillist.com*, February 24, 2018, https://www.thrillist.com/news/
nation/usa-medal-count-women-winning-more-than-men.

3. HONORING OUR WOMEN ATHLETES

1. "20 sports quotes by women," *Gal's Guide*, August 2, 2018, https://
galsguide.org/2018/08/02/20-sports-quotes-by-women/.

2. "NBC's prime time Olympic broadcast features more male athletes by
significant margin: Olympics' gender coverage gap worse than 2014 Sochi
Games," *Fiveringtv.com*, February 19, 2018, https://fiveringtv.com/2018/02/18/
nbcs-primetime-olympic-broadcast-features-male-athletes-by-a-significant-
margin-after-the-first-10-days/.

3. K. Lebel and K. Danlchuk, "Generation Y's perceptions of women's
sport in the media," *International Journal of Sport Communication* 2, no. 2
(2009).

4. T. Scheadler and A. Wagstaff, "Exposure to women's sports: Changing
attitudes toward female athletes," *Sport Journal*, June 5, 2018, http://
thesportjournal.org/article/exposure-to-womens-sports-changing-attitudes-
toward-female-athletes/.

5. D. Paramo, "Gender inequality in sports broadcasting apparent to viewers," *Daily Evergreen* (Washington State University), October 5, 2017, https://
dailyevergreen.com/17571/sports/women-broadcaster-column/.

6. J. Peters, "How women in sports media are cheering each other on,"
News Media Alliance, March 27, 2018, https://www.newsmediaalliance.org/
women-in-sports-media/.

7. "Women's sport: New research finds more than 80 percent of sports fans are interested," *BBC Sports*, October 4, 2018, https://www.bbc.com/sport/45737718.

8. D. Berri, "Some popular sports sites appear to cover more animals than women," *Forbes*, November 29, 2017, https://www.forbes.com/sites/davidberri/2017/11/29/some-popular-sports-sites-appear-to-cover-more-animals-than-women/?curator=SportsREDEF.

9. K. Danika, "Why are women's sports still not covered in the media?" *Women's Media Center*, March 6, 2016, http://www.womensmediacenter.com/fbomb/why-are-womens-sports-still-not-covered-in-the-media.

10. B. de la Cretaz, "Blackout goals: How sports media locks out women athletes," *Bitchmedia*, March 8, 2018, https://www.bitchmedia.org/article/sports-media-erases-women-athletes.

11. A. Alvarez, "Should female athletes sue the networks for equal coverage?" *Guardian*, April 14, 2018, https://www.theguardian.com/sport/2018/apr/14/womens-athletes-lawsuit-equal-coverage-title-ix.

12. J. Luther, "The more women's sports are covered, the more popular they will be," *Huffington Post*, March 3, 2018, https://www.huffpost.com/entry/opinion-luther-women-basketball_n_5ac27206e4b09712fec34663.

13. "World fame 100: Meet the 25 most famous women athletes in the world," *ESPN.com*, May 22, 2018, http://www.espn.com/espnw/culture/article/23337210/world-fame-100-25-most-famous-women-athletes.

14. E. N. Kendall, "Female athletes often face the femininity police—especially Serena Williams," *Guardian*, July 14, 2015, https://www.theguardian.com/commentisfree/2015/jul/14/serena-williams-female-athletes-femininity-police.

15. M. Santos, "Appearance and athleticism: Perception, reality, and changing the narrative," *Victory Press*, August 9, 2016, https://victorypress.org/2016/08/09/perceived-attractiveness-and-femininity-still-dominates-the-conversation-about-female-athletes-2/.

16. Kendall, "Female athletes often face the femininity police."

17. "Aesthetics over athletics when it comes to women in sport," *University of Cambridge*, August 12, 2016, https://www.cam.ac.uk/research/news/aesthetics-over-athletics-when-it-comes-to-women-in-sport.

18. M. Burton, "This reporter sexism needs to go," *OZY*, August 29, 2018, https://www.ozy.com/opinion/this-sports-reporter-sexism-needs-to-go/88992.

19. C. Schilken, "Girl with short hair kicked out of soccer tournament: 'They only did it because I look like a boy,'" *Los Angeles Times*, June 6, 2017, https://www.latimes.com/sports/sportsnow/la-sp-girl-disqualified-soccer-20170606-story.html.

20. K. Collins, "U.S. trapshooter wins bronze medal—there are immediately cries of sexism," *Daily Caller*, August 9, 2016, https://dailycaller.com/2016/08/09/u-s-trapshooter-wins-bronze-medal-there-are-immediately-cries-of-sexism/.

21. A. Patel, "Headline about Olympic swimmers Katie Ledecky and Michael Phelps called sexist," *Huffington Post*, October 17, 2016, https://www.huffingtonpost.ca/2016/08/16/sexist-headline-olympics_n_11544838.html.

22. C. Taibi, "TV ignores women's sports now more than it did 20 years ago," *Huffington Post*, June 9, 2015, https://www.huffpost.com/entry/womens-sports-tv_n_7535766?guccounter=1&guce_referrer=aHR0cHM6Ly93d3cuZ29vZ2xlLmNvbS8&guce_referrer_sig=AQAAALo55J-XggaqGMLt-Xo29zZmOMbFykAUyrMi94vitB_fkMeSXoPaBDPIJXAJIZohXWYCbTFTPzuxbuDia306kWhRdFwDG5Ha1xCoO4dWC6dEwGGjPDO_nT8KuL6botWghOUlV08TcnwyPpuXu8c_eGOAeuOX-PODewN-Yx6Z8FrRK.

23. M. Molloy, "Olympic sexism? Twitter is very angry about this headline," *Telegraph*, August 15, 2016, https://www.telegraph.co.uk/olympics/2016/08/15/olympic-sexism-twitter-is-very-angry-about-this-headline/.

24. G. Myre, "U.S. women are the biggest winners at the Rio Olympics," *NPR*, August 21, 2016, https://www.npr.org/sections/thetorch/2016/08/21/490818961/u-s-women-are-the-biggest-winners-in-rio-olympics.

25. Peters, "How women in sports media are cheering each other on."

26. B. Clapp, "Working in sports journalism as a woman," *WorkinSports.com*, November 14, 2016, https://www.workinsports.com/blog/working-in-sports-journalism-as-a-woman/.

27. J. Dicaro, "Safest bet in sports: Men complaining about a female announcer's voice," *New York Times*, September 18, 2017, https://www.nytimes.com/2017/09/18/sports/nfl-beth-mowins-julie-dicaro.html.

4. THE POLITICS OF WOMEN'S SPORT

1. R. Reichard, "12 Sonia Sotomayor quotes that will inspire Latinas to keep blazing throughout 2019," *Fierce*, June 25, 2018, https://fierce.wearemitu.com/politics/sonia-sotomayor-quotes-that-will-inspire-latinas-to-blaze-forever/.

2. J. Kassouf, "USWNT players file gender discrimination lawsuit against U.S. Soccer," *Equalizer*, March 8, 2019, https://equalizersoccer.com/2019/03/08/uswnt-lawsuit-gender-discrimination-28-players-details-documents/.

3. "Athletic Equality Index," *Athlete Ally*, 2017, https://www.athleteally.org/wp-content/uploads/2017/09/AEI-Final-Draft.pdf.

4. L. Smith, "Women have more stamina and muscle endurance than men, study suggests," *Independent*, August, 25, 2017, https://www.indepen dent.co.uk/news/science/women-more-stamina-muscle-endurance-exercise-sport-men-science-study-university-of-british-columbia-a7911776.html.

5. M. Brown, "The longer the race, the stronger we get," *Outside,* April 11, 2017, https://www.outsideonline.com/2169856/longer-race-stronger-we-get.

6. M. Mertens, "Women cyclists still aren't allowed to ride as far as the men," *ESPN.com*, July 21, 2016, http://www.espn.com/espnw/culture/feature/article/17113949/women-cyclists-allowed-ride-far-men.

7. Mertens, "Women cyclists still aren't allowed to ride as far as the men."

8. J. Foudy, "Ahead of Women's World Cup draw, FIFA's actions speak louder than words," *ESPN.com*, December 6, 2018, http://www.espn.com/espnw/voices/article/25460147/fifa-actions-speak-louder-words-ahead-women-world-cup-draw.

9. A. D. Madkour, "Women in sports media cite progress, obstacles," *Sports Business Journal*, March 6, 2017, https://www.sportsbusinessdaily.com/Journal/Issues/2017/03/06/Opinion/From-The-Executive-Editor.aspx.

10. R. Harris, "World Cup cash inequality persists after women's prize rises," *Associated Press*, October 26, 2018, https://www.apnews.com/91c2fb6e832845d8b30b6fd6b70d2b1b.

11. R. Lapchick, "The 2018 Associated Press Sports Editor Racial and Gender Report Card," *Tides: The Institute for Diversity and Ethics in Sport*, May 2, 2018, http://nebula.wsimg.com/2b640482e881dddc4dfb39e6aca52c2e?AccessKeyId=DAC3A56D8FB782449D2A&disposition=0&alloworigin=1.

12. J. McKenzie and L. Fisher, "Female sports journalists react to Cam Newton, share their own sexist experiences," *ABC News*, October 5, 2017, https://abcnews.go.com/Entertainment/female-sports-journalists-react-cam-newton-share-sexist/story?id=50304858.

13. J. Brady, "ESPN shows progress, faces challenges, regarding women in sports," *ESPN.com*, December 20, 2017, http://www.espn.com/blog/ombudsman/post/_/id/906/espn-shows-progress-faces-challenges-regarding-women-in-sports.

14. K. Close, "Five Reasons Why Tennis Should Keep Paying Men and Women Equally," *Money.com*, March 22, 2016, http://time.com/money/4265912/equal-pay-tennis-djokovic-williams/.

15. D. Levitt, "State of pay: Tennis has huge gender gap in earning power," *Guardian*, July 14, 2018, https://www.theguardian.com/sport/ng-interactive/2018/jul/14/tennis-pay-gap-shouldnt-be-gender-based.

16. C. Clarey, "Many athletes found their voices," *New York Times*, December 22, 2017, https://www.nytimes.com/2017/12/20/sports/year-sports-protests.html.

17. L. Rock, "As women's sport grows, athletes find they can't stay silent in the era of Trump," *Guardian*, July 29, 2017, https://www.theguardian.com/sport/2017/jul/29/womens-sport-activism-and-political-protest-planned-parenthood.

18. K. Best, "Megan Rapinoe's new focus: Make soccer inclusive for LGBTQ kids," *SBNation*, June 7, 2018, https://www.outsports.com/2018/6/7/17435834/megan-rapinoe-soccer-lgbtq-kids-project.

19. J. Sit, "Misty Copeland: Why this ballet superstar is fighting for diversity," *CNN.com*, April 5, 2018, https://www.cnn.com/2018/04/05/world/misty-copeland-ballet-fight-diversity/index.html.

20. M. Anthony, "Mike Anthony: Megan Rapinoe has played her way onto a world platform she's using wisely," *Hartford Courant*, July 29, 2018, https://www.courant.com/sports/hc-sp-megan-rapinoe-us-womens-soccer-column-20180728-story.html.

21. M. Lasher, "Breanna Stewart used her ESPY moment to speak out against inequality," *Time*, July 14, 2016, https://time.com/4406421/breanna-stewart-equality/.

22. Lasher, "Breanna Stewart used her ESPY moment to speak out against inequality."

23. Lasher, "Breanna Stewart used her ESPY moment to speak out against inequality"; "Release: WNBA invites to 'Take a Seat, Take a Stand' for women and girls during the 2018 season," *WNBA.com*, May 17, 2018, https://www.wnba.com/news/wnba-take-a-seat-take-a-stand-women-girls-2018-season.

24. B. Strauss, "How the WNBA stood up to Trump and won fans," *Politico Magazine*, August, 4, 2018, https://www.politico.com/magazine/story/2018/08/04/wnba-trump-protest-politics-sports-219155.

25. Strauss, "How the WNBA stood up to Trump and won fans."

26. A. Glass, "The WNBA's Best Fans," *Forbes*, September 26, 2018, https://www.forbes.com/sites/alanaglass/2018/09/26/the-wnbas-best-fans/#192eaab4192b.

27. Brady, "ESPN shows progress, faces challenges, regarding women in sports."

5. SPEAKING UP AND PROMOTING
WOMEN COACHES

1. Coach poster, *Zazzle*, https://www.zazzle.com/coach_thank_you_poster-228011491752114100.

2. R. Lapchick, "2017 College Sport Racial and Gender Report Card," *Institute for Diversity and Ethics in Sport*, February 2018, https://www.insidehighered.com/sites/default/server_files/media/2017%20College%20Sport%20Racial%20and%20Gender%20Report%20Card.pdf.

3. B. Cook, "Lack of presence for female coaches extends to kids' games," *Forbes*, November 28, 2018, https://www.forbes.com/sites/bobcook/2018/11/28/lack-of-presence-for-female-coaches-extends-to-kids-games/#b07a14b49386.

4. S. Jenkins, "Geno Auriemma: 'Not as many women want to coach.' His daughter: 'DAD. WALK IT BACK,'" *Chicago Tribune*, March 31, 2017, https://www.chicagotribune.com/sports/college/ct-geno-auriemma-female-coaches-sally-jenkins-20170331-story.html.

5. L. Flanagan, "The field where men still call the shots," *Atlantic*, July 28, 2017, https://www.theatlantic.com/education/archive/2017/07/the-field-where-men-still-call-the-shots/535167.

6. H. Weaver, "Watch Notre Dame coach Muffet McGraw make a strong case for gender equality," *Elle*, April 6, 2019, https://www.elle.com/culture/celebrities/a27062036/muffet-mcgraw-speaks-out-gender-equality/.

7. E. Strout, "American running needs more female coaches," *Outside*, September 14, 2018, https://www.outsideonline.com/2342711/why-we-need-more-female-coaches.

8. "U.S. road race participation numbers hold steady for 2017," *Running USA*, June 27, 2018, https://runningusa.org/RUSA/News/2018/U.S._Road_Race_Participation_Numbers_Hold_Steady_for_2017.aspx.

9. N. LaVoi, "Tucker Center releases annual Women in Coaching Report Card," *University of Minnesota*, February 7, 2018, http://wcs.umn.edu/news/tucker-center-releases-annual-women-coaching-report-card.

10. LaVoi, "Tucker Center releases annual Women in Coaching Report Card."

11. K. Fominykh, "New study from Morgan State explores how black female athletes navigate racism and sexism to excel," *Baltimore Sun*, June 27, 2018, https://www.baltimoresun.com/sports/bs-sp-morgan-state-black-female-athlete-study-20180625-story.html.

12. S. Ryan, "College sports needs more women—and women of color—in coaching ranks," *Chicago Tribune*, April 17, 2017, https://

www.chicagotribune.com/sports/ct-womens-college-coaching-diversity-ryan-spt-0419-20170417-column.html.

13. "Playing in the closet: Homophobia in sports," Women's Sports Foundation, June 11, 2011, http://www.womenssportsfoundation.org/home/research/articles-and-reports/lgbt-issues/playing-in-the-closet.

14. E. Nelson, "The dynamics of women coaching men and gender stereotypes," *Sport in American History*, July 9, 2018, https://ussporthistory.com/2018/07/09/the-dynamics-of-women-coaching-men-and-gender-stereotypes/.

15. K. Suigura, "Attorney for MaChelle Joseph amid investigation of Tech's men's program: 'Hypocrisy is stunning.'" *Atlanta Journal-Constitution*, March 15, 2019, https://www.ajc.com/sports/basketball/attorney-for-machelle-joseph-amid-investigation-tech-men-program-hypocrisy-stunning/nFy-LO4BsuPugRBmFyR7aSO/.

16. L. Torres, "MTSU volleyball coach Chuck Crawford suspended after claims of player mistreatment," *Daily News Journal*, April 12, 2019, https://www.dnj.com/story/sports/college/mtsu/2019/04/12/mtsu-volleyball-chuck-crawford-chris-massaro/3331811002/.

17. C. Gomex-Gonzalez, H. Dietl, and C. Nesseler, "Does performance justify the underrepresentation of women's coaches? Evidence from professional women's soccer," *Sports Management Review*, September 8, 2018, https://www.sciencedirect.com/science/article/abs/pii/S1441352317301857.

18. N. LaVoi, @DrSportPsych, Twitter, January 16, 2019.

19. R. Lapchick, B. Estrella, and N. Bredikhina, "The 2017 Racial and Gender Report Card: College Sport," *Institute for Diversity and Ethics in Sport, University of Central Florida*, February 28, 2018, http://docplayer.net/73853405-2017-college-sport-racial-gender-report-card-by-richard-e-lapchick-edited-by-brett-estrella-with-nataliya-bredikhina.html.

20. Lapchick, Estrella, and N. Bredikhina, "The 2017 Racial and Gender Report Card: College Sport,"

21. "WNBA receives 'A' on race and gender report card," *USA Today*, November 15, 2017, https://www.usatoday.com/story/sports/wnba/2017/11/15/wnba-receives-a-on-race-and-gender-report-card/107716184/.

22. R. Lapchick, "WNBA score record marks for hiring practices," *ESPN.com*, October 25, 2018, http://www.espn.com/wnba/story/_/id/25075162/wnba-once-again-sets-record-high-marks-diversity-their-hiring-practices.

23. D. Ditota, "Felisha Legette-Jack making most of second chance many women coaches don't get," *Syracuse.com*, October 10, 2018, https://www.syracuse.com/sports/index.ssf/2018/10/felisha_legette-jacks_rise_from_devasting_job_loss_to_advocate_for_second_chance.html.

24. F. Legette-Jack, "2018 Sweet 16 – Buffalo Postgame," *YouTube*, March 24, 2018, https://www.youtube.com/watch?v=PWPM3FeCLd4.

25. K. Whiteside, "Muffet McGraw says she won't hire a man on her coaching staff. Let her tell you why," *New York Times*, April 4, 2019, https://www.nytimes.com/2019/04/04/sports/womens-final-four-muffet-mcgraw.html.

26. P. Kennedy, "U.S. Soccer signs eight-figure sponsorship deal with VW," *SoccerAmerica Daily*, January 14, 2019, https://www.socceramerica.com/publications/article/80987/us-soccer-signs-eight-figure-sponsorship-deal-wi.html.

27. N. LaVoi, "Why women matter in sport coaching," *University of Minnesota College of Education and Human Development*, March 13, 2015, https://cehdvision2020.umn.edu/blog/why-women-matter-in-sport-coaching/.

6. THE #METOO MOVEMENT IN SPORTS

1. J. L. Herman, *Trauma and Recovery: The Aftermath of Violence—from Domestic Abuse to Political Terror* (New York: Basic Books, 1997), 116.

2. H. Freeman, "How was Larry Nassar able to abuse so many gymnasts for so long?" *Guardian*, January 26, 2018, https://www.theguardian.com/sport/2018/jan/26/larry-nassar-abuse-gymnasts-scandal-culture.

3. "Media kit on sexual assault," *Institut National de Sante Publique*, 2018, https://www.inspq.qc.ca/en/sexual-assault/media/sexual-assault-and-media.

4. C. Ballentine, "Olympian alum Nancy Hogshead-Makar takes on sexual harassment, assault," *Chronicle*, April 4, 2018, https://www.dukechronicle.com/article/2018/04/olympian-alum-nancy-hogshead-makar-takes-on-sexual-harassment-assault.

5. J. Ryan, *Little Girls in Pretty Boxes* (New York: Grand Central Publishing, 1995; reprint, 2018).

6. C. Chavez, "Victims share stories of abuse at former USA Gymnastics doctor Larry Nassar's sentencing," *Sports Illustrated*, January 18, 2018, https://www.si.com/olympics/2018/01/16/Larry-nassar-sentencing-victims-abuse-stories.

7. J. Dator, "A comprehensive timeline of the Larry Nassar case," *SBNation*, December 21, 2018, https://www.sbnation.com/2018/1/19/16900674/larry-nassar-abuse-timeline-usa-gymnastics-michigan-state.

8. Chavez, "Victims share stories of abuse at former USA Gymnastics doctor Larry Nassar's sentencing."

9. Chavez, "Victims share stories of abuse at former USA Gymnastics doctor Larry Nassar's sentencing."

10. D. Nyad, "Diana Nyad: My life after sexual assault," *New York Times*, November 9, 2017, https://www.nytimes.com/2017/11/09/opinion/diana-nyad-sexual-assault.html.

11. L. Gibbs, "This WNBA team took a risk and stood up for Planned Parenthood," *ThinkProgress*, July 19, 2017, https://thinkprogress.org/wnba-planned-parenthood-rally-8967bc1ce66c/.

12. S. Gregory, "How the #MeToo Movement is about to change pro sports," *Time*, December 19, 2017, http://time.com/5064703/how-the-metoo-movement-is-about-to-change-pro-sports/.

13. N. Hogshead-Makar, "#TimesUpSports/@Hogshead3Au," Twitter, December 30, 2018.

14. J. Macur, "Olympic Committee alerted to sex abuse in gymnastics years ago, court filing says," *New York Times*, November 22, 2018, https://www.nytimes.com/2018/11/22/sports/gymnastics-abuse-.html.

15. "Olympic Committee knew about sexual abuse in gymnastics since the 1990s, according to court filings," *Women in the World*, November 26, 2018, https://womenintheworld.com/2018/11/26/olympic-committee-knew-about-sexual-abuse-in-gymnastics-since-the-1990s-according-to-court-filings/.

16. S. Reid, "Steve Penny banned by USA Gymnastics but not the only focus of investigations into alleged Nassar cover-up," *Orange County Register*, October 18, 2018, https://www.ocregister.com/2018/10/18/steve-penny-not-the-only-focus-of-investigations-into-alleged-nassar-cover-up/.

17. N. Armour and R. Axon, "House committee wants answers from sports organizations on sexual abuse," *USA Today*, January 26, 2018, https://www.usatoday.com/story/sports/olympics/2018/01/26/house-committee-wants-answers-sports-organizations-sexual-abuse/1070016001/.

18. Freeman, "How was Larry Nassar able to abuse so many gymnasts for so long?"

19. A. Loudin, "Talking to your young athletes about sex abuse," *ESPN.com*, January 16, 2018, http://www.espn.com/espnw/voices/article/18979442/talking-your-young-athletes-sexual-abuse.

20. C. Brackenridge, D. Bishop, S. Moussali, and J. Tapp, "The characteristics of sexual abuse in sport: A multidimensional scaling analysis of events described in media reports," *International Journal of Sport and Exercise Psychology* 6, no. 4 (2008): 23.

21. K. Fasting and C. Brackenridge, "Coaches, sexual harassment, and education," *Sport, Education, and Society Journal* 14, no. 1 (2009): 21.

22. A. Starr, "As USA Swimming grapples with sexual abuse, athletes cite lack of female coaches," *NPR*, July 4, 2018, https://www.npr.org/2018/07/04/623540000/as-usa-swimming-grapples-with-sexual-abuse-athletes-cite-lack-of-female-coaches.

23. S. Ladika, "Sports and sexual assault: Can colleges and pro leagues curb abuse by athletes?" *CQ Press*, April 28, 2017, https://library.cqpress.com/cqresearcher/document.php?id=cqresrre2017042800.

24. "Preventing child abuse: New federal requirement facing youth sports," *Philadelphia Insurance Companies*, February 16, 2018, https://www.phly.com/rms/blog/NewAbusePreventionLaw.aspx.

25. "Who we are: Collaborating to create a positive sport culture," *SafeSport*, 2017, https://safesport.org/who-we-are.

26. S. Parent and G. Demers, "Sexual abuse in sport: A model to prevent and protect athletes," *Child Abuse Review* 20, no. 2 (March 2011): 120–33.

27. Fasting and Brackenridge, "Coaches, sexual harassment, and education."

28. Committee to Restore Integrity to the USOC, "Our recommendations for an "athletes-first" Olympic committee," *Around the Rings*, January 21, 2019, http://aroundtherings.com/site/A__75538/title__the-committee-to-restore-integrity-to-the-usoc-our-recommendations-for-an-athletes-first-olympic-committee/292/Articles.

7. DOUBLE STANDARDS

1. "Top 10 Jackie Joyner-Kersee quotes," *BrainyQuote*, https://www.brainyquote.com/lists/authors/top_10_jackie_joynerkersee_quotes.

2. C. Frisby, "A content analysis of Serena Williams and Angelique Kerber's racial and sexist microaggressions," *Open Journal of Social Sciences* 5 (2017): 263–81, https://file.scirp.org/pdf/JSS_2017052316172687.pdf.

3. E. Smith, "Jessica Ennis coach hits out at UK Athletics for labeling her 'fat,'" *Guardian*, May 12, 2012, https://www.theguardian.com/sport/2012/may/24/jessica-ennis-fat-olympics.

4. M. Lawrence Corbett, "The problem with the conversation surrounding Serena Williams," *Bleacher Report*, September 3, 2015, https://bleacherreport.com/articles/2550762-the-problem-with-the-conversation-surrounding-serena-williams.

5. J. Steidinger, "What Martina Navratilova and Mary Carillo got wrong," *AfterEllen*, September 20, 2018, https://www.afterellen.com/general-news/564533-what-martina-navratilova-and-mary-carillo-got-wrong.

6. "Kimberle Crenshaw on intersectionality, more than two decades later," *Columbia Law School*, June 8, 2017, https://www.law.columbia.edu/ptbr/news/2017/06/kimberle-crenshaw-intersectionality.

7. H. Pressley, "It's been 40 years since Title IX, but there's still more work to be done," *Girls on the Run*, June 22, 2017, https://www.girlsontherun.org/remarkable/331/Its-Been-40-Years-Since-Title-IX-and-Theres-Stil.

8. Pressley, "It's been 40 years since Title IX."

9. B. Cook, "It's tough for low-income kids, especially girls, to participate in sports," *Forbes*, January 6, 2017, https://www.forbes.com/sites/bobcook/2017/01/06/its-tough-for-low-income-kids-especially-girls-to-participate-in-sports/#733b49f9622c.

10. National Women's Law Center, Poverty and Race Research and Action Council, "Finishing last: Girls of color and school sports opportunities," *PRRAC.org*, 2015, https://prrac.org/pdf/GirlsFinishingLast_Report.pdf.

11. P. J. Giddings, "What the dominance of black female athletes means to American culture," *ESPN.com*, February 24, 2017, http://www.espn.com/espnw/culture/article/18750694/what-dominance-black-female-athletes-means-american-culture.

12. "History of Black Women in Sport Foundation," *Black Women in Sport Foundation*, https://www.blackwomeninsport.org.

13. "History of Black Women in Sport Foundation."

14. Lawrence Corbett, "The problem with the conversation surrounding Serena Williams."

15. "Green to headline the Institute for Sport and Social Justice 'Invisible Women in Sports' podcast," GoCrimson, October 18, 2018, https://www.gocrimson.com/sports/wten/2018-19/releases/20181016k2fdfp.

16. B. A. Larsen, D. Pekmezi, B. Marquez, T. J. Benitez, and B. H. Marcus, "Physical activity in Latinas: Social and environmental influences," *Women's Health* 9, no. 2 (2013): 201–13, https://www.ncbi.nlm.nih.gov/pmc/articles/PMC3868363/.

17. P. Ruffins, "Latinos not yet scoring with college athletics," *Minority News*, February 18, 2019, https://www.blackradionetwork.com/latinos_not_yet_scoring_with_college_athletics.

18. J. Fan, "Kim Yo Jong, Chloe Kim, and the shifting images of Asia and Asian American women at the Olympics," *New Yorker*, February 15, 2018, https://www.newyorker.com/news/daily-comment/kim-yo-jong-chloe-kim-shifting-images-asian-women-olympics.

19. National Women's Law Center, Poverty and Race Research and Action Council, "Finishing last: Girls of color and school sports opportunities," PRRAC.org, 2015, https://prrac.org/pdf/GirlsFinishingLast_Report.pdf.

20. R. Lapchick, "The WNBA leads all sports leagues in diversity and inclusion," *ESPN.com*, November 16, 2017, http://www.espn.com/espnw/sports/article/21434534/the-wnba-scores-high-marks-comes-diversity-hiring-practices.

8. THE LGBTQ COMMUNITY

1. P. Griffin and N. Caple, "The times they are a-changin' for LGBTQ people in sports," *Huffington Post*, February 2, 2016, https://www.huffpost.com/entry/the-times-they-are-achang_b_4986048.

2. "184 people in sports who came out publicly in the media in 2017," *SBNation*, January 4, 2018, https://www.outsports.com/2018/1/4/16666278/2017-list-out-gay-lesbian-bisexual-transgender-athletes.

3. R. Picheta and J. Masters, "Martina Navratilova dropped by LGTB group over trans athletes row," *CNN.com*, February 20, 2019, https://www.cnn.com/2019/02/20/tennis/martina-navratilova-dropped-lgbt-group-scli-spt-intl/index.html.

4. E. Andersen, R. Bullingham, and R. Magrath, "Out in sport: The experiences of openly gay and lesbian athletes in competitive sport," *ResearchGate*, January 2016, https://www.researchgate.net/publication/303434435_Out_in_sport_The_experiences_of_openly_gay_and_lesbian_athletes_in_competitive_sport.

5. R. Niolon, "The stages of coming out," *PsychPage*, http://www.psychpage.com/learning/library/gay/comeout.html.

6. E. Braidwood, "Pro golfer Mel Reid comes out as gay: 'Be proud of who you are,'" *Pink News*, December 11, 2018, https://www.pinknews.co.uk/2018/12/11/pro-golfer-mel-reid-comes-out-gay/.

7. T. Bella, "NCAA relents: Lesbian college athlete, disowned by parents, can get outside help," *Washington Post*, November 19, 2018, https://www.washingtonpost.com/nation/2018/11/19/ncaa-relents-lesbian-college-athlete-disowned-by-parents-can-get-outside-help/?noredirect=on.

8. Bella, "NCAA relents."

9. Vote for Equality: Billie Jean King. *Freedom to Marry Campaign*. November 11, 2009. http://www.freedomtomarry.org/blog/entry/voice-for-equality-billie-jean-king.

10. C. Zeigler, "Moment #2: Martina Navratilova comes out," *SBNation*, October 3, 2011, https://www.outsports.com/2011/10/3/4051944/moment-2-martina-navratilova-comes-out.

11. Picheta and Masters, "Martina Navratilova dropped by LGBT group over trans athletes row."

12. D. Leung, "Jennifer Azzi comes out as gay, announces marriage to her USF assistant coach," *San Jose Mercury News*, August 11, 2016, https://www.mercurynews.com/2016/03/31/jennifer-azzi-comes-out-as-gay-announces-marriage-to-her-usf-assistant-coach/.

13. L. Haldane, "Megan Rapinoe is an open book," *ESPN.com*, November 28, 2012, http://www.espn.com/espnw/news-commentary/article/8684043/

women-soccer-star-megan-rapinoe-coming-future-women-soccer-espn-maga-zine-interview-issue.

14. M. Flynn, "Seattle sports stars Sue Bird and Megan Rapinoe are first same-sex couple on cover of ESPN's Body Issue," *Washington Post*, June 26, 2018, https://www.washingtonpost.com/news/morning-mix/wp/2018/06/26/seattle-sports-stars-sue-bird-and-megan-rapinoe-are-first-same-sex-couple-on-cover-of-espn-body-issue/.

15. C. Zeigler, "Elena Delle Donne hopes her gay wedding can help others," *SBNation*, October 25, 2017, https://www.outsports.com/2017/10/25/16551830/elena-delle-donne-wedding-amanda-clifton.

16. S. Rankin and D. Merson, "2012 LGBTQ National College Athlete Report," *Campus Pride/Stand Up Foundation*, 2012, https://www.campuspride.org/wp-content/uploads/CampusPride-Athlete-Report-Exec-Summary.pdf.

17. C. Zeigler, "Seimone Augustus talks to ESPN about coming out as lesbian on Minnesota Lynx," *SBNation*, August 8, 2012, https://www.sbnation.com/london-olympics-2012/2012/8/8/3227355/seimone-augustus-talks-to-espn-about-coming-out-as-lesbian-on.

18. "Play to Win: Improving the lives of LGBTQ youth in sports," *Human Rights Campaign*, 2018, https://assets2.hrc.org/files/assets/resources/PlayToWin-FINAL.pdf?_ga=2.37765539.1429494980.1552423600-599741926.1514587348.

19. "The experiences of LGBT students in school athletics," *GLSEN*, 2013, https://www.glsen.org/sites/default/files/The%20Experiences%20of%20LGBT%20Students%20in%20Athletics.pdf.

20. D. Malone, "Q&A with Pat Griffin: 'Grandmother of the LGBTQ sports movement' discusses Derrick Gordon's decision to come out," *MassLive*, April 10, 2014, https://www.masslive.com/umassbasketball/2014/04/q_a_pat_griffin_grandmother_of.html.

21. "Trans athletes make great gains, yet resentment still flares," *NBC News*, February 25, 2019, https://www.nbcnews.com/feature/nbc-out/trans-athletes-make-great-gains-yet-resentment-still-flares-n975646.

22. P. Griffin and H. Carroll, "NCAA Inclusion of Transgender Student-Athletes," *NCAA*, April 2010, https://www.ncaa.org/sites/default/files/Transgender_Handbook_2011_Final.pdf.

23. R. A. Peike, R. Tucker, and E. Boye, "Scientific integrity and the IAAF testosterone regulations," *Science Daily*, February 2019, https://www.sciencedaily.com/releases/2019/02/190212160030.htm.

24. Peike, Tucker, and Boye, "Scientific integrity and the IAAF testosterone regulations."

25. LGBT SportSafe: Making the World of Sport Safe for All, https://lgbtsportsafe.com/#benefits.

26. Peike, Tucker, and Boye, "Scientific integrity and the IAAF testosterone regulations."

27. J. Levitt, "Halala! Caster Semenya voted most influential young South African," *Herald Live*, March 6, 2019, https://www.heraldlive.co.za/news/2019-03-06-halala-caster-semenya-voted-most-influential-young-south-african/.

28. "Mission statement," *You Can Play*, March 4, 2012, http://www.youcanplayproject.org/pages/mission-statement.

29. "Vision," *LGBT SportSafe*, March 2014, https://lgbtsportsafe.com/#vision.

30. B. Whitehead, "Cajon High's Layshia Clarendon featured in Adidas campaign championing girls, women in sport," *Sun*, March 11, 2019, https://www.sbsun.com/2019/03/11/cajon-highs-layshia-clarendon-featured-in-adidas-campaign-championing-girls-women-in-sport/.

31. Griffin and Carrol, "NCAA Inclusion of Transgender Student-Athletes."

9. A GLOBAL CHALLENGE

1. N. Mandela, "Speech by Nelson Mandela at the Inaugural Laureus Lifetime Achievement Award, Monaco, 2000," *Nelson Mandela Foundation*, May 25, 2000, http://db.nelsonmandela.org/speeches/pub_view.asp?pg=item&ItemID=NMS1148.

2. L. Puri, "Remarks by UN secretary-general and UN women deputy executive director at 'The Value of Hosting Mega Sport Events as a Social, Economic, and Environmental Sustainable Development Tool' event," *UN Women*, February 16, 2016, http://www.unwomen.org/en/news/stories/2016/2/lakshmi-puri-speech-at-value-of-hosting-mega-sport-event.

3. M. Marinosdottir, "Gender equality in sports," *Ministry of Welfare Iceland*, presentation at the 11th annual Transnational Working Group for the Study of Gender and Sport, August 15, 2018, https://rm.coe.int/gender-equality-in-sports-iceland/16807b8a8b.

4. "Zambia: NOWSPAR wins UN praise," *Times of Zambia*, February 27, 2012, https://allafrica.com/stories/201202271114.html.

5. J. Sejablsigo, "Violence against women remains high," *Daily News (Botswana)*, May 15, 2013, http://www.dailynews.gov.bw/news-details.php?nid=2781.

6. P. B. Massao and K. Fasting, "Race and racism: Experiences of black Norwegian athletes," *International Review for the Sociology of Sport* 45, no. 2

(June 2010): 147–62, https://www.researchgate.net/publication/
258142830_Race_and_Racism_Experiences_of_Black_Norwegian_Athletes.

7. A. Tornkvist, "Swedish female athletes face discrimination: Women in
sport do not get equal treatment despite the country's feminist reputation," *Al
Jazeera*, April 2, 2016, https://www.aljazeera.com/indepth/features/2016/03/
swedish-female-athletes-face-discrimination-160315110758946.html.

8. M. Hytner, "Research reveals over half of Australians follow women's
sport," *Guardian*, February 15, 2019, https://www.theguardian.com/sport/
2019/feb/16/research-reveals-over-half-of-australians-follow-womens-sport.

9. S. Chalkley-Rhoden, "Decline of women's sports coverage in Australia 'a
tragedy'; report shows drop in coverage," *ABC News Australia*, April 12, 2015,
https://www.abc.net.au/news/2015-04-12/decline-of-women-sports-coverage-
in-australia-a-tragedy/6359786.

10. T. Bruce, "Women's sport: Less talk more action," *Newsroom*, March 9,
2018, https://www.newsroom.co.nz/@lockerroom/2018/03/08/95196/womens-
sport-rhetoric-must-become-reality.

11. "Fast four questions: Kirikaiahi Mahutariki, executive manager, Maori
financial solutions, ASB Bank Limited," *Global Women*, June 29, 2017, https://
www.globalwomen.org.nz/developing-leaders/fast-four-questions-kirikaiahi-
mahutariki-executive-manager-maori-financial-solutions-asb-bank-limited/.

12. R. Lopez D'Amico and T. Benn, *Women and Sport in Latin America*
(New York: Routledge, 2016).

13. M. Sandoval, Women's Football in Latin America. Latin American Post,
June 30, 2017.

14. A. E. Mayer, "Law and women in the Middle East," *Cultural Survival*,
June 1984, https://www.culturalsurvival.org/publications/cultural-survival-
quarterly/law-and-women-middle-east.

15. Mayer, "Law and women in the Middle East."

16. M. Hamilton, "Defying a cultural taboo, Saudi women are running—
and they're not going to stop," *Runner's World*, September 7, 2018, https://
www.runnersworld.com/women/a22773825/defying-a-cultural-taboo-saudi-
women-are-runningand-theyre-not-going-to-stop/.

17. Hamilton, "Defying a cultural taboo, Saudi women are running."

18. C. Culpepper, "Middle Eastern women were once discouraged from
sport. A new generation now chases glory," *Washington Post*, July 11, 2016,
https://www.washingtonpost.com/sports/olympics/muslim-women-were-once-
forbidden-from-sport-a-new-generation-now-chases-olympic-glory/2016/07/
11/ec01b4a6-2cb6-11e6-9de3-6e6e7a14000c_story.html?utm_term=.b40605
a8e850.

19. S. A. Harvard, "Meet these 14 incredible Muslim women athletes who
won medals at the 2016 Rio Olympics," *Mic Network*, August 22, 2016, https://

mic.com/articles/152257/meet-these-14-incredible-muslim-women-athletes-who-won-medals-at-the-2016-rio-olympics#.LXdyU4agy.

20. Ladies Mountain League, http://www.ladiesmountainleague.com/.

21. Moving the Goalposts SA, https://mtgk.org/.

22. Girls and Football SA.org, http://www.girlsandfootball.org/.

23. NOWSPAR, www.nowspar.org.

24. "Hidden gender: Women's sport in developing nations," *Globalsportsjobs.com*, October 5, 2016, https://www.globalsportsjobs.com/article/hidden-gender-women-s-sport-in-developing-nations/.

25. "The UK's attitudes towards women in sport," *Insure4sport*, April 5, 2018, https://ww.insure4sport.co.uk/blog/the-uks-attitudes-towards-women-in-sport.

26. "The UK's attitudes towards women in sport."

27. "The UK's attitudes towards women in sport."

28. "Annamarie Phelps CBE interview: 'I love what I do; I've viewed it as a privilege,'" *British Rowing*, March 29, 2018, https://www.britishrowing.org/2018/03/annamarie-phelps-cbe-interview-i-love-i-ive-viewed-privilege/.

29. "Women in sport: Fueling a lifetime of participation," *Canadian Association for the Advancement of Women and Sport and Physical Activity*, March 2016, https://www.caaws.ca/e/wp-content/uploads/2016/03/FWC_ResearchPublication_EN_7March2016.pdf.

30. "Women in sport."

31. R. Picheta and K. Mirchandi, "Only six countries have equal rights for men and women, World Bank finds," *CNN.com*, March 2, 2019, https://www.cnn.com/2019/03/02/europe/world-bank-gender-equality-report-intl/index.html.

10. TIME'S UP

1. A. Das, "U.S. women's soccer team sues U.S. Soccer for gender discrimination," *New York Times*, March 8, 2019, https://www.nytimes.com/2019/03/08/sports/womens-soccer-team-lawsuit-gender-discrimination.html.

2. "Ernst and Young to launch leadership network for elite female athletes to address unmet global need," *DiversityInc*, March 13, 2013, https://www.diversityinc.com/ernst-young-to-launch-leadership-network-for-elite-female-athletes-to-address-unmet-global-need/.

3. K. Elsesser, "Here's why women's teams are coached by men," *Forbes*, March 1, 2019, https://www.forbes.com/sites/kimelsesser/2019/03/01/heres-why-womens-teams-are-coached-by-men/#268116c3b3f9.

4. Elsesser, "Here's why women's teams are coached by men."

5. C. Herreria, "California lawmakers fight for equal pay for athletes in contests on state land," *Huffington Post*, February 26, 2019, https://www.huffpost.com/entry/california-athletes-equal-pay_n_5c71b472e4b00eed0834d8dc.

6. E. Sanchez and L. Rodriguez, "These are the best and worst countries to be a woman in 2018," *Global Citizen*, December 18, 2018, https://www.globalcitizen.org/en/content/best-worst-countries-for-women-2018-list-ranking/.

7. "Jackie Joyner-Kersee quotes," *Thought Company*, https://www.thoughtco.com/jackie-joyner-kersee-quotes-3530110.

BIBLIOGRAPHY

"184 people in sports who came out publicly in the media in 2017." *SBNation*, January 4, 2018, https://www.outsports.com/2018/1/4/16666278/2017-list-out-gay-lesbian-bisexual-transgender-athletes.

Adriaanse, J. "Women are missing in sport leadership, and it's time that changed." *Conversation*, December 11, 2016, http://theconversation.com/women-are-missing-in-sport-leadership-and-its-time-that-changed-69979 .

"Aesthetics over athletics when it comes to women in sport." *University of Cambridge*, August 12, 2016, https://www.cam.ac.uk/research/news/aesthetics-over-athletics-when-it-comes-to-women-in-sport.

Alvarez, A. "Should female athletes sue the networks for equal coverage?" *Guardian*, April 14, 2018, https://www.theguardian.com/sport/2018/apr/14/womens-athletes-lawsuit-equal-coverage-title-ix.

Amuchie, N. "How black women shaped the law banning sex discrimination in education." *Rewire.News*, February 28, 2018, https://rewire.news/article/2018/02/28/black-women-shaped-law-banning-sex-discrimination-education/ .

Andersen, E., R. Bullingham, and R. Magrath. "Out in sport: The experiences of openly gay and lesbian athletes in competitive sport." *ResearchGate*, January 2016, https://www.researchgate.net/publication/303434435_Out_in_sport_The_experiences_of_openly_gay_and_lesbian_athletes_in_competitive_sport.

"Annamarie Phelps CBE interview: 'I love what I do; I've viewed it as a privilege.'" *British Rowing*, March 29, 2018, https://www.britishrowing.org/2018/03/annamarie-phelps-cbe-interview-i-love-i-ive-viewed-privilege/.

Anthony, M. "Mike Anthony: Megan Rapinoe has played her way onto a world platform she's using wisely." *Hartford Courant*, July 29, 2018, https://www.courant.com/sports/hc-sp-megan-rapinoe-us-womens-soccer-column-20180728-story.html.

Armour, N., and R. Axon. "House committee wants answers from sports organizations on sexual abuse." *USA Today*, January 26, 2018, https://www.usatoday.com/story/sports/olympics/2018/01/26/house-committee-wants-answers-sports-organizations-sexual-abuse/1070016001/.

"Athletic Equality Index." *Athlete Ally*, 2017, https://www.athleteally.org/wp-content/uploads/2017/09/AEI-Final-Draft.pdf.

Badenhausen, K. "The highest-paid female athletes 2018." *Forbes*, August 21, 2018, https://www.forbes.com/sites/kurtbadenhausen/2018/08/21/the-highest-paid-female-athletes-2018/#7e41a733405f.

Ballantine, C. "Olympian alum Nancy Hogshead-Makar takes on sexual harassment, assault." *Chronicle*, April 4, 2018, https://www.dukechronicle.com/article/2018/04/olympian-alum-nancy-hogshead-makar-takes-on-sexual-harassment-assault .

Belzer, J. "The most powerful women in U.S. sports 2018." *Forbes*, March 27, 2018, https://www.forbes.com/sites/jasonbelzer/2018/03/27/the-most-powerful-women-in-u-s-sports-2018/#54443889423f .

Berkman, S. "U.S. women's team strikes a deal with U.S.A. Hockey." *New York Times*, March 28, 2017, https://www.nytimes.com/2017/03/28/sports/hockey/usa-hockey-uswnt-boycott.html.

Berri, D. "Some popular sports sites appear to cover more animals than women." *Forbes*, November 29, 2017, https://www.forbes.com/sites/davidberri/2017/11/29/some-popular-sports-sites-appear-to-cover-more-animals-than-women/?curator=SportsREDEF .

Best, K. "Megan Rapinoe's new focus: Make soccer inclusive for LBGTQ kids." *SBNation*, June 7, 2018, https://www.outsports.com/2018/6/7/17435834/megan-rapinoe-soccer-lgbtq-kids-project.

"Beyond x's and o's: Gender bias and coaches of women's college sports." *Women's Sport Foundation*, September 2, 2016, https://files.eric.ed.gov/fulltext/ED570470.pdf .

Blum, S. "American women are winning more medals than men for Team USA." *Thrillist.com*, February 24, 2018, https://www.thrillist.com/news/nation/usa-medal-count-women-winning-more-than-men .

Brackenridge, C., D. Bishop, S. Moussali, and J. Tapp. "The characteristics of sexual abuse in sport: A multidimensional scaling analysis of events described in media reports." *International Journal of Sport and Exercise Psychology* 6, no. 4 (2008): 385–406.

Brady, J. "ESPN shows progress, faces challenges, regarding women in sports." *ESPN.com*, December 20, 2017, http://www.espn.com/blog/ombudsman/post/_/id/906/espn-shows-progress-faces-challenges-regarding-women-in-sports.

Braidwood, E. "Pro golfer Mel Reid comes out as gay: 'Be proud of who you are.'" *Pink News*, December 11, 2018, https://www.pinknews.co.uk/2018/12/11/pro-golfer-mel-reid-comes-out-gay/.

Brown, M. "The longer the race, the stronger we get." *Outside*, April 11, 2017, https://www.outsideonline.com/2169856/longer-race-stronger-we-get.

Bruce, T. "Women's sport: Less talk more action." *Newsroom*, March 9, 2018, https://www.newsroom.co.nz/@lockerroom/2018/03/08/95196/womens-sport-rhetoric-must-become-reality.

Burton, L. J. "Underrepresentation of women in sport leadership: A review of research." *Sport Management Review* 18, no. 2 (March 2014): 155–65, https://daneshyari.com/article/preview/140857.pdf.

Burton, M. "This reporter sexism needs to go." *OZY*, August 29, 2018, https://www.ozy.com/opinion/this-sports-reporter-sexism-needs-to-go/88992.

Chalkley-Rhoden, S. "Decline of women's sports coverage in Australia 'a tragedy'; report shows drop in coverage." *ABC News Australia*, April 12, 2015, https://www.abc.net.au/news/2015-04-12/decline-of-women-sports-coverage-in-australia-a-tragedy/6359786.

Chavez, C. "Victims share stories of abuse at former USA Gymnastics doctor Larry Nassar's sentencing." *Sports Illustrated*, January 18, 2018, https://www.si.com/olympics/2018/01/16/Larry-nassar-sentencing-victims-abuse-stories.

Clapp, B. "Working in sports journalism as a woman." *WorkinSports.com*, November 14, 2016, https://www.workinsports.com/blog/working-in-sports-journalism-as-a-woman/.

Clarey, C. "Many athletes found their voices." *New York Times*, December 22, 2017, https://www.nytimes.com/2017/12/20/sports/year-sports-protests.html.

Close, K. "Five Reasons Why Tennis Should Keep Paying Men and Women Equally." *Money.com*, March 22, 2016, http://time.com/money/4265912/equal-pay-tennis-djokovic-williams/.

Coles, T. "Famous Olympic quotes to get inspired about the games." *Huffpost*, February 7, 2014, https://www.huffingtonpost.ca/2014/02/07/famous-olympic-quotes_n_4745472.html.

Collins, K. "U.S. trapshooter wins bronze medal—there are immediately cries of sexism." *Daily Caller*, August 9, 2016, https://dailycaller.com/2016/08/09/u-s-trapshooter-wins-bronze-medal-there-are-immediately-cries-of-sexism/.

Committee to Restore Integrity to the USOC. "Our recommendations for an 'athletes-first' Olympic committee." *Around the Rings*, January 21, 2019, http://aroundtherings.com/site/A__75538/title__the-committee-to-restore-integrity-to-the-usoc-our-recommendations-for-an-athletes-first-olympic-committee/292/Articles.

Cook, B. "It's tough for low-income kids, especially girls, to participate in sports." *Forbes*, January 6, 2017, https://www.forbes.com/sites/bobcook/2017/01/06/its-tough-for-low-in-come-kids-especially-girls-to-participate-in-sports/#733b49f9622c.

———. "Lack of presence for female coaches extends to kids' games." *Forbes*, November 28, 2018, https://www.forbes.com/sites/bobcook/2018/11/28/lack-of-presence-for-female-coaches-extends-to-kids-games/#b07a14b49386.

Culpepper, C. "Middle Eastern women were once discouraged from sport. A new generation now chases glory." *Washington Post*, July 11, 2016, https://www.washingtonpost.com/sports/olympics/muslim-women-were-once-forbidden-from-sport-a-new-generation-now-chases-olympic-glory/2016/07/11/ec01b4a6-2cb6-11e6-9de3-6e6e7a14000c_story.html?utm_term=.b40605a8e850.

Danika, K. "Why are women's sports still not covered in the media?" *Women's Media Center*, March 6, 2016, http://www.womensmediacenter.com/fbomb/why-are-womens-sports-still-not-covered-in-the-media.

Das, A. "Long days, Google docs, and anonymous surveys: How the U.S. soccer team forged a deal." *New York Times*, April 5, 2017, https://www.nytimes.com/2017/04/05/sports/soccer/uswnt-us-soccer-labor-deal-contract.html .

———. "U.S. women's soccer team sues US Soccer for gender discrimination." *New York Times*, March 8, 2019, https://www.nytimes.com/2019/03/08/sports/womens-soccer-team-lawsuit-gender-discrimination.html.

Dator, J. "A comprehensive timeline of the Larry Nassar case." *SBNation*, December 21, 2018, https://www.sbnation.com/2018/1/19/16900674/larry-nassar-abuse-timeline-usa-gymnastics-michigan-state.

de la Cretaz, B. "Blackout goals: How sports media locks out women athletes." *Bitchmedia*, March 8, 2018, https://www.bitchmedia.org/article/sports-media-erases-women-athletes.

Dicaro, J. "Safest bet in sports: Men complaining about a female announcer's voice." *New York Times*, September 18, 2017, https://www.nytimes.com/2017/09/18/sports/nfl-beth-mowins-julie-dicaro.html.

Ditota, D. "Felisha Legette-Jack making most of 2nd chance many women coaches don't get." *Syracuse.com*, October 10, 2018, https://www.syracuse.com/sports/index.ssf/2018/10/felisha_legette-jacks_rise_from_devasting_job_loss_to_advocate_for_second_chance.html.

Dosh, K. "Why women's college basketball might be stuck in the red." *SB Nation*, November 12, 2013, https://www.swishappeal.com/2013/11/12/5090384/ncaa-womens-college-basketball-profits-donations .

Doubek, J. "'We don't have enough women in power': Notre Dame coach Muffet McGraw goes viral." *NPR*, April 6, 2019, https://www.npr.org/2019/04/06/710539614/we-don-t-have-enough-women-in-power-notre-dame-coach-muffet-mcgraw-goes-viral .

Dunbar, G. "FIFA to 'significantly' raise prize money for Women's World Cup." *CBC Sports*, September 20, 2018, https://www.cbc.ca/sports/soccer/fifa-to-raise-womens-world-cup-prize-money-1.4831379.

———. "FIFA to upgrade flights, raise prize money for Women's WCup." Associated Press, September 20, 2018, https://www.apnews.com/e78eb030fd9347adb449f7e2e607493a.

Elsesser, K. "Here's why women's teams are coached by men." *Forbes*, March 1, 2019, https://www.forbes.com/sites/kimelsesser/2019/03/01/heres-why-womens-teams-are-coached-by-men/#268116c3b3f9.

Emmert, M. "Griesbaum on lawsuit against Iowa: I tried to represent the coaching profession." *Des Moines Register*, May 22, 2017, https://www.hawkcentral.com/story/sports/

2017/05/22/tracey-griesbaum-her-lawsuit-vs-iowa-i-tried-represent-coaching-profession/
337109001/.

———. "In Lawsuit against UIowa, Jane Meyer details the firing of her partner, and the
fallout." *Des Moines Register and Iowa City Press-Citizen*, April 20, 2017, https://
www.hawkcentral.com/story/sports/college/iowa/2017/04/20/jane-meyer-tells-fateful-
meeting-gary-barta/305737001/.

"Ernst and Young to launch leadership network for elite female athletes to address unmet
global need." *DiversityInc*, March 13, 2013, https://www.diversityinc.com/ernst-young-to-
launch-leadership-network-for-elite-female-athletes-to-address-unmet-global-need/.

"The experiences of LGBT students in school athletics." *GLSEN*, 2013, https://
www.glsen.org/sites/default/files/The%20Experiences%20of%20LGBT%20Students
%20in%20Athletics.pdf.

Fan, J. "Kim Yo Jong, Chloe Kim, and the shifting images of Asia and Asian American
women at the Olympics." *New Yorker*, February 15, 2018, https://www.newyorker.com/
news/daily-comment/kim-yo-jong-chloe-kim-shifting-images-asian-women-olympics.

"Fast four questions: Kirikaiahi Mahutariki, executive manager, Maori financial solutions,
ASB Bank Limited." *Global Women*, June 29, 2017, https://www.globalwomen.org.nz/
developing-leaders/fast-four-questions-kirikaiahi-mahutariki-executive-manager-maori-fi-
nancial-solutions-asb-bank-limited/.

Fasting, K., and C. Brackenridge. "Coaches, sexual harassment, and education." *Sport, Education, and Society Journal* 14, no. 1 (2009): 21–35.

Flanagan, L. "The field where men still call the shots." *Atlantic*, July 28, 2017, https://
www.theatlantic.com/education/archive/2017/07/the-field-where-men-still-call-the-shots/
535167.

Flynn, M. "Seattle sports stars Sue Bird and Megan Rapinoe are first same-sex couple on
cover of ESPN's Body Issue." *Washington Post*, June 26, 2018, https://
www.washingtonpost.com/news/morning-mix/wp/2018/06/26/seattle-sports-stars-sue-
bird-and-megan-rapinoe-are-first-same-sex-couple-on-cover-of-espn-body-issue/.

Fominykh, K. "New study from Morgan State explores how black female athletes navigate
racism and sexism to excel." *Baltimore Sun*, June 27, 2018, https://
www.baltimoresun.com/sports/bs-sp-morgan-state-black-female-athlete-study-20180625-
story.html.

Foudy, J. "Ahead of Women's World Cup draw, FIFA's actions speak louder than words."
ESPN.com, December 6, 2018, http://www.espn.com/espnw/voices/article/25460147/fifa-
actions-speak-louder-words-ahead-women-world-cup-draw.

Fowler, S. "Cam Newton's sexist comment to Observer reporter wasn't one bit funny."
Charlotte Observer, October 4, 2017, https://www.charlotteobserver.com/sports/spt-
columns-blogs/scott-fowler/article177107336.html.

Freeman, H. "How was Larry Nassar able to abuse so many gymnasts for so long?" *Guardian*, January 26, 2018, https://www.theguardian.com/sport/2018/jan/26/larry-nassar-
abuse-gymnasts-scandal-culture.

Frisby, C. "A content analysis of Serena Williams and Angelique Kerber's racial and sexist
microaggressions." *Open Journal of Social Sciences* 5 (2017): 263–81, https://file.scirp.org/
pdf/JSS_2017052316172687.pdf.

Gentile, L. "Playing a sport can get women to the c-suite." *Fortune*, January 23, 2016, https://
fortune.com/2016/01/23/sport-women-c-suite/.

Gibbs, L. "This WNBA team took a risk and stood up for Planned Parenthood." *ThinkProgress*, July 19, 2017, https://thinkprogress.org/wnba-planned-parenthood-rally-
8967bc1ce66c/.

Giddings, P. J. "What the dominance of black female athletes means to American culture."
ESPN.com, February 24, 2017, http://www.espn.com/espnw/culture/article/18750694/
what-dominance-black-female-athletes-means-american-culture.

Glass, A. "The WNBA's Best Fans." *Forbes*, September 26, 2018, https://www.forbes.com/
sites/alanaglass/2018/09/26/the-wnbas-best-fans/#192eaab4192b.

Gomex-Gonzalez, C., H. Dietl, and C. Nesseler. "Does performance justify the underrepresentation of women's coaches? Evidence from professional women's soccer." *Sports Man-*

agement Review, September 8, 2018, https://www.sciencedirect.com/science/article/abs/pii/S1441352317301857.

"Green to headline the Institute for Sport and Social Justice 'Invisible Women in Sports' podcast." *GoCrimson*, October 18, 2018, https://www.gocrimson.com/sports/wten/2018-19/releases/20181016k2fdfp.

Gregory, S. "How the #MeToo Movement is about to change pro sports." *Time*, December 19, 2017, http://time.com/5064703/how-the-metoo-movement-is-about-to-change-pro-sports/.

Griffin, P., and H. Carroll. "NCAA Inclusion of Transgender Student-Athletes." *NCAA*, April 2010, https://www.ncaa.org/sites/default/files/Transgender_Handbook_2011_Final.pdf.

Griffin, P., and N. Caple. "The times they are a-changin' for LGBTQ people in sports." *Huffington Post*, February 2, 2016, https://www.huffpost.com/entry/the-times-they-are-achang_b_4986048.

Haldane, L. "Megan Rapinoe is an open book." *ESPN.com*, November 28, 2012, http://www.espn.com/espnw/news-commentary/article/8684043/women-soccer-star-megan-rapinoe-coming-future-women-soccer-espn-magazine-interview-issue.

Hamilton, M. "Defying a cultural taboo, Saudi women are running—and they're not going to stop." *Runner's World*, September 7, 2018, https://www.runnersworld.com/women/a22773825/defying-a-cultural-taboo-saudi-women-are-runningand-theyre-not-going-to-stop/.

Harris, R. "World Cup cash inequality persists after women's prize rises." Associated Press, October 26, 2018, https://www.apnews.com/91c2fb6e832845d8b30b6fd6b70d2b1b .

Harvard, S. A. "Meet these 14 incredible Muslim women athletes who won medals at the 2016 Rio Olympics." *Mic Network*, August 22, 2016, https://mic.com/articles/152257/meet-these-14-incredible-muslim-women-athletes-who-won-medals-at-the-2016-rio-olympics#.LXdyU4agy.

Hastie, E. "Despite progress made under Title IX, gender inequalities still persist in high school sports." *Buffalo News*, November 9, 2017, https://buffalonews.com/2017/11/09/despite-progress-made-under-title-ix-gender-inequalities-still-persist-in-high-school-sports/.

———. "Gender inequality persists in high school sports." *Athletic Business*, November 2017, https://www.athleticbusiness.com/high-school/gender-inequality-persists-in-high-school-sports.html .

Herreria, C. "California lawmakers fight for equal pay for athletes in contests on state land." *Huffington Post*, February 26, 2019, https://www.huffpost.com/entry/california-athletes-equal-pay_n_5c71b472e4b00eed0834d8dc.

Hershman, B. "The WNBA is scoring new fans: Merchandise sales up 50 percent, viewership up 35 percent in 2018." Benzinga.com, August 9, 2018, https://www.benzinga.com/news/18/08/12177369/the-wnba-is-scoring-new-fans-merchandise-sales-up-50-viewership-up-35-in-2018 .

"Hidden gender: Women's sport in developing nations." *Globalsportsjobs.com*, October 5, 2016, https://www.globalsportsjobs.com/article/hidden-gender-women-s-sport-in-developing-nations/.

Howard, J. "With deal reached, U.S. women's national hockey team will play at world championships." *ESPN.com*, March 29, 2017, https://www.espn.com/olympics/story/_/id/19026627/usa-hockey-us-women-national-team-reach-agreement-avoid-boycott.

Hytner, M. "Research reveals over half of Australians follow women's sport." *Guardian*, February 15, 2019, https://www.theguardian.com/sport/2019/feb/16/research-reveals-over-half-of-australians-follow-womens-sport.

Jenkins, S. "Geno Auriemma: 'Not as many women want to coach.' His daughter: "DAD. WALK IT BACK."" *Chicago Tribune*, March 31, 2017, https://www.chicagotribune.com/sports/college/ct-geno-auriemma-female-coaches-sally-jenkins-20170331-story.html.

Jimbo, S. B. "Geno was asked about Muffet not hiring male assistants." *Ndnation.com*, April 4, 2019, https://ndnation.com/boards/showpost.php?b=mcgraw;pid=70019;d=all .

Kassouf, J. "USWNT players file gender discrimination lawsuit against U.S. Soccer." *Equalizer*, March 8, 2019, https://equalizersoccer.com/2019/03/08/uswnt-lawsuit-gender-discrimination-28-players-details-documents/.

Kay, K., and C. Shipman. "The confidence gap." *Atlantic*, May 2014, https://www.theatlantic.com/magazine/archive/2014/05/the-confidence-gap/359815/#_blank.

Kendall, E. N. "Female athletes often face the femininity police—especially Serena Williams." *Guardian*, July 14, 2015, https://www.theguardian.com/commentisfree/2015/jul/14/serena-williams-female-athletes-femininity-police.

Kennedy, P. "U.S. Soccer signs eight-figure sponsorship deal with VW." *SoccerAmerica Daily*, January 14, 2019, https://www.socceramerica.com/publications/article/80987/us-soccer-signs-eight-figure-sponsorship-deal-wi.html.

"Kimberley Crenshaw on intersectionality, more than two decades later." *Columbia Law School*, June 8, 2017, https://www.law.columbia.edu/pt/br/news/2017/06/kimberle-crenshaw-intersectionality.

Ladika, S. "Sports and sexual assault: Can colleges and pro leagues curb abuse by athletes?" *CQ Press*, April 28, 2017, https://library.cqpress.com/cqresearcher/document.php?id=cqresrre2017042800.

Lapchick, R. "2017 College Sport Racial and Gender Report Card." *Institute for Diversity and Ethics in Sport*, February 2018, https://www.insidehighered.com/sites/default/server_files/media/2017%20College%20Sport%20Racial%20and%20Gender%20Report%20Card.pdf.

———. "The 2018 Associated Press Sports Editor Racial and Gender Report Card." *Tides: The Institute for Diversity and Ethics in Sport*, May 2, 2018, http://nebula.wsimg.com/2b640482e881dddc4dfb39e6aca52c2e?AccessKeyId=DAC3A56D8FB782449D2A&disposition=0&alloworigin=1.

———. "The WNBA leads all sports leagues in diversity and inclusion." *ESPN.com*, November 16, 2017, http://www.espn.com/espnw/sports/article/21434534/the-wnba-scores-high-marks-comes-diversity-hiring-practices.

———. "WNBA score record marks for hiring practices." *ESPN.com*, October 25, 2018, http://www.espn.com/wnba/story/_/id/25075162/wnba-once-again-sets-record-high-marks-diversity-their-hiring-practices.

———, B. Estrella, and N. Bredikhina. "The 2017 Racial and Gender Report: College Sport." *Institute for Diversity and Ethics in Sport, University of Central Florida*, February 28, 2018, http://docplayer.net/73853405-2017-college-sport-racial-gender-report-card-by-richard-e-lapchick-edited-by-brett-estrella-with-nataliya-bredikhina.html.

Larsen, B. A., D. Pekmezi, B. Marquez, T. J. Benitez, and B. H. Marcus. "Physical activity in Latinas: social and environmental influences." *Women's Health* 9, no. 2 (2013): 201–13, https://www.ncbi.nlm.nih.gov/pmc/articles/PMC3868363/.

Lasher, M. "Breanna Stewart used her ESPY moment to speak out against inequality." *Time*, July 14, 2016, https://time.com/4406421/breanna-stewart-equality/.

LaVoi, N. "Tucker Center releases annual Women in Coaching Report Card," *University of Minnesota*, February 7, 2018, http://wcs.umn.edu/news/tucker-center-releases-annual-women-coaching-report-card.

———. "Why women matter in sport coaching." *University of Minnesota College of Education and Human Development*, March 13, 2015, https://cehdvision2020.umn.edu/blog/why-women-matter-in-sport-coaching/.

———, ed. *Women in Sports Coaching*. New York: Routledge, 2016.

Lawrence Corbett, M. "The problem with the conversation surrounding Serena Williams." *Bleacher Report*, September 3, 2015, https://bleacherreport.com/articles/2550762-the-problem-with-the-conversation-surrounding-serena-williams.

Lebel, K., and K. Danlchuk. "Generation Y's perceptions of women's sport in the media." *International Journal of Sport Communication* 2, no. 2 (2009): 146–63.

Legette-Jack, F. "2018 Sweet 16 – Buffalo Postgame." *YouTube*, March 24, 2018, https://www.youtube.com/watch?v=PWPM3FeCLd4.

Leung, D. "Jennifer Azzi comes out as gay, announces marriage to her USF assistant coach." *San Jose Mercury News*, August 11, 2016, https://www.mercurynews.com/2016/03/31/jennifer-azzi-comes-out-as-gay-announces-marriage-to-her-usf-assistant-coach/.

Levitt, D. "State of pay: tennis has huge gender gap in earning power." *Guardian*, July 14, 2018, https://www.theguardian.com/sport/ng-interactive/2018/jul/14/tennis-pay-gap-shouldnt-be-gender-based.

Levitt, J. "Halala! Caster Semenya voted most influential young South African." *Herald Live*, March 6, 2019, https://www.heraldlive.co.za/news/2019-03-06-halala-caster-semenya-voted-most-influential-young-south-african/.

Lewis, M. "Going Solo: U.S. goalkeeper sues U.S. Soccer over pay discrimination." *Front Row Soccer*, August 25, 2018, https://www.frontrowsoccer.com/2018/08/25/going-solo-ex-u-s-goalkeeper-sues-u-s-soccer-over-pay-discrimination/ .

Lloyd, C. "Why I'm fighting for equal pay." *New York Times*, April 10, 2016, https://www.nytimes.com/2016/04/11/sports/soccer/carli-lloyd-why-im-fighting-for-equal-pay.html?action=click&module=RelatedCoverage&pgtype=Article&region=Footer .

Lopez D'Amico, R., and T. Benn. *Women and Sport in Latin America*. New York: Routledge, 2016.

Loudin, A. "Talking to your young athletes about sex abuse." *ESPN.com*, January 16, 2018, http://www.espn.com/espnw/voices/article/18979442/talking-your-young-athletes-sexual-abuse.

Lough, N. "The case for boosting WNBA player salaries." *Conversation*, August 9, 2018, https://theconversation.com/the-case-for-boosting-wnba-player-salaries-100805 .

Lovelin, M., and M. Hanold. "Female sport leaders' perception of leadership and management: Skills and attitudes for success." *Global Sport Business Journal* 2, no. 1 (2014): 14–29, http://www.gsbassn.com/Journal/Vol2-1/14-29.pdf.

Luther, J. "The more women's sports are covered, the more popular they will be." *Huffington Post*, March 3, 2018, https://www.huffpost.com/entry/opinion-luther-women-basketball_n_5ac27206e4b09712fec34663.

Macur, J. "Olympic Committee alerted to sex abuse in gymnastics years ago, court filing says." *New York Times*, November 22, 2018, https://www.nytimes.com/2018/11/22/sports/gymnastics-abuse-.html.

Madkour, A. D. "Women in sports media cite progress, obstacles." *Sports Business Journal*, March 6, 2017, https://www.sportsbusinessdaily.com/Journal/Issues/2017/03/06/Opinion/From-The-Executive-Editor.aspx.

Malone, D. "Q&A with Pat Griffin: 'Grandmother of the LGBTQ sports movement' discusses Derrick Gordon's decision to come out." *MassLive*, April 10, 2014, https://www.masslive.com/umassbasketball/2014/04/q_a_pat_griffin_grandmother_of.html.

Marinosdottir, M. "Gender equality in sports." *Ministry of Welfare Iceland*, presentation at the 11th annual Transnational Working Group for the Study of Gender and Sport, August 15, 2018, https://rm.coe.int/gender-equality-in-sports-iceland/16807b8a8b.

Massao, P. B., and K. Fasting. "Race and racism: Experiences of black Norwegian athletes." *International Review for the Sociology of Sport* 45, no. 2 (June 2010): 147–62, https://www.researchgate.net/publication/258142830_Race_and_Racism_Experiences_of_Black_Norwegian_Athletes.

Mayer, A. E. "Law and women in the Middle East." *Cultural Survival Quarterly Magazine*, June 1984, https://www.culturalsurvival.org/publications/cultural-survival-quarterly/law-and-women-middle-east.

McKenzie, J., and L. Fisher. "Female sports journalists react to Cam Newton, share their own sexist experiences." *ABC News*, October 5, 2017, https://abcnews.go.com/Entertainment/female-sports-journalists-react-cam-newton-share-sexist/story?id=50304858.

"Media kit on sexual assault." *Institut National de Sante Publique*, 2018, https://www.inspq.qc.ca/en/sexual-assault/media/sexual-assault-and-media.

Mertens, M. "Women cyclists still aren't allowed to ride as far as the men." *ESPN.com*, July 21, 2016, http://www.espn.com/espnw/culture/feature/article/17113949/women-cyclists-allowed-ride-far-men.

Molloy, M. "Olympic sexism? Twitter is very angry about this headline." *Telegraph*, August 15, 2016, https://www.telegraph.co.uk/olympics/2016/08/15/olympic-sexism-twitter-is-very-angry-about-this-headline/.

Myre, G. "U.S. women are the biggest winners at the Rio Olympics." *NPR*, August 21, 2016, https://www.npr.org/sections/thetorch/2016/08/21/490818961/u-s-women-are-the-biggest-winners-in-rio-olympics.

National Women's Law Center, Poverty and Race Research and Action Council. "Finishing last: Girls of color and school sports opportunities." *PRRAC.org*, 2015, https://prrac.org/pdf/GirlsFinishingLast_Report.pdf .

"NBC's prime time Olympic broadcast features more male athletes by significant margin: Olympics' gender coverage gap worse than 2014 Sochi Games." *Fiveringtv.com*, February 19, 2018, https://fiveringtv.com/2018/02/18/nbcs-primetime-olympic-broadcast-features-male-athletes-by-a-significant-margin-after-the-first-10-days/ .

Nelson, E. "The dynamics of women coaching men and gender stereotypes." *Sport in American History*, July 9, 2018, https://ussporthistory.com/2018/07/09/the-dynamics-of-women-coaching-men-and-gender-stereotypes/.

Niolon, R. "The stages of coming out." *PsychPage*, http://www.psychpage.com/learning/library/gay/comeout.html.

Nyad, D. "Diana Nyad: My life after sexual assault." *New York Times*, November 9, 2017, https://www.nytimes.com/2017/11/09/opinion/diana-nyad-sexual-assault.html.

"Olympic Committee knew about sexual abuse in gymnastics since the 1990s, according to court filings." *Women in the World*, November 26, 2018, https://womenintheworld.com/2018/11/26/olympic-committee-knew-about-sexual-abuse-in-gymnastics-since-the-1990s-according-to-court-filings/ .

Paramo, D. "Gender inequality in sports broadcasting apparent to viewers." *Daily Evergreen* (Washington State University), October 5, 2017, https://dailyevergreen.com/17571/sports/women-broadcaster-column/ .

Parent, S., and G. Demers. "Sexual abuse in sport: A model to prevent and protect athletes." *Child Abuse Review* 20, no. 2 (March 2011): 120–33.

Patel, A. "Headline about Olympic swimmers Katie Ledecky and Michael Phelps called sexist." *Huffington Post*, October 17, 2016, https://www.huffingtonpost.ca/2016/08/16/sexist-headline-olympics_n_11544838.html.

Peike, R. A., R. Tucker, and E. Boye. "Scientific integrity and the IAAF testosterone regulations." *Science Daily*, February 2019, https://www.sciencedaily.com/releases/2019/02/190212160030.htm.

Peters, J. "How women in sports media are cheering each other on." *News Media Alliance*, March 27, 2018, https://www.newsmediaalliance.org/women-in-sports-media/ .

Picheta, R., and J. Masters. "Martina Navratilova dropped by LGTB group over trans athletes row." *CNN.com*, February 20, 2019, https://www.cnn.com/2019/02/20/tennis/martina-navratilova-dropped-lgbt-group-scli-spt-intl/index.html.

Picheta, R., and K. Mirchandi. "Only six countries have equal rights for men and women, World Bank finds." *CNN.com*, March 2, 2019, https://www.cnn.com/2019/03/02/europe/world-bank-gender-equality-report-intl/index.html.

"Play to win: Improving the lives of LGBTQ youth in sports." *Human Rights Campaign*, 2018, https://assets2.hrc.org/files/assets/resources/PlayToWin-FINAL.pdf?_ga=2.37765539.1429494980.1552423600-599741926.1514587348.

"Playing in the closet: Homophobia in sports." *Women's Sports Foundation*, June 11, 2011, http://www.womenssportsfoundation.org/home/research/articles-and-reports/lgbt-issues/playing-in-the-closet.

Pressley, H. "It's been 40 years since Title IX, but there's still more work to be done." *Girls on the Run*, June 22, 2017, https://www.girlsontherun.org/remarkable/331/Its-Been-40-Years-Since-Title-IX-and-Theres-Stil.

"Preventing Child Abuse: New Federal Requirement Facing Youth Sports." *Philadelphia Insurance Companies*, February 16, 2018, https://www.phly.com/rms/blog/NewAbusePreventionLaw.aspx.

"Prize money: 2018 Cincinnati Masters 1000." *Tennis Planet.me*, August 13, 2018, https://www.tennisplanet.me/blog/2018/08/prize-money-2018-cincinnati-masters-1000.html.

Puri, L. "Remarks by UN secretary-general and UN women deputy executive director at The Value of Hosting Mega Sport Events as a Social, Economic, and Environmental Sustainable Development Tool' event." *UN Women*, February 16, 2016, http://www.unwomen.org/en/news/stories/2016/2/lakshmi-puri-speech-at-value-of-hosting-mega-sport-event.

Rankin, S., and D. Merson. "2012 LGBTQ National College Athlete Report." *Campus Pride/Stand Up Foundation*, 2012, https://www.campuspride.org/wp-content/uploads/Campus-Pride-Athlete-Report-Exec-Summary.pdf.

Reid, S. "Steve Penny banned by USA Gymnastics but not the only focus of investigations into alleged Nassar cover-up." *Orange County Register*, October 18, 2018, https://www.ocregister.com/2018/10/18/steve-penny-not-the-only-focus-of-investigations-into-alleged-nassar-cover-up/.

"Release: WNBA invites to "Take a Seat, Take a Stand" for women and girls during the 2018 season." *WNBA.com*, May 17, 2018, https://www.wnba.com/news/wnba-take-a-seat-take-a-stand-women-girls-2018-season.

Reliable Source. "How Venus Williams got equal pay for women at Wimbledon." *Washington Post*, July 2, 2013, https://www.washingtonpost.com/news/reliable-source/wp/2013/07/02/how-venus-williams-got-equal-pay-for-women-at-wimbledon/?noredirect=on .

Rock, L. "As women's sport grows, athletes find they can't stay silent in the era of Trump." *Guardian*, July 29, 2017, https://www.theguardian.com/sport/2017/jul/29/womens-sport-activism-and-political-protest-planned-parenthood.

Ruffins, P. "Latinos not yet scoring with college athletics." *Minority News*, February 18, 2019, https://www.blackradionetwork.com/latinos_not_yet_scoring_with_college_athletics.

Ryan, J. *Little Girls in Pretty Boxes*. New York: Grand Central Publishing, 1995; reprint, 2018.

Ryan, S. "College sports needs more women—and women of color—in coaching ranks." *Chicago Tribune*, April 17, 2017, https://www.chicagotribune.com/sports/ct-womens-college-coaching-diversity-ryan-spt-0419-20170417-column.html.

Sanchez, E., and L. Rodriguez. "These are best and worst countries to be a woman in 2018." *Global Citizen*, December 18, 2018, https://www.globalcitizen.org/en/content/best-worst-countries-for-women-2018-list-ranking/.

Santos, M. "Appearance and athleticism: Perception, reality, and changing the narrative." Victory Press, August 9, 2016, https://victorypress.org/2016/08/09/perceived-attractiveness-and-femininity-still-dominates-the-conversation-about-female-athletes-2/.

Scheadler, T., and A. Wagstaff. "Exposure to women's sports: Changing attitudes toward female athletes," *Sport Journal*, June 5, 2018, http://thesportjournal.org/article/exposure-to-womens-sports-changing-attitudes-toward-female-athletes/.

Schilken, C. "Girl with short hair kicked out of soccer tournament: 'They only did it because I look like a boy.'" *Los Angeles Times*, June 6, 2017, https://www.latimes.com/sports/sportsnow/la-sp-girl-disqualified-soccer-20170606-story.html.

Sejablsigo, J. "Violence against women remains high." *Daily News (Botswana)*, May 15, 2013, http://www.dailynews.gov.bw/news-details.php?nid=2781.

Settimi, C. "Maya Dodd, one of soccer's most powerful women, isn't done playing." *Forbes*, March 27, 2018, https://www.forbes.com/sites/christinasettimi/2018/03/27/moya-dodd-one-of-footballs-most-powerful-women-isnt-done-playing/#310bb3af458c .

Sit, J. "Misty Copeland: Why this ballet superstar is fighting for diversity." *CNN.com*, April 5, 2018, https://www.cnn.com/2018/04/05/world/misty-copeland-ballet-fight-diversity/index.html.

Smith, E. "Jessica Ennis coach hits out at UK Athletics for labeling her 'fat.'" *Guardian*, May 12, 2012, https://www.theguardian.com/sport/2012/may/24/jessica-ennis-fat-olympics.

Smith, L. "Women have more stamina and muscle endurance than men, study suggests." *Independent*, August 25, 2017, https://www.independent.co.uk/news/science/women-more-stamina-muscle-endurance-exercise-sport-men-science-study-university-of-british-columbia-a7911776.html.

Starr, A. "As USA Swimming grapples with sexual abuse, athletes cite lack of female coaches." *NPR*, July 4, 2018, https://www.npr.org/2018/07/04/623540000/as-usa-swimming-grapples-with-sexual-abuse-athletes-cite-lack-of-female-coaches.

Steidinger, J. "What Martina Navratilova and Mary Carillo got wrong." *AfterEllen*, September 20, 2018, https://www.afterellen.com/general-news/564533-what-martina-navratilova-and-mary-carillo-got-wrong.

Strauss, B. "How the WNBA stood up to Trump and won fans." *Politico Magazine*, August, 4, 2018, https://www.politico.com/magazine/story/2018/08/04/wnba-trump-protest-politics-sports-219155.

Strout, E. "American running needs more female coaches." *Outside*, September 14, 2018, https://www.outsideonline.com/2342711/why-we-need-more-female-coaches.

Suigura, K. "Attorney for MaChelle Joseph amid investigation of Tech's men's program: 'Hypocrisy is stunning.'" *Atlanta Journal-Constitution*, March 15, 2019, https://www.ajc.com/sports/basketball/attorney-for-machelle-joseph-amid-investigation-tech-men-program-hypocrisy-stunning/nFyLO4BsuPugRBmFyR7aSO/.

Swiatek, J. "Sports scholarships most often received by male gender." *HawkHeadlines*, April 21, 2016, https://hawkheadlines.net/news/2016/04/21/sports-scholarships-most-often-received-by-male-gender/.

Taibi, C. "TV ignores women's sports now more than it did 20 years ago." *Huffington Post*, June 9, 2015, https://www.huffpost.com/entry/womens-sports-tv_n_7535766?guccounter=1&guce_referrer=aHR0cHM6Ly93d3cuZ29vZ2xlLmNvbVS8&guce_referrer_sig=AQAAALo55J-XggaqGMLtXo29zZmOMbFykAUyrMi94vitB_fkMeSXoPaBDPIJXAJIZohXWYCbTFTPzuxbuDia306kWhRdFwDG5Ha1xCoO4dWC6dEwGGjPDO_nT8KuL6botWghOUlV08TcnwyPpuXu8c_eGOAeuOX-PODewN-Yx6Z8FrRK.

Toporek, B. "Gender gap grows in high school sports, report says." *Education Week*, October 10, 2012, http://blogs.edweek.org/edweek/schooled_in_sports/2012/10/gender_gap_grows_in_high_school_sports_over_past_decade_report_says.html.

Tornkvist, A. "Swedish female athletes face discrimination: Women in sport do not get equal treatment despite the country's feminist reputation." *Al Jazeera*, April 2, 2016, https://www.aljazeera.com/indepth/features/2016/03/swedish-female-athletes-face-discrimination-160315110758946.html.

Torres, L. "MTSU volleyball coach Chuck Crawford suspended after claims of player mistreatment." *Daily News Journal*, April 12, 2019, https://www.dnj.com/story/sports/college/mtsu/2019/04/12/mtsu-volleyball-chuck-crawford-chris-massaro/3331811002/.

"Trans athletes make great gains, yet resentment still flares." *NBC News*, February 25, 2019, https://www.nbcnews.com/feature/nbc-out/trans-athletes-make-great-gains-yet-resentment-still-flares-n975646.

Tucker, J. "Oakland schools' blunder shows larger issue: Girls' sport stuck at second." *San Francisco Chronicle*, September 2, 2018, https://www.sfchronicle.com/education/article/Oakland-schools-blunder-shows-larger-issue-13199449.php#photo-16098893 .

"The UK's attitudes towards women in sport." *Insure4sport*, April 5, 2018, https://ww.insure4sport.co.uk/blog/the-uks-attitudes-towards-women-in-sport.

"U.S. road race participation numbers hold steady for 2017." *Running USA*, June 27, 2018, https://runningusa.org/RUSA/News/2018/U.S._Road_Race_Participation_Numbers_Hold_Steady_for_2017.aspx.

"U.S. women's team files wage-discrimination action vs. U.S. Soccer." *ESPN.com*, April 1, 2016, http://www.espn.com/espnw/sports/article/15102506/women-national-team-files-wage-discrimination-action-vs-us-socccer-federation .

Weaver, H. "Watch Notre Dame coach Muffet McGraw make a strong case for gender equality." *Elle*, April 6, 2019, https://www.elle.com/culture/celebrities/a27062036/muffet-mcgraw-speaks-out-gender-equality/.

Whitehead, B. "Cajon High's Layshia Clarendon featured in Adidas campaign championing girls, women in sport." *Sun*, March 11, 2019, https://www.sbsun.com/2019/03/11/cajon-highs-layshia-clarendon-featured-in-adidas-campaign-championing-girls-women

-in-sport/.

Whiteside, K. "Muffet McGraw says she won't hire a man on her coaching staff. Let her tell you why." *New York Times*, April 4, 2019, https://www.nytimes.com/2019/04/04/sports/womens-final-four-muffet-mcgraw.html.

"Who succeeds NOCZ boss Miriam Moyo?" *Zambia Daily Mail*, December 9, 2017, http://www.daily-mail.co.zm/who-succeeds-nocz-boss-miriam-moyo/ .

"Who we are: Collaborating to create a positive sport culture." *SafeSport*, 2017, https://safesport.org/who-we-are .

"WNBA receives 'A' on race and gender report card." *USA Today*, November 15, 2017, https://www.usatoday.com/story/sports/wnba/2017/11/15/wnba-receives-a-on-race-and-gender-report-card/107716184/.

Wojnarowski, A. "Pacers hire Kelly Krauskopf as NBA's first woman assistant GM." *ESPN.com*, December 17, 2018, http://www.espn.com/espnw/story/_/id/25559938/indiana-pacers-hire-kelly-krauskopf-nba-first-female-assistant-general-manager.

"Women's sport: New research finds more than 80 percent of sports fans are interested." *BBC Sports*, October 4, 2018, https://www.bbc.com/sport/45737718.

Wong, A. "Where girls are missing out on high school sports." *Atlantic*, June 26, 2015, https://www.theatlantic.com/education/archive/2015/06/girls-high-school-sports-inequality/396782/ .

"World fame 100: Meet the 25 most famous women athletes in the world." *ESPN.com*, May 22, 2018, http://www.espn.com/espnw/culture/article/23337210/world-fame-100-25-most-famous-women-athletes.

"Zambia: NOWSPAR wins UN praise." *Times of Zambia*, February 27, 2012, https://allafrica.com/stories/201202271114.html.

Zeigler, C. "Elena Delle Donne hopes her gay wedding can help others." *SBNation*, October 25, 2017, https://www.outsports.com/2017/10/25/16551830/elena-delle-donne-wedding-amanda-clifton.

———. "Moment #2: Martina Navratilova comes out." *SBNation*, October 3, 2011, https://www.outsports.com/2011/10/3/4051944/moment-2-martina-navratilova-comes-out.

———. "Seimone Augustus talks to ESPN about coming out as lesbian on Minnesota Lynx." *SBNation*, August 8, 2012, https://www.sbnation.com/london-olympics-2012/2012/8/8/3227355/seimone-augustus-talks-to-espn-about-coming-out-as-lesbian-on.

INDEX

ABOUT THE AUTHOR AND CONTRIBUTORS

Joan Steidinger, CMPC, is a licensed psychologist, sport psychologist, and certified mental performance consultant administered by the Association of Applied Sports Psychology. She specializes in sports and peak performance, sport injuries, executive coaching, depression and anxiety, life transitions, and sports stress/posttraumatic stress disorders (PTSD), especially for female athletes who have experienced sexual harassment and abuse. Her first book, *Sisterhood in Sports: How Female Athletes Collaborate and Compete* (2014), won five literary awards.

Steidinger has worked with both pro and amateur athletes in such sports as running, cycling (both road and mountain), soccer, football, softball, basketball, rugby, volleyball, boxing, tennis, triathlon, and golf. She also works with musicians, dancers, and other performing artists focusing on performance, injury concerns and adjustments, and personal issues.

Steidinger has graduate degrees from the University of San Diego, the University of LaVerne, and CSPP-Berkeley. On the USOC Registry of Sport Psychology, she is a member of the Marin County Psychologists Association and the American Psychological Association. She taught sports psychology at University of California, Berkeley, as well as San Francisco State University, and continuing education to her peers throughout California.

A columnist for Moremarin.com, *Psychology Today*, and SFGate.com, Steidinger has also been featured in *The Station Game*

On. Her interviews include for the *Bleacher Report*, the *Frankie Boyer Show*, *Conversations Radio*, *Book Journeys*, and the *Women's Round Table*. Steidinger has presented at such important venues as the Commonwealth Club in San Francisco, the IWG on Women in Sport conference in Botswana, and the Caribbean Sports Conference in Barbados.

Steidinger played competitively in badminton and tennis in high school. A competitive ultrarunner, she was a Ride and Tie equestrian competitor and double century cyclist. (An ultrarunner covers any distance longer than marathon length, 26.2 miles.) She was on the first Tamalpa Runners Club's women's ultrarunning team, which placed first in the Pacific Region's Ultra Grand Prix series, and she placed third in the open division of that same series. In 2011, she and her husband climbed a 20-kilometer peak in Leh, India, and they annually participate in a three-day stage race in Nepal, raising funds for the educational costs of a small orphanage in Kathmandu. They go to Nepal annually to support the orphanage and participate in either a trek or race.

Having worked with sport psychology clients for more than 30 years, Steidinger has been in private practice for 30 years and has an office in Mill Valley, California.

❀ ❀ ❀

Much gratitude and many thanks to the "village" of leaders in women's sport from throughout the world whose generosity of spirit and information are contained in this book:

Alpha Alexander—fitness director at Walter State Community College, chair of the Morristown Tennessee Diversity Committee, and cofounder and vice president of the Black Women in Sport Foundation.

Heather Barbour—associate professor at the University of New Hampshire; researcher on sport psychology, motivation of girls and women in sports, and homophobia and closeted athletes and coaches in sport; member of the USOC Registry of Sports Psychologists; and consultant to U.S. Youth Soccer.

Dave Berri—sports economist and professor of economics at Southern Utah University, past president of the North American Association of Sport Economists, and member of the editorial boards of the *Journal of Sports Economics* and the *International Journal of Sport Finance*.

Wendy Borlabi—high-performance coach for the NBA Chicago Bulls and a consultant for the NBA; former employee of the USOC at San Diego Training Center (six years); and cofounder of Acumen Performance Group, together with six Navy Seals.

Helen Carroll—Second Godmother of Women in the LGBT, well-known coach whose basketball team from the University of North Carolina won a national championship, athletic director of Mills College for 12 years, advocate for LBGTQ equality in sports, and sports project director for the National Center of Lesbian Rights.

Stiliani "Ani" Chroni—former alpine ski racer and coach, president of Women Sport International and the Sport Psychology Council, professor in the Department of Sports and Physical Education in sports psychology and coaching at the Inland Norway University of Applied Sciences, and technical delegate for the International Ski Federation.

Rosa Lopez D'Amico—former member of the Venezuelan artistic gymnastics team, founder of the Latin American Association for Sport Management, president of the International Association of Physical Education and Sport for Girls and Women (IAPESGW), NGO representative on the IWG Global Executive Board, professor at Universidad Pedagogica Experimental Libertador, and lead editor of *Women and Sport in Latin America*.

Lilamani de Soysa—former member of the Sri Lankan national table tennis team, co-opted expert on international sport relations and development of the IWG on Women in Sport, founder of the International Table Tennis Federation's Women's Development Programme, researcher at Tsukyba International University's Academy for Sports Studies "Tokyo 2020 and the Internationalization of Sport Education."

Kisha Ford-Torres—former member of the Georgia Tech Yellow Jackets basketball team, inductee to the Georgia Tech Sports Hall of Fame, former WNBA player, and deputy sheriff.

Julie Foudy—former American midfielder on the U.S. women's national soccer team for 17 years (captain for the 2004 and 2007 Olympic Games, played in three Olympic Games, winning two golds and one silver), 1991 and 1999 FIFA Women's World Cup champion, TV sports analyst for ESPN and ABC, founder of the Julie Foudy Sports Leadership Academy in 2006 (now also featuring water polo and basketball).

Nikki Franke—former Olympic foil fencer on the 1976 and 1980 Olympic fencing teams; the United States Fencing Association's (USFA) national foil champion in 1975 and 1980; participant in two Pan American Games (silver in 1975 and bronze in 1979); associate professor in the Department of Public Health at Temple University; coach of Temple University's women's fencing teams for more than 40 years; United States Fencing Coaches Association Women's Fencing Coach of the Year four times; and inductee to the International Sports Hall of Fame in 2002, Temple University's Athletics Hall of Fame 1995, and the United States Hall of Fame in 1998.

Laura Gentile—three-time All-ACC field hockey player at Duke University; senior vice president of marketing for ESPN and cofounder of ESPNW; cocreator, along with the Women's Sport Foundation, of Sports 4 Life (a "national grant program to increase participation and retention of African American and Hispanic girls in sport"); and member of the Global Sports Mentoring Program, the U.S. Department of State's Council to Empower Women and Girls through Sports, and the Women's Sports Foundation Advisory Panel.

Georgia Gould—U.S. Olympic bronze medalist in cross-country mountain biking at the 2012 London Games, winner of five national mountain biking championships, an outspoken advocate for women in cycling, and a member of the Union Cycliste Internationale's Athletes' Commission.

Traci Green—former national-level tennis player, first black female tennis coach at Harvard and first black female head coach at an Ivy League school in 2007, and first black Harvard coach to win an Ivy League title.

Tracey Griesbaum—former field hockey player at West Chester University, two-time All-American, three-time regional All-American, former field hockey head coach at the University of Iowa for 14 years and former field hockey assistant coach at the University of Iowa for seven years (including six NCAA Tournament appearances and three Big Ten Conference Women's Field Hockey Tournament championships [2006, 2007, and 2008]), two-time National Field Hockey Coaches Association West Region Coach of the Year honoree, 2000 United States Field Hockey Coach of the Year, and 2004 Big Ten Coach of the Year.

Pat Griffin—grandmother of the LGBT movement in sports through activism and education; lifelong athlete (field hockey, basketball, and swimming); member of the 1971 U.S. field hockey team; professor emerita and professor in the Social Justice Education Program at the University of Massachusetts Amherst; author of *Strong Women, Deep Closets: Lesbians and Homophobia in Sport*; founder of Changing the Game: The GLSEN Sports Project; former director of the Women's Sports Foundation's It Takes a Team project; recipient of a honorary doctoral degree from Laval University in Quebec in 2017; recipient of the Honor Award by the Women Leaders in College Sports.

Wendy Hilliard—first African American rhythmic gymnast on the U.S. women's national gymnastics team, for which she appeared nine times, twice as team captain; four-time coach of the U.S. national team; founder of the Wendy Hilliard Gymnastics Foundation (WHGF); former president of the Women's Sports Foundation (the first African American and the first gymnast to hold the position); recipient of the Rings of Gold from the U.S. Olympic Committee; founding member the Sports and Arts in Schools Foundation and Women in Sports and Events (WISE); and television and radio gymnastics commentator.

Nancy Hogshead-Makar—attorney; three-time U.S. Olympic gold medalist and one-time silver medalist in swimming; former president of the Board of Trustees, legal advisor, and senior director of advocacy for the Women's Sport Foundation; CEO and president of Champion Women; advocate of bringing Title IX in compliance with sexual harassment, abuse, assault, employment, pregnancy, and LGBTQ discrimination; worked to establish the Protecting Young Victims from Sexual Abuse and Safe Sport Authorization Act; and coleader of Team Integrity.

Nada Knorre—former national-level gymnastics competitor for 10 years; coach, judge, and member of the Czech Official Board of Gymnastics; vice president of Women Sport International; board member of the Czech Olympic Committee for 23 years; and established the Women and Sport Committee for the Czech Republic in 1997.

Vikki Krane—former collegiate runner; professor of human movement, sport, and leisure studies at Bowling Green State University; director and graduate coordinator of the women's studies program at Bowling Green State University; Outstanding Contributor to Graduate Education at the Graduate Student Senate Awards Ceremony at Bowling Green State University; 2015 recipient of the Professor of Teaching Excellence award bestowed by Bowling Green State University; and past president, fellow, and former CC-AASP of the Association of Applied Sports Psychology.

Nicole LaVoi—former intercollegiate tennis player at Gustavus Adolphus College, winning the NCAA-III national team championships in 1990; women's tennis head coach at Wellesley College; director of the Tucker Center for Research on Girls and Women in Sport; senior lecturer in the School of Kinesiology at the University of Minnesota; member of the Board of Directors for WeCOACH; faculty member of the NCAA Women Coaches Academies; and author of *Women in Sports Coaching* (2016) and the annual *Women in Collegiate Coaching Report Card*.

Donna Lopiano—six-time national champion, nine-time All-American, and three-time ASA Softball MVP; former CEO of the Women's Sports Foundation; and one the "10 Most Powerful Women in Sports" and one of the "100 Most Influential People in Sports."

Kirikaiahi Mahutariki—board member of Women in Sport Aotearoa and host of the 2022 IWG secretariat in New Zealand.

Jane Meyer—former senior associate athletic director at the University of Iowa and, in a landmark gender discrimination suit, sued the University of Iowa for gender and sexual discrimination, winning $4 million in a jury trial.

Thomas Newkirk—attorney who successfully litigated the case of Coach Tracey Griesbaum and former senior associate athletic director Jane Meyer versus the University of Iowa.

Carole Oglesby—godmother of sports psychology; former softball player; professor at Temple University for 26 years and Cal State University, Northridge for six years; member of the American Alliance for Health, Physical Education, and Recreation and Dance for 49 years; member of the Association of Applied Sport Psychology; former trustee and project consultant for the Women's Sports Foundation; and cochair of the IWG on Women in Sport from 2014 to 2018.

Margaret Ottley—former high school field hockey player and member of the national field hockey team for Trinidad and Tobago; professor of sport and exercise psychology at West Chester University; and certified teacher in the Trinidad and Tobago Ministry of Education, CMPC, monitored by AASP.

Allison Overholt—editor in chief at ESPNW and the first female editor in chief for a major national sports magazine, *ESPN The Magazine*; general editor of *ESPN The Magazine*; senior editor (special projects) of *ESPN The Magazine*; and adjunct professor at the Preston Robert Tisch Center for Hospitality, Tourism, and Sports Management at New York University.

Marcia Oxley—former competitor in track and field, and netball; manager of the Barbados Netball Team for Women XIII World Championship 2011, in Singapore; educator at Barbados Community College from 2003 to present; regional manager of the Caribbean Commonwealth Sport Development Programme; and assistant professor at Norfold State University.

Annamarie Phelps—former Olympic lightweight rower and member of world champion British rowing team, vice chair for the British Olympic Association, Olympic rower, and former chair of Britain's Olympic Rowing Association.

Mark Purdy—adjunct lecturer at San Jose State University, sports journalist for the *San Jose Mercury News* for 23 years, adjunct lecturer at Santa Clara University, and sports columnist/sports editor for the *Cincinnati Enquirer* for 19 years.

Melodie Robinson—first female sports journalist in New Zealand; first international female broadcaster for rugby; former international player for New Zealand's women's national rugby union team; general manager of sport and events for the 2019 Rugby World Cup; sports broadcaster for Sky TV for 14-plus years; commentator; corporate communications manager; and founder of the "Wonderful Group," providing advocacy for women's sport.

Joan Ryan—award-winning pioneering woman in sports journalism; author of *Little Girls in Pretty Boxes*, featured on *Oprah*, and three other books; winner of 13 Associated Press awards, the Women's Sports Foundation Journalism Award, and the National Headliner Award; writer for the *San Francisco Chronicle* for 22 years; and founding member of Coaching Corps, a nonprofit organization that uses the power of sport to help low-income youth.

Allison Sandmeyer-Graves—CEO of the Canadian Association for the Advancement of Women and Sport and Physical Activity (CAAWS) and director of Development (Annual and Major Gifts) and coordinator of International Programs and Development for Free the Children.

Tina Sloan Green—pioneering athlete in field hockey and lacrosse; the first African American woman on the women's national lacrosse team, in 1969; the first African American lacrosse collegiate coach at Temple University, from 1975 to 1992, leading the Temple Owls to three national championships and 11 consecutive Final Four appearances; and cofounder of the Black Women in Sport Foundation (BWSF) in 1992, to combat the underrepresentation of women of color in nontraditional sports.

Nefertiti Walker—former collegiate basketball player, recipient of a master's in business administration, associate dean for an inclusive organization, director of Diversity and Inclusion for the Isenberg School of Management, and associate professor of sport management at the University of Massachusetts Amherst.

Peter Westbrook—American fencing legend in sabre; member of the U.S. Olympic fencing team from 1976 to 1996, winning bronze in 1984, and the first African American to win a fencing medal, winning the U.S. National Individual Sabre Championship 13 times; inductee to the U.S. Fencing Hall of Fame in 1989; and founder of the Peter Westbrook Foundation in 1991, to help underprivileged and children of color develop positive attitudes and life skills through fencing.

Mike Woitalia—executive editor of *Soccer America* magazine and coauthor of *More Than Goals: The Journey from Backyard Games to World Cup Competition*, with former U.S. women's national soccer team captain Claudio Reyna.